CULTURAL REPRODUCTION

The idea of cultural reproduction was first developed by Bourdieu (1973) who sees the function of the education system as being to reproduce the culture of the dominant classes, thus helping to ensure their continued dominance. Through his concepts of 'cultural capital' and 'habitus', Bourdieu's influence spread into other areas of socialisation and high culture. However, despite the complex of influences that contribute to Bourdieu's method, sociologists of culture and students of cultural studies seem to have picked up on the negative and critical elements in the work. In particular, they developed the metaphor of reproduction as copy or imitation rather than reproduction as regeneration and synthesis. As a consequence 'cultural reproduction' has become part of the orthodoxy of studies in the theory of ideology and neo-Marxism. While still addressing this well-established theme of ideology and structural determinacy in cultural reproduction theory, this collection of original essays seeks also to explore other possibilities in terms of ethnomethodology, Durkheimianism, structuralism and post-structuralism. Many of the arguments put forward also confront the contemporary challenges presented by postmodernism. The papers address an unusually wide spectrum of cultural formations, including gender roles, fine art, film, journalism, education, consumerism, style, language and sociology itself. The introduction discusses the origin and development of the concept of cultural reproduction and shows the variety of analytic possibilities within several traditions of social theorising, all later expanded in the body of the text.

Most of the contributors are academics working in the area of sociology of communication studies. All of them have taught in and have continuing research interests in the sociology of culture and cultural studies.

Chris Jenks is Senior Lecturer and Deputy Head of the Department of Sociology, Goldsmiths' College, University of London.

CULTURAL REPRODUCTION

Edited by
Chris Jenks

London and New York

First published in 1993
by Routledge
11 New Fetter Lane, London EC4P 4EE

Simultaneously published in the USA and Canada
by Routledge
29 West 35th Street, New York, NY 10001

Typeset in Baskerville by LaserScript, Mitcham, Surrey
Printed and bound in Great Britain by
Mackays of Chatham PLC, Chatham, Kent

British Library Cataloguing in Publication Data
A catalogue record for this book is available from the British Library.

Library of Congress Cataloging in Publication Data
  Cultural reproduction/edited by Chris Jenks.
  p. cm.
  Includes bibliographical references and index.
  1. Culture. 2. Social change. 3. Social structure.
  4. Social control. I. Jenks, Chris.
  HM101.C892   1993
  306 – dc20   92-28808
                                                        CIP

ISBN 0–415–07182–8
      0–415–07183–6 (pbk)

CONTENTS

CONTENTS

CONTRIBUTORS

Malcolm Barnard is Senior Lecturer in Visual Culture at the University of Derby. He studied philosophy and sociology at the Universities of York and Warwick. His doctorate explored deconstructionist theory and his current research is into the philosophical bases of visual knowledge.

James Donald is Senior Lecturer in Media Studies at the University of Sussex. His previous publications include: *Politics and Ideology* (Milton Keynes, Open University Press, 1986); *Fantasy and the Cinema* (London, BFI Publishing, 1989); *Psychoanalysis and Cultural Theory: Thresholds* (London, Macmillan, 1992); and *Sentimental Education: Schooling, Popular Culture and the Regulation of Liberty* (London, Verso, 1992).

Stephen Featherstone is currently Management Research Officer for the Leisure Services department of Calderdale Metropolitan Borough Council. He studied sociology at Teesside Polytechnic, and the Universities of York and Leeds. His doctorate was in the area of culture and mass communication. He has a range of research interests connected with the theory/practice of service provision in local government.

Dick Hebdige is Reader in Communication Studies at Goldsmiths' College, University of London. He has published extensively in the area of cultural studies and postmodernism. His major works include: *Subculture: The Meaning of Style* (London, Methuen, 1979); *Cut 'N' Mix* (London, Comedia, 1987); and *Hiding in the Light* (London, Routledge, 1988).

Ian Heywood is Principal Lecturer and Course Leader in Fine Art at Leeds Polytechnic. He studied fine art at Rochdale and Maidstone

Colleges of Art and sociology at Goldsmiths' College, University of London and at York University. His doctorate concerned the sociology of art. He is awaiting publication of *Discourses, Art and the City.*

Chris Jenks is Senior Lecturer and Deputy Head of Sociology at Goldsmiths' College, University of London. His major publications include: *Worlds Apart – Readings for a Sociology of Education* (London, Collier-Macmillan, 1976); *Toward a Sociology of Education* (New Brunswick, NJ, Transaction Books, 1977); *Rationality, Education and the Social Organization of Knowledge* (London, Routledge & Kegan Paul, 1977); *The Sociology of Childhood* (London, Batsford, 1982; Gregg, 1992); *Durkheim, Art and Representation* (forthcoming); and *Culture* (London, Routledge, forthcoming). His current research is into child abuse and the city.

Justin Lorentzen teaches sociology at Goldsmiths' College, University of London. He studied sociology at Portsmouth Polytechnic and at Goldsmiths' College, where he is currently engaged in postgraduate research into the sociology of transgression.

Michael Phillipson was, until recently, Senior Lecturer in Sociology at Goldsmiths' College, University of London; he is now Honorary Fellow to the department. His previous publications include: *Sociological Aspects of Crime and Delinquency* (London, Routledge & Kegan Paul, 1971); *New Directions in Sociological Theory* (London, Collier-Macmillan, 1972); *Paining, Language and Modernity* (London, Routledge & Kegan Paul, 1985); and *In Modernity's Wake* (London, Routledge, 1989).

David Silverman is Professor of Sociology at Goldsmiths' College, University of London. He has published widely in the areas of organisation theory, language, sociological theory and, more recently, the sociology of health and illness. His major publications include *The Theory of Organizations* (London, Heinemann, 1970); *Organizational Work* (London, Collier-Macmillan, 1975); *The Material Word* (London, Routledge & Kegan Paul, 1980); *Qualitative Methodology and Sociology* (Aldershot, Gower, 1985); and *Communication and Medical Practice* (London, Sage, 1987).

Don Slater is Lecturer in Sociology at Goldsmiths' College, University of London. His main research interests include advertising and marketing, history and theories of consumption and consumer culture, and photographic theory and practice. He is currently embarking on research into the development of consumer culture in Czechoslovakia.

John A. Smith is currently a School Teacher having also taught at Goldsmiths' College, University of London. He studied fine art at Grimsby and the Royal College of Art, and sociology at Goldsmiths' College. His doctorate was in the sociology of art. His current research is into the phenomenology of neo-classicism, modernism and postmodernism. He awaits publication of *Durkheim, Art and Representation* (with C. Jenks).

David Walsh is Senior Lecturer in Sociology at Goldsmiths' College, University of London. He has published in the areas of sociological theory and the sociology of science. He is co-author (with M. Phillipson) of *New Directions in Sociological Theory* (London, Collier-Macmillan, 1972). He is awaiting publication of a collection of original papers on Durkheim's contribution to contemporary social and cultural thought.

1

INTRODUCTION
The analytic bases of cultural reproduction theory

Chris Jenks

'Cultural reproduction', though currently not a fashionable concept, is a particularly fertile area for social theory which this volume seeks to revivify. The idea of cultural reproduction makes reference to the emergent quality of experience of everyday life – albeit through a spectrum of interpretations. That is to say that the concept serves to articulate the dynamic process that makes sensible the utter contingency of, on the one hand, the stasis and determinacy of social structures and, on the other, the innovation and agency inherent in the practice of social action. Cultural reproduction allows us to contemplate the necessity and complementarity of continuity and change in social experience.

Although this zone of concern has been a permanent preoccupation of social theorising since its inception the modern critical conceptualisation of the problem, around the concept of cultural reproduction, was first developed by the French sociologist and cultural theorist Pierre Bourdieu in the early 1970s. The initial empirical context of Bourdieu's work was education in modern society: he saw the function of the education system being to 'reproduce' the culture of the dominant classes, thus helping to ensure their continued dominance and to perpetuate their covert exercise of power. Such ideas resonated with Althusser's notions of 'ideological state apparatuses' which were emerging about the same period. Through his central concepts of 'cultural capital' and 'habitus' Bourdieu's own work and his influence upon the research of others spread into an examination of other areas of concern such as socialisation, high culture and artistic practice, and style and mannerism in social relations. I will expand on these and other of Bourdieu's ideas later in this chapter.

At this stage, in terms of the history of ideas, it is both

1

interesting and important to note that despite the complex of traditions and influences which contribute to Bourdieu's method of analysis the British tradition of the sociology of culture and cultural studies seems to have picked up on and crystallised around the largely negative and critical elements of the thesis. To this end the majority of contributions to this field have developed the metaphor of reproduction as copy or imitation rather than as regeneration or synthesis. As a consequence 'cultural reproduction' has become subsumed under the orthodoxy of studies in the theory of ideology and neo-Marxisms.[1-3] Other different and significant bodies of work continued to develop the positive side, such as Bernstein's extended studies of the role of socio-linguistic codes in revealing the character of the relation between the social structure and the symbolic order, and Cicourel's research into cognitive sociology which revolved around the acquisition of interpretive procedures. Despite these important initiatives, and others, the central concept of cultural reproduction has become seemingly highjacked.

While still addressing the well-established theme of ideology and structural determinacy in cultural reproduction theory, the collection of essays gathered here endeavours to open up other possibilities from a variety of perspectives less familiar in this area of study like, for example, reflexive sociology, Durkheimian sociology, ethnomethodology, structuralism and post-structuralism. Inevitably, given the historical-intellectual context of our work, many of the arguments put forward also confront the most contemporary challenges presented by postmodernism.

Substantively, the chapters address an unusually broad sweep of cultural formations including gender roles, visual art, mass communication, consumerism, education, film, philosophy and language itself. All the chapters attest to the analytic character of their topic: they aim to theorise the field and not leave it to a supposed saturation by ethnography – what Parsons once referred to as an attempt to construct reality through a 'mosaic atomism' – description serves, then, largely to adorn the work.

All sociological explanations begin with some concept of *structure* which, following Durkheim, appears as typical to all societal members; that is, it stands as the normal, the mundane, it has a series of taken-for-granted manifestations. Structure is also constraining upon the conduct of members either overtly or, more successfully, through a network of covert strategies. Finally,

2

structure is to be recognised as ultimately independent of the will
or caprice of particular individuals. It is, then, a determinate form,
intangible but real, and always real in its consequences. Structure
provides the supra-individual source of causality in sociological
reasoning whether it is experienced by members (or constituted by
theorists) as economic, political, moral, cognitive or even physical
in its orientation. From these various conceptions (or formu-
lations) stem the dynamics in social theory that we might call
process. Culture and particularly cultural reproduction are precisely
dynamics that we would gather within this notion of process.
Indeed, the idea of culture emerges from the noun 'process', in
the sense of nurture, growth and bringing into being – in fact, to
cultivate in an agricultural or horticultural sense.[4] Culture, as
process, is emergent, it is forthcoming, it is continuous in the way
of reproducing, and as all social processes it provides the grounds
and the parallel context of *social action* itself.

Any social action, within sociology, appears not in isolation but
rather depends upon its context or a sense of competence for its
meaning. In this way it stands as an index of the social occasion
from which it arose.[5] Action therefore inevitably relates back to the
original, but perhaps unspoken, social structure for its coherence
and intelligibility. Two important points emerge from this
exposition: firstly, that sociology has a perpetually ambivalent
relationship with the centrality and efficacy of subjectivity – selves
become movements within culture or parts of cultural units – and
secondly, that sociology appears to generate one sense of a causal
chain, but what we have essentially is a teleology, a circuit of
explanation.

Perhaps the most significant analytic point is that the patterning
of the modalities *structure, process* and *social action* is not descriptive,
although in some epistemological guises, like, for example,
positivism, it passes itself off as if it were wholly descriptive. But I
repeat, this patterning is not descriptive, rather it is metaphoric.
The metaphors become our analytic topic. Those cultural signs or
conventions as metaphors become our topic. Our choice of metaphors and our choice through cultural metaphors expresses our
interests, our intentions and our moral relation to the world.
Nietzsche tells us that 'truth is nothing but the solidification of old
metaphors'. The use of different metaphors in our analysis displays our attitude to a knowledge of the social world; it reveals our
vision and that also of our tradition. It is, or should be by now,

commonplace to attend critically to the invocation of the masculine form 'man' to summon up images of all human kind in Western reason though perhaps less routine to acknowledge the empiricist legacy of the centrality of the senses, particularly vision, in much social theory that 'looks at', 'sees' and specifically 'observes' its phenomena. We may note further the technical and commercial metaphoricity that has permeated much contemporary sociology, even in the often bureaucratic prose of such theorists as Habermas when he is, ironically, levelling a critique at the penetration of the discourse of science and technology into the life-world thus militating against a free democracy. Therefore different metaphors unconsciously, or in the case of reflexive theorising consciously, display our varieties of moral commitment and thus our different perspectives on social life. In this gathering of ideas, in this process of signification, our central metaphors are 'culture' and 'reproduction', and to play with these metaphors, seriously, as Merleau-Ponty might recommend, is to liberate their potential into the range of interpretations that this collection of writings displays, and beyond.

We have already introduced culture in relation to process and growth – culture is becoming. But we also need to know what is culture as distinct from society, or do the terms duplicate? Malinowski[6] tells us that culture is '. . . inherited artefacts, goods, technical process, ideas, habits and values'. He included within his definition a notion of social structure which, he felt, could not be understood apart from culture. He further states that culture '. . . obviously is the integral whole consisting of the implements and consumer goods, of constitutional charters for the various social groupings, of human ideas and crafts, beliefs and customs', and he continues that '. . . the essential fact of culture as we live it and experience it, as we observe it scientifically, is the organisation of human beings into permanent groups'.

Firth,[7] another eminent anthropologist, distinguishes firmly between social structure and culture and defines the latter as '. . . the component of accumulated resources, immaterial as well as material, which a people inherit, employ, transmute, add to and transmit; it is all learned behaviour which has been socially acquired'.

Bottomore[8] concludes my inventory of definitions with the proposition that 'By culture we mean the ideational aspects or social life, as distinct from the actual relations and forms of relationship between individuals; and by *a* culture the ideational aspects of *a* particular society'.

The concept of culture, then, implies a relationship with the accumulated shared symbols representative of and significant within a particular community – a context-dependent semiotic system. Culture, however, is not simply a residue, it is in progress; it processes and reveals as it structures and contains. Culture is the way of life and the manner of living of a people. It is often conflated with the idea of high culture, but this is an understanding both too restrictive and too exclusive, yet high culture is our topic also.

What now can we make of this concept 'reproduction'? A phenotypical reading of the term, or what I have previously referred to as a 'negative' definition, invokes all of the modern and sterile resonances of mechanicism and technicism, it speaks of a crafted or rather fashioned reproduction. At its strongest we have a copy or repeat, whereas at its most dilute an imitation or a likeness – throughout this reading we are presented with reproduction as replication, this is a metaphor of constraint. In relation to the social, such reproduction must be an affirmation of the 'ancien régime', a system which extols a symbolic violence through its containment of choice in the present.[9] The symbolism of such an order is condensed, opaque and referential of convention, form and demise.

A genotypical reading of reproduction is, in juxtaposition, positive and vibrant – it brings to mind the excitement and newness of sexual and biological reproduction. Here the image is generative rather than replicative and it offers the possibilities of change and new combinations. The very idea of birth that stems from such a formulation is innovative and necessarily creative. Here is the theorising of the new or coming order and the social is conceived of through change, reformation or even revolution. The symbolism is diffuse and elusive, it lives within rules-in-use as meaning is depicted in the later Wittgenstein.

These two readings, which are well rehearsed by Williams,[10] can be taken to relate to other pervasive binary combinations in social theory such as continuity and change, consensus and conflict, structure and agency, and determinism and freewill. The fluidity that exists in the space between these pairs of pattern variables is itself infinitely reproductive and generative of varieties of theorising. It is also this territory left vacant amidst the avenues of post-Enlightenment dichotomies that is being colonised by the polysemy of postmodern critique.

Cultural reproduction is, then, a theme that has arisen from within a diversity of forms of contemporary social investigation, all of which variously but inevitably refer to a sense of social continuity achieved through modalities of change. Now in one dominant form this appears as a classical Marxist dichotomy between *essence* (continuity) and *appearance* (as change) and indeed, as previously suggested, much of the British work on cultural reproduction emerges from a Marxist tradition – but by no means all, as this volume shows. Our work here is, at one level, an attempt to liberate the concept back into the wider arena of sociological debate. But let us look briefly at the constitution of a Marxist method in terms of essence and appearance – an epistemology initiated in *The German Ideology*, refined in *The Introduction to the Critique of Political Economy* and *The Grundrisse*, and one reaching its fruition in *Das Kapital*. A classical example of this method derives from Volume 1 of .the latter source in the section on 'Wages'. Wages, Marx argues, produce a distorted and distorting image of the relationship between people in the market place. One group, the owners of the means of production, appears to offer wages to the working group in return for the exercise of its labour – labour, then, is treated as if it were like any other commodity: it is objective and it can be assigned an exchange value. Labour, however, is unlike any other commodity: it is subjective, it is part of our species being *Homo laborens*, and its consumption generates a value in excess of its original unmobilised state. This property of labour is called 'labour power'.

Thus despite the *appearance* of wages as fair exchange for the consumption of labour what is actually being appropriated is 'labour power'; it is generating a 'surplus value' or profit for its consumer. The *essence* of the wages relation is, then, the true relation of 'exploitation' and whatever changes occur in the appearance of wages (Trade Union bargaining, pay increases, improved conditions of service). The mechanism of exploitation, as the essence, is always reproduced. So in Marxist terms we have an elementary example of how components of a market culture are reproduced such that the real relations that befit the old order remain intact and hidden. The linking concept for this contradiction or discrepancy between appearance and essence is, of course, ideology. Ideology becomes the process both conscious, but largely unconscious, through which a distortion, blurring, generalising and decontextualising of realities occurs.

This model provides a pattern and a battery of concepts for the analysis of any cultural phenomenon from the material, like property, artefacts or commodities (things in themselves), to the ideational, like language, knowledge and subjectivity itself. Indeed, Althusser's concept of 'interpellation' provides precisely the possibility of identity and subjectivity emerging from the ideological process. Ideology being a constant variable in social life, it hails and elects individuals, it incorporates them and provides them with purpose and a sense of self. The determinacy of distortion is complete; the realm of the private is invaded and inhabited by the grinding inevitability of ideological necessity.

Although, as we have become even more poignantly aware due to recent events in Eastern Europe, Marxism as a concrete economic and political policy has generated a series of social structures which manifest oppression and, at the personal level, despair, in the context of Western theorising the tradition has always provided for the possibility of freedom, emancipation and authenticity as intellectual principles. Nevertheless, in the context of cultural analysis in terms of cultures' reproducibility, such work provides a vision of pessimism, of regret and of fallenness. Thus its often unspoken recommendations provide the grounds for upheaval and conflict. As a form of analysis, Marxist theory espouses a democracy which is, however, overseen and directed by the hidden expert, the defiler of reified images and the revealer of distortions.

Cultural reproduction theory finds another, relatively underexercised, resource in Durkheimian sociology. This tradition centres on an unashamed expert who wishes to 'speak louder than common sense'.[11] Indeed, at an early stage of *The Rules of Sociological Method* Durkheim tells us that we must 'eradicate all preconceptions', which Hirst[12] has interpreted as an assault on the ideology of common sense; it is without question a demand for a form of discourse that is disciplined, unconventional and reflexive upon the commonplace. Durkheim directs us to proceed from the local and the particular experience of everyday life, the individual manifestation, to the real, the typical, the collective representation. From this realm of phenomena we can generate an altruistic commitment to the development of a truly moral science. Morality in Durkheim refers to that which binds people together, the essential adhesion or bond which must reproduce from moment to moment in order to sustain any experience of cohesion or indeed sociality itself.

For Durkheim the problem with social and cultural reproduction is not to reveal its occurrence behind the distorted ideological mask of change but rather to search for the appropriate collective secular credo that will ensure reproduction of solidarity in the face of change. Durkheim offers us this thesis, which is fundamental to all of his writings,[13] in *The Division of Labour*. It is in this seminal work that he provides the two pervasive models of integration, across the axis of modernity, in the form of 'mechanical' and 'organic' solidarity. Mechanical solidarity is a societal form based on sameness, on compact, shared beliefs, on an ill-defined division of labour and on an intensely other-directed collective consciousness. The transition to organic solidarity, which occurs through 'moral density' accompanying the passage of modernity, brings about a steady and debilitating enfeeblement of this collective consciousness which has a knock-on effect on the other features of the society. The division of labour becomes clearly demarcated and rigorously policed, belief systems diffuse and dissemble, and the point of recognition becomes utter difference. The change might be summarised, within a science of ethics, as a movement away from altruism into the ascendence of egoism. Durkheim's purpose, and his legacy, is to produce a theory of benign reproduction, a theory that will locate the binding force in the face of potential fragmentation, an impulsion to reconstruct difference as interdependence. Here, then, Durkheim is informing us of the very necessity of cultural reproduction, the necessity of conformity through change. Some systems simply must reproduce – his societal forms are, after all, not evolutionary but morphological. The Durkheimian tradition views reproduction with an optimism, indeed a positivism; its metaphors are consensual rather than divisive and its motivation is integrative.

Another source of cultural reproduction theory, namely ethnomethodology, may be seen instructively in the wake of the Durkheimian tradition. Garfinkel, though notably influenced by Schutzian phenomenology, Parsonian systems theory and Wittgenstein's linguistic philosophy, is also very much in debt to Durkheim's realisation of a 'collective consciousness'; this is clearly paraded in Garfinkel's early paper on *Conditions for Successful Degradation Ceremonies*. Ethnomethodology relies upon a strong sense of a collective but inarticulate consensus in its explanations of human conduct which it describes ironically, in the context of its contest with positivist rhetoric, as the 'normal'. This normal implies not the normative against which we can judge the deviant or pathological but the routine, the taken-for-granted, that which we all must know in order to assume the status of a member in everyday culture. Cultural reproduction, for ethnomethodologists, is almost a necessary process. Indeed, it is a purpose. The artful practices of members that ethnomethodology reveals and celebrates for us in the intricate ethnographic detail of, most usually, conversational exchange is dedicated (though not determined) to make sense of its context by reflexively reproducing the conditions of its own occurrence. Thus reproduction for members is both intentional and integrative. It is a constant reaffirmation of collective life through what Giddens[14] might refer to as the process of structuration. A major departure for ethnomethodology is the dissolution of the theorist as expert – the sociologist in accounting for the character of social life is exercising the same skills and practices as the lay member, it is just that the sociologist is reflexive back upon these practices. Whatever the status of this utopian democratic claim on behalf of this body of work it reiterates the necessary role of both theorist and lay member as agents in the reproduction of a continuous and shared symbolic network that we can call culture.

A final, but compelling, input to cultural reproduction theory is to be found in that internally divisive spectrum or attitudes towards human affairs that has come to be known as structuralism. Structuralism contains and combines many elements of the previously mentioned approaches but reworks the classical epistemological dichotomy between *essence* and *appearance* in terms of the continuum between *depth* and *surface*. Lévi-Strauss, who was primarily instrumental in exercising this geological metaphor, likens the formation of cultural phenomena to their layering as in strata, and the understanding of such phenomena in terms of the excavation of these strata and an exposure of their patterns of interrelation. Elements of a culture, as we experience them, are the surface appearances or manifestations of underlying patterns at a deeper level – both within time, the 'synchronic', and through time, the 'diachronic'. What de Saussure has provided, and what stands as perhaps the most significant and binding element of all structuralisms, is that the underlying pattern or structure of any cultural phenomenon is to be understood in terms of a linguistic metaphor. We may come to know the structures that comprise a culture as if they were a language. The lexical terms or items of

9

vocabulary within such a language are provided for by the symbols that exist within social life, that is, the representations that attach to or arise from the tangible state of things or materiality itself. The grammatical rules of this metaphoric language are provided for by the act, the continuous and habitual act, of signification. So the variety of ways that we make sense in different cultures variously articulates and therefore gives rise to the different 'languages' that our cultural symbols comprise. The complexity of this system of meaning is compounded by the essentially arbitrary relation between any particular object or state of affairs and the symbolic (linguistic) device that is employed to signify its being. Thing-like-ness, then, as objective and recognisable within any culture, derives not from any correspondence between name and named but from a delicately poised structuring of otherness in our contained network of ideas. Things are not so much what they are but emerge from a knowledge of what they are not, in fact a system of oppositions; the principle at the core of any binary code. Now the fragility of this structuring of otherness remains unthreatened, indeed, it appears as robust through the very practice of sociality, through the persistence and reproduction of that tenuous relation at each and every turn within a culture. Meaning, then, within a particular culture, emerges from convention overcoming the arbitrary relation between the signifier and the signified. Convention reproduces culture, and culture is contingent upon reproduction within structuralism.

If we now look to the work of Bourdieu we find elements of each of the major traditions considered above emergent in his writing and integrated seemingly without conflict or ambiguity.

Bourdieu is committed to the development of a critical yet appreciative theory of culture and as such his ideas provide an important contribution to our understanding of both power and authority within our society. He began from an analysis of the education system and the part that its institutions play in the constitution and transmission of what counts as legitimate knowledge and forms of communication:

> . . . the cultural field is transformed by successive restructurations rather than by radical revolutions, with certain themes being brought to the fore while others are set to one side without being completely eliminated, so that continuity of communication between intellectual generations remains

possible. In all cases, however, the patterns informing the thought of a given period can be fully understood only by reference to the school system, which is alone capable of establishing them and developing them, through practice, as the habits of thought common to a whole generation.[15]

In this sense Bourdieu is forging a positive link between the symbolic order and the state of the social structure. He is showing how forms and patterns of communication both reflect and perpetuate particular communities. In this way his work has much in common with Bernstein's theory of socio-linguistic codes and both serve to blur the distinction between cultural reproduction and social reproduction.

It is here that he reveals elements of a Durkheimian epistemology through his interest in the sustaining character of cultural representations, the production and maintenance of a social consensus (a concept parallel in importance to the idea of a 'collective consciousness'), and through the assumption of the social origins and persistence of knowledge classifications. He is, however, critical of what he sees as Durkheim's positivism in that it depends upon stasis, and also that Durkheim considers the functions of the education system to be anticipated.[16]

Within the context of education Bourdieu conceptualises all pedagogic practice as, at one level, a style of inculcation that perpetuates a more general social tendency towards repression – a symbolic violence. Repression, for Bourdieu, becomes a 'natural' mode of human adaptation within a culture that is pervasively oppressive. All forms of socialisation and en-culturation are seen to contribute to this alienating adaptation. Here we see his obvious continuity with the tradition of Marxism. Bourdieu bears witness to a society based on constraint, not a just or equitable constraint, but one organised in terms of the unequal distribution of power in relation to the economic order. He looks towards the sets of interests that ground particular social groupings and the selections of what constitute the culturally located sense of reality of their members. He is critical of the structures and institutions that engender, embody and project images of 'what is the case' and he wishes to look beyond to reveal the true conditions hidden by these mechanisms of distortion.

Bourdieu's structuralism is apparent throughout. He regards society as a surface structure of illusions from which his analysis will reveal the actual set of relations existing at the deep structural level. The transition between the levels will uncover homologies between previously disparate elements of the cultural system but simultaneously the individual actor will recede as a source of agency and intentionality in the construction of history.

A major contribution of Bourdieu's thought has been his development of a series of forceful metaphors to articulate the subtle relation of power and domination at work in the social world and through the stratification of culture. Most notable is that which he draws from political economy when he speaks of *cultural capital*: '. . . there is, diffused within a social space a cultural capital, transmitted by inheritance and invested in order to be cultivated.'[17]

Stratified socialisation practices and the system of education function to discriminate positively in favour of those members of society who, by virtue of their location within the class system, are the 'natural' inheritors of cultural capital. This is no crude conspiracy theory of a conscious manipulation, rather what is being explored here is the possibility of a cultural process that is self-sustaining and self-perpetuating. This process is regarded as carrying with it a context of anticipation and tolerance of stratification and privilege. In this way Bourdieu moves from the ideological function of culture into an awareness of the peculiar efficacy of culture in that it is seen as structuring the system of social relations by its functioning.

Within the analysis the education system thus comes to be treated as the means by which social privilege is allocated and confirmed, and it is the myth of pedagogic practice as value-free that enables this process to complete. This myth is all-engrossing in its opacity, that is, it envelopes all groups within society and thus produces complementary versions of the 'natural' order. Neither dominant nor oppressed groups suspect this latent function of the educational system and consequently perfect integrity is maintained at the level of each individual consciousness. 'School serves to transform the collective heritage into the common individual unconscious.'[18]

Therefore, as Bourdieu makes clear, even within a democratic society this manifestation of a disguised machinery continues to re-establish the inequalities of a social order which is pre-democratic in character and anti-democratic in essence.

Bourdieu includes within his definition of culture all semiotic

12

systems, ranging from language as a communicative network, through science to art and literature; all instances of a symbolic universe. He argues that all societal members actively involved in the creation and expressive reconstruction of such systems do so against the assumed backdrop of freedom and neutrality. This he points to as a grand illusion that is disguising the true political function of culture. As all members assume and become aware of reality through and within culture, they inevitably and unknowingly have the structure of existing power relations thrust upon them. This is a clear instance of what Bourdieu refers to as symbolic violence. The particular status groups who confer cultural legitimacy, like teachers and critics, conduct their professional roles and distribute merit with reference to an absolute index of intrinsic worth. This index and its acceptance mystifies the actual political situation, that cultural judgements and ranking are grounded in the protection of particular interests – indices of worth speak not of an absolute but of power and domination. The area of creative and artistic freedom is accounted for by Bourdieu through linking its emergence with the historical development and automisation of the system of production and consumption of cultural goods. This historical process generates what Bourdieu refers to as an *intellectual field*. Young clearly summarises this concept as follows:

> He (Bourdieu) conceives of the 'intellectual field' as the mediating set of agencies in which various groups of producers compete for cultural legitimacy. In elaborating on the idea of 'intellectual field' Bourdieu suggests the social and economic context for three aspects of the literary and art 'worlds' that are normally taken for granted. (1) The belief in 'art for art's sake'. (2) The assumption of the public's incompetence and the consequent refusal of artists to respond to public demands. (3) The growth of a group of critics who interpret artistic work for the public and give it legitimacy. Bourdieu refers to the 'creative project' as the activity in which the demands of the 'intellectual field' and the external context of the social and economic order of the time are joined in the work of art itself. Thus he suggests works of art and literature are formed in the context of public categories of definitions like 'nouvelle vague' and 'new novel' in terms of which the artist is defined and defines himself.[19]

Another important concept in Bourdieu's work is that of the *habitus*. This idea provides a link between the structuring of social relationships and the culture of a society. The habitus constitutes 'the principle that regulates the act'; it is typified as 'the system of modes of perception, of thinking, of appreciation and of action'.[20] The habitus is a concept that seems to take meaning at a number of different levels: it is in one sense the metaphor for membership of a community grounded in intellectual or aesthetic considerations yet it is also available as a key to integration into a Durkheimian creed of solidarity, a key that is acquired in early socialisation. So, for example, language can be considered as a habitus – certain ways of speech provide for membership of particular communities. These forms of speech, which instance membership, are far more than mere media for communication – they speak more than they can say. Such forms of speech are totemic, they are emblems, they symbolise the particular group, they carry with them the group's particular interests and orientations, and they display the group's thought style. At its most concrete, and yet still remarkably subtle, a sense of habitus may be rendered as 'style' – an idea foreign to most British social analysts (even after Hebdige) yet one absolutely central to the deep and painful recognition of class variations through accents, knots in ties, ways of holding cutlery, recognising appropriate wine glasses and so on.

Again, not unlike Bernstein's codes, certain habitus stand in disjunction with the habitus of the dominant group – the latter carrying with it a self-structuring sense of 'good taste', 'appropriate style', 'expressiveness' and so on, all of which are deemed meretricious within the institutions of the intellectual field. The possessors of the dominant group habitus are the inheritors of cultural capital, their form of reality and cognition is always appropriate . . . 'you can always tell a gentleman . . .' So different habitus constitute different forms of programming or equipping individuals such that they naturally gravitate towards their eventual, and proper, location in the stratification hierarchy . . . 'class will out . . .'

> It may be assumed that every individual owes to the type of schooling he has received a set of basic, deeply interiorised master-patterns on the basis of which he subsequently acquires other patterns, so that the system of patterns by

which his thought is organised owes its specific character not only to the nature of the patterns constituting it but also to the frequency with which these are used and to the level of consciousness at which they operate, these properties being probably connected with the circumstances in which the most fundamental intellectual patterns were acquired.[21]

Education and different socialisation variants function to transmit cultural capital in the form of particular valued signs and the styles of their presentation. Other habitus are consequently relegated to the status of stigma. Common sense representations come to realise different social locatedness through differential talent (or even 'blood'). School failure and indeed social stratification are rendered 'naturally' intelligible and the political differentiating function of the education system and family structure is obscured through the fog of public consensus. Bourdieu's other major concept of the *cultural unconscious* resonates strongly with the notion of habitus and also the Durkheimian 'collective consciousness'. It is intangible and made real through external referents. It refers to the tacit, assumed and unspoken grounds which precondition any cultural production. Within Bourdieu's model the cultural unconscious has an elective affinity with the dominant social interests of the epoch.

I will leave the chapters that follow to introduce themselves . . .

NOTES

1 M. Barrett, *et al. Ideology and Cultural Production*, London, Croom Helm, 1979.
2 T. Bennett, *et al. Culture, Ideology and Social Process*, Batsford, Open University, 1981.
3 M. Apple, *Cultural and Economic Reproduction in Education*, London, Routledge & Kegan Paul, 1982.
4 R. Williams, *Keywords*, Glasgow, Fontana, 1976.
5 H. Garfinkel, *Studies in Ethnomethodology*, Englewood Cliffs, NJ, Prentice-Hall, 1967.
6 B. Malinowski, *A Scientific Theory of Culture*, North Carolina, Chapel Hill, 1944, p. 17.
7 R. Firth, *Elements of Social Organisation*, London, Tavistock, 1971, p. 27.
8 T. Bottomore, *Sociology*, London, Unwin, 1962, p. 125.
9 P. Bourdieu, 'Symbolic power', in D. Gleeson (ed.) *Identity and Structure*, trans. C. Wringe, Humberside, Driffield, Nafferton, 1977.
10 R. Williams, *Culture*, Glasgow, Fontana, 1981.
11 E. Durkheim, *The Rules of Sociological Method*, New York, Free Press, 1938.

12 P. Hirst, *Durkheim, Bernard and Epistemology*, London, Routledge, 1975.
13 J. Smith and C. Jenks, *Durkheim, Art and Representation* (forthcoming).
14 A. Giddens, *The Constitution of Society: Outline of a Theory of Structuration*, Cambridge, Polity, 1984.
15 P. Bourdieu, 'Systems of education and systems of thought', in M.F.D. Young, *Knowledge and Control*, London, Collier-Macmillan, 1971, p. 192.
16 J. Kennett, 'The sociology of Pierre Bourdieu', *Educational Review*, 1973, vol. 25, pp. 237–49.
17 Bourdieu, 1971, op. cit., p. 201.
18 Bourdieu, 1971, op. cit., p. 200.
19 M.F.D. Young, *Knowledge and Control*, London, Collier-Macmillan, 1971, pp. 10–11.
20 P. Bourdieu, 'Intellectual field and creative project', in M.F.D. Young, 1971, op. cit., p. 184.
21 Ibid, pp. 192–3.

BIBLIOGRAPHY

Althusser, L. (1971) 'Ideological and repressive state apparatuses', *Lenin and Philosophy and Other Essays*, London, New Left Books.
Bernstein, B. (1971–3) *Class, Codes and Control*, Vols 1, 2 and 3, London, Routledge & Kegan Paul.
Bourdieu, P. (1977a) *Outline of a Theory of Practice*, Cambridge, Cambridge University Press.
—— (1977b) *Reproduction: In Education, Society and Culture*, London, Sage.
—— (1984) *Distinction: A Social Critique of the Judgement of Taste*, London, Routledge & Kegan Paul.
Cicourel, A. (1973) *Cognitive Sociology*, Harmondsworth, Penguin.
de Saussure, F. (1966) *Course in General Linguistics*, New York, McGraw-Hill.
Habermas, J. (1971) *Toward a Rational Society*, London, Heinemann.
Hebdige, D. (1979) *Subculture: The Meaning of Style*, London, Methuen.
Lévi-Strauss, C. (1976) *Triste Topique*, Harmondsworth, Penguin.
Merleau-Ponty, M. (1964) *The Primacy of Perception*, Evanston, Northwestern University Press.
Nietzsche, F. (1966) *Beyond Good and Evil*, New York, Vintage Books.
Parsons, T. (1968) *The Structure of Social Action*, New York, Free Press.
Wittgenstein, L. (1967) *Philosophical Investigations*, Oxford, Blackwell.

2

ECONOMY AND STRATEGY
The possibility of feminism
Malcolm Barnard

INTRODUCTION

The inclusion of a chapter on feminism's involvement with phallocentrism in a text dealing with cultural reproduction might seem entirely appropriate, even if, as here, it has been written by a man. And the inclusion of a chapter on Derrida's entanglements with logocentrism in such a text might seem wildly inappropriate, no matter who had written it. So a chapter linking Derrida's entanglements with logocentrism to feminism's involvement with phallocentrism might seem out of place wherever it appeared.

That phallocentrism and logocentrism are accomplices[1] and that there is some relationship between feminism and deconstruction may be taken as improper suggestions in some quarters. Some will say that the relationship must be a 'union forever deferred'[2] due to irreconcilable differences. Others will suspect priapic and duplicitous deconstruction of using feminism for its own gratification. There will be those who see cocky, cosmopolitan feminism moving out and setting up with deconstruction over at its place. And there may even be those who see deconstruction behaving very properly, proposing marriage to a flattered and blushing feminism.[3]

This chapter will explore the idea that deconstruction and feminism are always already living together. It will argue that logocentrism, one of Derrida's pseudonyms for the concern with appropriation and identification,[4] represents 'the masculine concern'.[5] If this is the case, then the attempt to critique the production of meaning and value in logocentric economy will by definition be a 'feminine operation'.[6] Thus the matter of identification and appropriation, including sexual identity, what is proper in sexual terms, is not to be subsumed into the domain of a general or fundamental ontology. To the contrary, 'propriation is more powerful than the question *ti esti*'; 'it is its process that organised both the totality of language's process and symbolic exchange in general'.[7]

The question, if it can still be said to be a question, of the proper is not a matter to be involved, as a regional ontology, in a larger or more fundamental ontology. To even ask the question 'What is?' is already to have decided the matter of propriation. To have decided this matter is the masculine concern. Moreover, to have decided the question of the proper is to have set in train the process that organises the economy of language and symbolic exchange in general. Culture, and its reproduction, then, are already governed by the values of the proper and identification. To this extent, it may be surprising that there are not more chapters in this volume dealing with Derrida's entanglements with logocentrism. Similarly, if the concepts and values that would seem to form sexual differences are based on a 'process of propriation',[8] then it cannot be any more or less improper for this chapter to have been written by a man.

Logocentrism, as the 'masculine concern', is thus phallocentrism, and Derrida does refer to 'phallogocentrism'.[9] The critique of phallocentrism, commonly or vulgarly[10] called feminism, is thus always already living with deconstruction, the critique of logocentrism. No longer a vulgar feminism, feminism has always already moved out of its own proper and private place[11] to be entangled at the limits of thought and language, where the question 'What *is* property? What *is* appropriation?' is no longer possible, where propriation is finally undecidable.[12] Non-vulgar feminism thus does not have its own place, nor does it have a proper set of concerns. What would be an improper suggestion and what would be a proper concern of feminism are thus open to question, the question of the possibility of feminism.

ECONOMY AND FEMINISM

This section will establish the problems facing feminism and deconstruction, phallocentrism and logocentrism, as matters of economy. Explaining economy as a relationship between identity, difference and opposition, it will thus elucidate Derrida's claim that phallocentrism and logocentrism are 'one and the same system'.[13] Having done this, the next section will look at the problems involved in adopting a strategy to critique or oppose that system or economy.

In *Positions*, Derrida says that 'differance is *the* economical concept and since there is no economy without differance, it is the most general structure of economy'.[14] He also says that what he calls metaphysics amounts to 'a subordination of the movement of differance in favour of a value or meaning supposedly antecedent to differance . . . governing it in the last analysis'.[15]

Where metaphysics posits the presence of a meaning or value as the source or origin of other values, Derrida attempts to indicate the work of the economy of differance, 'the non-full, non-simple "origin" . . . the structured and differing "origin"',[16] as the 'absolute production and destruction of value'.[17]

Differance is the absolute production of value in that it is the endless and eccentric interplay of oppositions in which elements relate and refer to one another and by means of which their value and meaning is generated. Insofar as differance may be conceived, for Derrida says that it is not a concept,[18] it may be conceived as a generalised and radicalised version of the diacriticity by means of which de Saussure holds that the value of the linguistic sign is produced. As the 'non-full, non-simple "origin" of differences', it is productive of the differences by means of which elements relate to one another and so come to have the value that they have.[19]

On the other hand, differance is the absolute destruction of value in that it would defer and postpone[20] the presence of any meaning or value that metaphysics might appeal to as the source or origin of value. It would show that the value which Derrida calls the 'transcendental signified'[21] or 'centre',[22] as supposed source of value, was always already inhabited by absence. As in de Saussure's diacriticity, that value would itself be part of an infinite play of deferring and differentiating relationships to other, absent, terms from which its value would derive. Where metaphysics posits a centre that is supposedly antecedent to the play of oppositive relations, Derrida's task is that of showing that the apparently self-present identity was already the result or product of those relations and would therefore be destroyed or deferred infinitely.

The 'common root'[23] of the conceptual oppositions of which language is built, differance is the 'structured and differing' origin of differences and thus of those conceptual oppositions. As structured, differance is the absolute production of value or identity

19

since it is the play of oppositions which, as seen in de Saussure, produces the value or identity of a particular term. As differing, it is the absolute destruction of value since it defers and postpones any full and simply present element in relation to which another element could be said to have value. Insofar as the economy of differance is not 'governed by'[24] but would rather destroy the self-present identity of the centre posited by metaphysics as the source of value, it may be called ec-centric economy.

Thus an identity or value only acquires that identity or value in the economy of differance. At the same time, however,[25] that value or identity is subverted or postponed. It is the relation to the other, to what is different and never present, that both constitutes and destroys or subverts value and identity in the economy of differance.

On the most general level, Derrida holds metaphysics to be the 'exigent, powerful, systematic and irrepressible desire for a transcendental signified'.[26] It is the desire for the 'subordination of the movement of differance in favour of the presence of a meaning or value supposedly antecedent to it'.[27] It could be said that metaphysics is indicative of a certain 'anxiety'[28] in the face of differance and the lack of full and simple origins that it entails. It is indicative of the desire to posit or possess some such source in order that the ec-centric free play of the economy of differance be curtailed and seen to issue from some stable and present source.

Supposedly antecedent to the economy of differance, the centre is held to provide a stable and fully present identity, the value of which is *not* produced through its relations with other not simply present values. The centre is thus a privileged term that has been set apart from or outside of the play of oppositive relations that would ultimately both produce and destroy its value.[29] This centre which is thus held to be outside the ec-centric economy of differance has at least two functions.

First, it is supposed to 'master', 'neutralise' or 'reduce'[30] the economy of differance. The economy of differance is 'neutralised or reduced . . . by . . . giving it a fixed centre or referring it to a point of presence, a fixed origin'. Thus the centre puts an end to the endless referral and deferral of differance. Second, the centre is to 'orient, balance and organise'[31] the economy that is established by the curtailing of differance. As such an entity, the centre provides some organising or governing principle in relation to which the other elements in the economy are said to have the value they have. In this sense, the centre is set up and privileged as being outside the differential relations that would at once produce and destroy value and identity. Thus it is held by metaphysics to be a stable and self-present identity that is the origin of value.

However, as Derrida says, metaphysics does not 'merely set up value oppositions around an ideal . . . limit',[32] it also subordinates those values to one another. In a given economy, there will be found such oppositions or subordinations as 'normal/abnormal, standard/parasite, fulfilled/void, serious/non-serious, literal/non-literal'. These, he says, reduce to a basic opposition or subordination – 'positive/negative and ideal/non-ideal'.[33] That is, while *all* the values produced within centred economy are held to be what they are by virtue of their relation to the centre, there are various terms that are held to be supplementary, to be secondary and thus subordinate, to the others.

These, then, are some of the major aspects of economy to be found in the work of Derrida. Derrida describes the operation whereby differance is reduced to centred economy as being performed by 'man as that being who, throughout the history of metaphysics . . . has dreamed of the full presence . . . the origin'.[34] This description of the desire to master the anxiety engendered by the lack of full and simple origins of value, however, raises explicitly a point that is significant for this essay and should be emphasised.

It is that, following Nietzsche,[35] Derrida calls the play of difference, as both the production and destruction of value, the feminine operation.[36] Similarly, he calls the setting up and workings of centred economy the masculine operation.[37] That is, at the 'moment' a centre is set up to order the various differences and regulate the production of value, any number of other centres are set up to organise other differences in other areas. The opernation is 'the same' in all these areas. As Derrida says, 'it is one and the same system: the erection of a paternal logos'.[38]

If, as Derrida says, differance is both the general structure and some sort of condition for economy,[39] and if the reduction of ec-centric economy involves 'motivations and relations of force',[40] then not only is that reduction a 'sexual operation but before it there was no sexuality'.[41] To reduce ec-centric economy to centred economy, of which sexuality is an example, is to decide what is properly sexual, as opposed to what is not sexual, and to decide the values and identities that have been constituted within that economy. An example of such a reduction would be Freud's 'demonstration' that children, who were supposed to be pre-eminently non-sexual beings, were actually part of sexual economy. There was no sexuality, in the sense in which it is familiar from within centred economy, before the operation that reduced ec-centric economy to centric economy because the ec-centric economy of differance would both produce and destroy the identity of whatever it was that was held to be properly sexual.

'Before' the reduction of ec-centric economy to centred economy, everything and nothing was properly sexual: identities and differences, motivations and forces, among which what are, in centred sexual economy, called sexual identities, differences and so on, are to be found in ec-centric economy but precisely *not* as organised in centred economy. As such, the identities, differences, motivations and forces of ec-centric economy are organised, their value as either sexual or non-sexual, for example, being decided in terms of the relation to the centre.

In this sense, then, the movement from ec-centric economy (differance) to centred economy (metaphysics, logocentrism) is a sexual operation that institutes sexuality. The identities, differences, motivations and forces that are referred to in centred economy 'exist' 'prior' to the reduction to centred economy but not as they are organised or referred to in centred economy. Thus the operation is sexual in a non-vulgar sense, a sense that is not familiar from the organisation of sexuality in centred economy.

As a sexual operation, the reduction of the economy of differance to centred economy is called masculine in what should be referred to as a vulgar sense. This is because differance, as the absolute production and destruction of value and identity, would defer and postpone all attempts to provide or ascribe a proper sense or identity. It would preclude the possibility of identifying an operation as properly masculine *or* feminine. The vulgar sense of masculine is that which is usual, the value of which has itself been produced in centred economy, an economy which involves the privileging of an identity, the centre.

Similarly, as a sexual operation, the effects of differance are termed the feminine operation in what must be understood as a non-vulgar sense. The feminine, as it indicates the subversive and identity-disrupting work of differance, is to be understood in a non-vulgar sense in the same way and for the same reasons as *écriture* in *Of Grammatology* is intended in a non-vulgar sense. Where *écriture* is not writing in the sense in which the logocentric tradition identifies and values it, but is rather the 'writing' that is interior to speech, so the 'feminine' operation is not the value or identity that the phallocentric tradition has generated. It is, rather, an operation that would show the disruptive undecidable within what is supposed to be a self-identity and from which it was supposed to have been excluded.

Insofar as vulgar masculinity has been identified with reason and logic, for example, and insofar as reason and logic are classically based upon the principle of identity, from which the laws of thought are held to follow, then the reduction of ec-centric economy to centred economy (of an economy which would subvert identity to one which privileges a particular identity as source of value) is termed the vulgarly masculine operation. And insofar as the value of non-vulgar femininity would not be produced in terms of one or other of the dichotomous poles of phallocentric economy (which would produce an identity that was either masculine or supplementary), then the effects of the economy of differance may be termed the non-vulgarly feminine operation. 'Not answering'[42] to phallocentrism, but rather producing and destroying value and identity, the economy of differance is called feminine in a non-vulgar sense.

Logocentrism and phallocentrism are 'one and the same system',[43] then, in that they both involve the reduction of differance to centred economy. They both 'curtail' the radical diacriticity of differance which is, at the same time, both the absolute production and the absolute destruction of value, by means of providing an organising principle. That organising principle, or centre, 'regulates' the restricted economy that is formed, providing a supposedly 'full' and simple value in terms of which terms within the economy are said to have meaning or value. In logocentrism, the centre is *logos*, the supposedly full and simple self-presence of the spoken word. It is *logos* that organises the economy of logocentrism and in terms of which logocrats like Husserl and de Saussure ascribe value to writing. And in phallocentrism, the centre is the phallus. It is the phallus that regulates the economy of phallocentrism, ascribing and organising the distribution of value.

One of Derrida's pseudonyms for the process of reducing the economy of differance is propriation. The history of thought or metaphysics, he says, 'like the history of the West',[44] may be

23

conceived 'as a series of substitutions of centre for centre'.[45] So the history of thought and truth may be conceived as a 'process of propriation',[46] a history of the various reductions of the economy of differance. Insofar as propriation is a sexual operation and insofar as phallocentrism and logocentrism are instances of propriation, then logocentrism and phallocentrism are 'accomplices'.[47] The move towards the reduction of differance is itself a sexual operation, for Derrida, and according to him it is the masculine concern to want to make this move. So, any attempt to critique or oppose that move, to adopt a critical stance with regard to propriation, will be 'feminist'.

Feminism and deconstruction, then, are always already living together. As the attempt to critique the reduction of ec-centric economy or differance, deconstruction is always already in feminism's place. However, deconstruction is what has been referred to as a 'non-vulgar' feminism; its value has not itself been produced in centred economy. Thus, while deconstruction is a form of feminism, not all feminisms are deconstructive. The next section will investigate the possibility of producing a critique of the masculine concern that will not be appropriated by that concern – the possibility of feminism.

ECONOMY AND STRATEGY

This section will consider the question of how to oppose or critique the operations of centred economy. It will look at how the nature of economy affects the chances of a discourse or practice that is attempting to oppose phallocentrism not being appropriated by that economy. The possibility of not being appropriated by that economy, not being rendered proper and thus harmless, by centred economy has been seen to be the possibility of feminism. The section will first look at the two types of what has been referred to as 'vulgar'[48] feminism, reversal and refusal. It will then assess their chances of successfully opposing or critiquing what has been identified as phallocentrism before examining some attempts at what might be called deconstructive feminism.

It will be recalled from the previous section that, in centred economy, values are not only 'set up . . . around an ideal',[49] they are also organised in such a way that one term of a dichotomous pair is supplementary or subordinate to the other.[50] There are two kinds of reversalist strategy. The first kind reverses the positions accorded the terms of the hierarchy on the grounds that the identity deemed appropriate to the supplementary term in phallocentric economy is at least as valuable as that deemed to justify the status of the superior term. Such a strategy would, then, privilege the hitherto supplementary term on the grounds that its identity in centred economy is at least as valuable and no less ideal than the identity of the superior term.

Thus, for example, Leghorn and Parker, exploring what they call 'the economy of the world of women',[51] make a list of some of the characteristics that women have traditionally been supposed to possess. This list of the properties that phallocentric society has ascribed to women also includes ideas as to the sorts of power relations that are supposed to be appropriate to women and is to be used as a guide 'in exploring the notion of a woman's culture'.[52]

From this list, one learns, among other things, that women are 'creators of life, nurturing and caring . . . clever at making something out of nothing . . . [and] getting round barriers erected to keep them back'.[53] These are some of the values which, on this form of feminist strategy, are to be privileged to provide the centre of a female value-based economy. They are those which had previously been supposed to justify women's supplementary status within the phallocentric economy that is being contested.

The sort of power relations to be instituted within this female value-based economy are also hinted at. They will involve the capacity to 'get round barriers' and they will be 'indirect'.[54] Such a notion of power 'does not imply coercion', but 'has more to do with creativity and cooperation'.[55] Again, such a notion of the operation of power is that which was considered appropriate to women within the original economy: this kind of reversal is intended to valorise and universalise it above the sort of power relations that were supposed to be appropriate to men.

Elements of the same strategy may also be found in the work of Duras and Chawaf. Duras considers women to have been associated with darkness and obscurity in phallocentric economy: 'women have been in darkness for centuries', she says, and 'women have never known what they were'. In the face of this, she advises 'making darkness the point of departure for judging what men call light' and making 'obscurity the point of departure for judging what men call clarity'.[56] That is, those things that women have been associated with or deemed to be in phallocentric economy are now to be made 'the point of departure' for a new female economy – they are to form the origin or centre of that economy.

Similarly, Chawaf considers that phallocentrism, in the guise of 'classicism and rationalism', has repressed the sensual, 'sensorial' and corporeal aspects of language.[57] Women have been associated with these long-repressed material aspects ('material language corresponds to our historical place', she says), and have been similarly repressed. The form that opposition is to take, according to Chawaf, is that of a feminine language which is 'in touch'[58] with those hitherto repressed aspects and which will 'disintellectualise' writing, bringing it back to an appreciation of the organic life of the word.

The second form of reversalist strategy would involve the privileging of the hitherto supplementary term on the grounds that it actually possessed the characteristics that were held to justify the superior term's or group's status. This form of strategy would attempt to show that the supposedly inferior term ought to be equally privileged because it was all the things, because it had all the properties, which it had been held to lack.

A version of this second form of reversalist strategy may be seen in what Kristeva summarises as 'the political demands of women, the struggles for equal pay for equal work, for taking power in social institutions on an equal footing with men and the rejection, where necessary, of the attributes traditionally considered feminine or maternal'.[59] This strategy attempts to demonstrate that women are all the things that men are supposed to be and demands their insertion into positions and relations of power that had traditionally been denied them. It also involves the acknowledgement that women, no less than men, are, in relation to the centre, phallomorphic values.

Thus, where in phallocentric society, the attributes of aggression, competitiveness and emotional distance, for example,[60] are privileged and held to be appropriate qualities for those in powerful and important positions, and where men are held to be particularly well suited for these positions, this strategy would attempt to show that women are also competitive and so on. It would attempt to show that women are 'the same as' men and support the insertion of women into those positions that had been held to be important on the grounds that women, too, could wield power.

These are the two kinds of reversalist strategy adopted by vulgar feminism. There are also two kinds of refusalist strategy. On the matter of economy, the first form of refusal would consist in the attempt to reject or step outside of all centrisms on the grounds that all are inherently phallocentric, based as they are on the privileging of self-present, self-identical values. Where it has been seen that the privileging of identity and the reduction of differance to centred economy is the masculine concern, this form of feminism would attempt to refuse all instances of centred economy. Such a strategy would support all attempts at resisting the ascription of properties to both supplementary and superior terms and would reject the notion of the production of identities in centred economy.

Such a form of refusal may also take the form of refusing all forms of philosophical or theoretical discourse. Philosophy and theoretical discourse being based on the privileging of identity, those discourses would be seen as instances of phallocentric economy and refused as such. The feminists noted by Clément may be used to illustrate such a form of refusal. At the 1975 Week of Marxist Thought, a group of feminists interrupted the speeches from the floor. Clément reports that the supposedly reasoned speeches from the stage were disrupted by 'shouts, mimicking, gestures and . . . piercing cries of "Hey, Hey" '.[61]

She explains that the feminists who interrupted considered articulated speech and theoretical discourse to be phallocentric. They would, presumably, have argued that 'language is always masculine' since, in order for sense to be made, there must be a centre to the economy of language. Thus those feminists were only 'allowed' shouted speech and 'could not use thought to help free themselves'[62] and other women from inclusion and repression within phallocentric economy.

The second form of refusal consists in the attempt to step outside of a particular economy. It aims at the institution of a specific alternative economy by means of which the original and offensive one could be opposed. It differs in this last respect from the first form of reversal, noted above, in that it attempts to set up an economy the centre of which is neither the value which the original economy privileged nor the value which was deemed to be supplementary. The centre of the economy to be set up on this view is rather a different value – one which is specific to the hitherto supplementary term but neither that which was privileged nor that which was supplementary in the previous economy.

There are difficulties in describing this form of feminist

strategy. The problem is that any feminism which asserts itself as creating a specifically feminine economy is always open to the charge of being centred precisely on those values which were held to be of supplementary value and thus not a specifically feminine economy at all. However, the work of Duras and Chawaf, along with the others who are concerned with the possibility of an *écriture feminine*, for example, may be described as attempts at creating such an economy. Kristeva also describes some of this sort of feminist when she speaks of those who are 'essentially interested in the specificity of female psychology . . . [and seeking] to give a language to the intra-subjective and corporeal experience left mute by culture in the past'.[63]

These are the basic elements of the two forms of vulgar feminism. The nature of economy determines their chances of successfully opposing or critiquing centred economy, phallo-centric economy. The problems likely to be faced by these forms of feminism can be simply enumerated.

In view of the nature of what Derrida calls metaphysics, centred economy, it may be said that the first form of reversal is hardly a form of opposition to metaphysics at all. Metaphysics involves centred economy, the production of stable value and identity by means of the relation to the centre, and the positing of properties by means of which supplementarity is justified; this strategy affects neither.

Moreover, the values on the basis of which the supplementary term is now to be privileged are precisely those laid down or ascribed by the economy that this strategy should be critiquing. Were it not a thoroughly metaphysical distinction, it could be said that this sort of feminism affects neither the form nor the content of centred economy since it retains the idea of centred economy (with the resulting positions of supplementarity and so on), and since the values it proposes to make the centre of the alternative economy are only those which had been held to be of supplementary value in the original economy.

The second form of reversalist strategy also admits of the objection that it operates wholly in terms of the original economy that is being opposed. To privilege the hitherto supplementary term on the grounds that it possesses the properties previously denied it affects neither the idea of centred economy nor the properties ascribed by that economy. This strategy simply shows that the supplementary term is of the same nature, the same metaphysically produced nature, as the superior term: it deals with neither production of the value of the centre nor the nature of centred economy.

The second type of feminism, refusal, fares little better in the matter of opposing centred economy. The question as to whether it is in fact possible to step outside of all centred economy can be raised. The question as to whether, even if it is possible, it would be a good thing to step outside of all centred economy can also be raised. If, as Derrida says, the centreless economy represents the unthinkable,[64] and if thought itself is centred economy, then it would seem plausible to suppose that it would be impossible even to conceive what it would be to refuse all centred economy, let alone communicate one's findings having refused it. Moreover, supposing that it was possible to refuse all centred economy, that incommunicability would be likely to condemn those who had accomplished it to even greater marginality than they enjoyed before.

The second type of refusal consists in the attempt to step outside phallocentric economy and set up some alternative economy. This alternative economy will privilege women, presumably, on the basis of the properties they are held to possess but which are not those that were ascribed in phallocentric economy. It attempts, then, to centre an economy on some specifically feminine values and oppose the original economy.

As such, it does not challenge the idea or practice of centred economy. An economy that has specifically feminine values, whatever they would be, as centre is no less a phallocentric economy in that it is the role or rule of the centre that has been seen to be the masculine concern. Kristeva comments on these forms of feminism: they 'revive a kind of naïve romanticism, a belief in identity', that is the reverse of phallocratism.[65] De Beauvoir objects analogously: 'it would be an error to make of [the female body] a value and think that the feminine body gives you a new vision of the world. It would be ridiculous and absurd . . . like constructing a counter-penis.'[66]

Secondly, and like the first form of refusal, this strategy runs the risk of condemning women to positions of even greater marginality or supplementarity. In a sense, the reception of some French feminism, if not French thought generally, in Anglophone countries may be said to illustrate this situation. Jardine comments, in her introduction to Kristeva's 'Woman's Time', that

29

many American feminists will experience 'vertiginous and difficult' problems with the text because it is written from an unfamiliar tradition and attempts to articulate unfamiliar problems.[67] The alternative centre and the values it is held to generate may be such that the 'dominant economy' can afford to ignore them; those values will therefore not affect the original economy in any way.

The third form of feminism consists in a version of Derrida's deconstructive strategies. Where Derrida's deconstructions have been claimed to be always already feminist in dealing with metaphysics or logocentrism, these feminisms adopt deconstructive strategies in dealing with phallocentrism. This form of feminism consists in the attempt to chart the movements of ec-centric economy, differance, in what is presented as centred economy. It attempts to show how the identities and values that are produced in centred economy are based on the occlusion and mastering of ec-centric, non-vulgarly feminist, economy.

In one way, versions of this form of feminism are hard to find in that they seem to admit of the objection that they simply take over the economy that was considered proper to women in the first place and then to privilege it over what was considered properly masculine. This form of feminism may be distinguished from vulgar reversal, however, by a 'doubled strategy'. 'First', it attempts to render identity and property problematic through the demonstration that what was thought to be proper to the supplementary term and held to justify its inferior status is no less, and no more, proper to the supposedly superior term. The second stage consists in what Derrida has referred to as the 'irruptive emergence'[68] of a third term which refuses to settle into an identity. This third term is thus held to defer the possibility of the normalising and appropriating *aufhebung* that characterises the third term found in dialectics.

Evidence of such a strategy may be found in the work of such feminists as Cixous, Irigaray and Kristeva. Irigaray, for example, has been concerned with the value or identity of female sexuality as it has been produced in phallocentric economy. She says 'female sexuality has always been theorised within masculine parameters'.[69] It has been organised in terms of the opposition '"virile" clitoral activity/"feminine" vaginal passivity' and in relation to the penis and castration.[70]

As such, and as the title of the work from which these comments are taken indicates, female sexuality is a sex 'which is not one'.

That is, female sexuality is not considered to be a proper or genuine sexuality within these masculine limits. In various accounts of female sexuality, in that of Freud, for example, the clitoris is not defined on its own terms, whatever they would be, but rather as a small penis, as homologous to the penis.[71]

Irigaray is keen to stress, though, that female sexuality is also 'not one' in another sense, in the sense that it is 'always at least double . . . plural'. Female sexuality cannot be defined as a unity, as a One, since it involves at least two lips which constantly touch and retouch each other in such a way that it is impossible 'to distinguish exactly what parts are touching each other'.[72] Irigaray can be read as attempting to establish and emphasise the affinity between female sexuality and Derrida's dissemination. Irigaray's version of female sexuality, like Derrida's dissemination, 'mutilates the unity of the signifier, that is, of the phallus'.[73]

So, there is no unity to female sexuality, it is an irreducible plurality and resists appropriation into phallocentric economy. This is held to be the case, not only on an anatomical level, but also at the level of pleasure. In addition to the vaginal caress, there are 'gently stroking the posterior wall of the vagina, lightly massaging the cervix etc', to 'evoke some of the more specifically feminine pleasures' and to disrupt the phallocentric economy of pleasure, which operates in terms of active and passive principles and is organised in terms of the *telos* of orgasm.[74] Thus, 'woman's pleasure . . . poses a problem for any current economy in that all computations that attempt to account for women's incalculable pleasure are irremediably destined to fail'. This is because female sexuality 'diverts the linearity of a project, undermines the target object of a desire, explodes the polarisation onto only one pleasure and disconcerts fidelity to only one discourse'.[75]

Thus where phallocentrism 'mercilessly represses the uncontrollable multiplicity of ambiguity, the disseminating play of writing, which irreducibly transgresses any unequivocal meaning',[76] Irigaray posits a radical plurality. This plurality, as Foss points out, is not to be confused with the casual use of a fashionable epithet.[77] Property and identity are foreign to this plurality, as Irigaray says, 'property and propriety are undoubtedly quite foreign to all that is female'.[78]

In Irigaray's account, then, female sexuality is ec-centric economy which resists identification and appropriation by phallocentric economy and which disrupts and decentres that economy. It does this in such a way, moreover, that it cannot be said that 'female sexuality is such and such a thing'. And, although there is no explicit mention of a third term, it is claimed that Irigaray's feminism may be seen as an example of deconstructive feminism in that it attempts the disconcerting of propriety and proper identity. Female sexuality itself may be thought of as a third term in that it is clearly not the sexuality formed in phallocentric economy and in that it would disrupt any such centred economy. It functions, then, much in the way that Derrida's undecidables function. 'Hymen', 'pharmakon' and *écriture* are also disrupting elements to which no property or propriety may be ascribed.[79]

It is claimed, then, that this third form of feminist strategy alone constitutes a critical or opposing practice that will not be simply appropriated and rendered harmless to phallocentric economy. In that it is neither a form of reversal, amounting, as Derrida says, to little more than a 'clamorous declaration of the antithesis',[80] nor a form of refusal, a simple opposition which, as opposition, is already swallowed up in the discourse it claims to have refused,[81] this form of feminism does not differ from and oppose phallocentric economy in the way that difference and opposition are organised in phallocentric economy. Consequently, it constitutes a non-vulgar feminism, a feminism the value and identity of which is not derived from its phallocentric difference from and opposition to the masculine concern.

That is, centred economy was said to be a matter of a relationship between identity, difference and opposition. These were organised in such a way that stable identities and values were generated by virtue of the relation to the centre which oriented the differences between the other terms by means of opposition and hierarchy. In that centred economy was traditionally or vulgarly associated with masculinity, this economic organisation was called phallocentric economy.

Phallocentric economy organised difference and opposition in a particular way. Thus any practice attempting to be different from and opposed to phallocentric economy which was different from it and opposed to it in the ways that phallocentric economy organised difference and opposition could not, ultimately, be critical of that economy. Insofar as differentiation and opposition were only those to be found in phallocentric economy, a practice that made use of them could only be a vulgar feminism. As such, it would only be another version of phallocentrism, the masculine concern. And, as *such*, it would already have been appropriated by, rendered harmless by because proper to, the masculine concern.

Thus the sort of difference and opposition exemplified by both forms of reversal consists, as their names suggest, in a reversal of the privilege accorded one of the two terms of the hierarchy. And the sort of difference and opposition exemplified in both forms of refusal consists in the rejection of the centre of the economy that is being contested. In both cases, difference and opposition are organised in relation to the value of the centre. Both forms of feminism, then, both forms of strategy, are vulgar feminisms.

CONCLUSION

This chapter[82] claims to have shown how phallocentrism and logo-centrism are 'accomplices'[83] – how they are one and the same system.[84] They are representatives of the masculine concern. Thus, non-vulgar feminism (feminism which is not different and opposi-tive in the way difference and opposition are organised in centred economy) is always already living with deconstruction. Decon-struction, as a form of feminism, as a critique of the move to centred economy, is therefore in a position to chart the pro-duction and destruction of meaning and value in places that may seem to be entirely inappropriate to feminism since to have decided what *is* appropriate, what is proper, is to have made the move to centred economy, the masculine concern.

NOTES

1 J. Derrida, 'Avoir l'oreille de la philosophie' quoted in J. Culler, *On Deconstruction*, London, Routledge & Kegan Paul, 1982, p. 172 (hereafter *OD*).
2 F. Bartowksy, 'Feminism and deconstruction: a union forever de-ferred', *Enclitic*, 1980, vol. 4, no. 2, p. 70.
3 See J. Derrida, *Spurs/Éperons*, trans. B. Harlow, Chicago, University of Chicago Press, 1979, p. 53 (hereafter *S/É*).
4 Ibid., pp. 103–5.
5 Ibid., pp. 59–61.
6 Ibid., p. 109.
7 Ibid., p. 111.
8 Ibid., p. 109.
9 Ibid., p. 97.
10 J. Derrida, *Of Grammatology*, trans. G.C. Spivak, Baltimore, Johns Hopkins University Press, 1977, p. 56 (hereafter *OG*).

11 J. Derrida, *S/É*, p. 113.
12 Ibid., p. 111.
13 Derrida, op. cit., *OD*.
14 J. Derrida, *Positions*, trans. A. Bass, Chicago, University of Chicago Press, 1981, p. 8 (hereafter *Pos*).
15 Ibid., p. 29.
16 J. Derrida, *Speech and Phenomena*, trans. D. Allison, Evanston, Northwestern University Press, 1973, p. 141 (hereafter *SP*).
17 J. Derrida, *Writing and Difference*, trans. A. Bass, Chicago, University of Chicago Press, 1978, p. 271 (hereafter *WD*).
18 Derrida, *SP*, p. 140.
19 Derrida, *Pos*, pp. 8–9; F. de Saussure, *Course in General Linguistics*, trans. W. Baskin, London, Fontana, 1974.
20 Derrida, *SP*, p. 152.
21 Derrida, *Pos*, pp. 20, 27.
22 J. Derrida, 'Structure sign and play' (hereafter *SSP*), in R. Macksey and E. Donato (eds) *The Structuralist Controversy*, Baltimore, Johns Hopkins University Press, 1972, p. 248 (hereafter *SC*).
23 Derrida, *Pos*, p. 9.
24 Ibid., pp. 29, 41, 44.
25 J. Derrida, *Dissemination*, trans. B. Harlow, Chicago, University of Chicago Press, 1982, p. 6.
26 Derrida, *OG*, p. 49.
27 Derrida, *Pos*, p. 29.
28 Derrida, *SSP*, p. 248.
29 Ibid.
30 Ibid., p. 247.
31 Ibid.
32 J. Derrida, 'Limited Inc', in *Glyph*, vol. 2, Baltimore, Johns Hopkins University Press, 1977, p. 236.
33 Ibid.
34 Derrida, *SSP*, pp. 264–5.
35 F. Nietzsche, *The Gay Science*, trans. W. Kaufmann, New York, Vintage, 1974, §339, pp. 271–2.
36 Derrida, *S/É*, p. 57.
37 Ibid., p. 59.
38 Derrida, op. cit., *OD*.
39 Derrida, *Pos*, p. 88.
40 Ibid., p. 71.
41 Derrida, *S/É*, p. 111, but see original French text.
42 Ibid., p. 97.
43 Derrida, op. cit., *OD*.
44 Derrida, *WD*, p. 279.
45 Ibid.
46 Derrida, *S/É*, p. 111.
47 Derrida, op. cit., *OD*.
48 Derrida, *OG*, p. 56.
49 Derrida, 1977, op. cit. (see note 32).
50 Ibid.

51 L. Leghorn and K. Parker, *Woman's Worth*, London, Routledge & Kegan Paul, 1981, pp. 4, 235.
52 Ibid., p. 240.
53 Ibid., p. 238.
54 Ibid., p. 239.
55 Ibid., p. 287.
56 M. Duras, 'From an interview', in E. Marks and I. DeCourtivron (eds), *New French Feminisms*, New York, Schocken Books, 1981, pp. 174–6 (hereafter *NFF*).
57 C. Chawaf, 'Smothered creativity', in *NFF*, p. 177.
58 Ibid.
59 J. Kristeva, 'Woman's time', *Signs*, 1981, vol. 7, no. 1, p. 18.
60 Leghorn and Parker, op. cit., p. 240.
61 C. Clément, 'Enslaved enclave', in *NFF*, p. 135.
62 Ibid.
63 Kristeva, 1981, op. cit., p. 19.
64 Derrida, *SSP*, in *SC*, p. 248.
65 J. Kristeva, 'Woman can never be defined', in *NFF*, pp. 137–41.
66 S. de Beauvoir, 'The Second Sex', in *NFF*, p. 153.
67 A. Jardine, 'Introduction to Woman's time', in *Signs*, 1981, vol. 7, no. 1, p. 6.
68 Derrida, *Pos*, p. 42.
69 L. Irigaray, in *NFF*, p. 99.
70 Ibid.
71 S. Freud, *On Sexuality*, Penguin Freud Library, vol. 7, ed. A. Richards, Harmondsworth, Penguin, 1977, p. 195.
72 L. Irigaray, in *NFF*, pp. 101–2.
73 J. Derrida, quoted by B. Johnson, in 'The frame of reference', in R. Young (ed.) *Untying the Text*, London, Routledge & Kegan Paul, 1981, p. 232.
74 Irigaray, in *NFF*, pp. 102–3.
75 Ibid., pp. 104–5.
76 B. Johnson, in Young (ed.) op. cit.
77 P. Foss, 'The lottery of life', in M. Morris and P. Patton (eds), *Michel Foucault, Power, Truth, Strategy*, Sydney, Feral, 1979, p. 171.
78 Irigaray, in *NFF*, p. 104.
79 B. Martin provides another example of deconstructive feminism which contrasts with Derrida's and those presented here in 'Feminism, criticism and Foucault', *New German Critique*, Fall, 1982, no. 27, pp. 3–30.
80 Derrida, *S/É*, p. 95.
81 Ibid., pp. 117–19. See also *SSP* in *SC*, 1972.
82 This chapter is a much reduced version of some arguments discussed in my PhD which unfortunately (for me) remains unpublished.
83 Derrida, op. cit., *OD*.
84 Ibid.

3

THE NATURAL MAN AND THE VIRTUOUS WOMAN

Reproducing citizens

James Donald

Cultural reproduction is impossible. At least, it is impossible in the sense that Freud ruefully acknowledged the limits and frustrations of his work in the last text he wrote: 'It almost looks as if analysis were the third of those "impossible" professions in which one can be sure beforehand of achieving unsatisfying results. The other two, which have been known much longer, are education and government.' Perhaps he was remembering an earlier philosopher's perplexity. 'There are two human inventions which may be considered more difficult than any others,' Kant had warned; 'the art of government, and the art of education; and people still contend as to their very meaning.'[1]

Why are education and government such difficult arts not only to do, but even to define? The justified bafflement of Freud and Kant undermines any notion of cultural reproduction based on reassuring sociological and psychological narratives about the 'outside' of society impinging on the 'inside' of the individual psyche. Implicit in Freud's 'impossibility' is the central enigma for any social or cultural theory; that is, the contingency and the evanescence of both 'human nature' and 'the social'.

Stated simply, the paradox that theories of reproduction seek to explain is this: people make society, and yet society makes people. People act in self-directed and intentional ways, and yet the patterns of consciousness, perception and desire that inform their actions are already aspects of social being. Personality is socially determined, and yet people do act effectively in and on social institutions. The challenge is therefore to see both how people's field of possible actions is structured; and also how these structures are negotiated in practice. The relationship is neither a one-way determination, nor even a dialectic; it is characterised by oscillation, slippage and unpredictable transformations.

This is, I think, the problem that Bourdieu addresses through his concept of *habitus*, at least when he defines it as 'the durably installed generative principle of regulated improvisations'.[2] That presupposes a picture of culture as a polylogic field of forces. Within this field, the domain of the social is instituted through the dissemination of intersubjective terms of authority by, for example, the apparatuses of government and education. At the same time, it is in the negotiation, recombination and *bricolage* of these structures – the *regulated improvisations* through which the norms of cultural authority are transgressed and reworked in the very moment they are instituted – that the identification of subjectivity and the individuation of agency emerge contiguously as boundaries. Where I suspect I part company from Bourdieu is in trying to understand this process. Identity cannot be derived from a homogeneous notion of collective identity (such as race, class or gender), any more than agency can be attributed to a transcendent individualism. Rather, individuation is achieved in the split between identity and agency, a split which then allows an articulation between the two. To be 'a citizen' in a modern liberal democracy, for example, is to be both a member of the imagined community of the nation *and* a self-conscious and self-monitoring ethical being. But the pedagogic status of 'British citizenship' (its claim to tell you who you are) is always put into doubt by the performativity of agency (which requires that you be author of your own utterances and actions).[3]

Although subjectivity and agency are effects of these pedagogic norms, then, they are never just their realisation. Bourdieu is therefore quite right to emphasise the unrecorded but resourceful improvisations of everyday life. But what makes cultural reproduction both necessary and impossible is the dynamic of authority and agency instituted through the post-Enlightenment aspiration to government through technologies of social adaptation. That is the story I want to tell here. Firstly, I draw out the social imaginary at work in Rousseau's writings on 'the child' and 'the citizen' and in his prescriptions for the forms of education appropriate to them. Secondly, I link this narrative of socialisation to a Foucauldian conception of government; which, thirdly, I critique from a more psychoanalytic perspective.

ENLIGHTENMENT AND EDUCATION
Kant saw education as a way of liberating 'man' from the tutelage and dependence to which ignorance condemned him. This liberty could only be achieved through socialisation, however, by learning to recover what is natural. 'Man can only become man by education', he wrote. 'He is merely what education makes him.' To be 'man' is to act freely. But to be able to act freely, to become what he already was in essence, 'man' has to go through a process of socialisation – which may be formalised as education or may be the sentimental education of biographical experience. In schooling, Kant insists, the child's capacity for independence and rationality can only be achieved through the imposition of restraint: 'we must prove to him that restraint is only laid upon him that he may learn in time to use his liberty aright, and that his mind is being cultivated so that one day he may be free; that is, independent of the help of others.' Liberty is managed. It is a form of conduct to be learned. It is not an Edenic state of absolute freedom beyond the demands and boundaries of the social, but a capacity for acting autonomously within social rules and forms.[4]

The paradox of individual freedom being achieved through the submission to pedagogic norms is most dramatically expressed by Rousseau. Indeed, at first sight he appears to be saying two quite contradictory things. In *Émile*, he argues passionately that the child needs to be protected from premature exposure to the corruptions of society if it is to have any chance of growing or developing naturally. And yet in *The Social Contract* he suggests with equal force that it is only through active participation in the business of society that man develops his intellectual and moral capacities:

> . . . although in civil society man surrenders some of the advantages that belong to the state of nature, he gains in return far greater ones: his faculties are so exercised and developed, his sentiments so ennobled, and his whole spirit so elevated that, if the abuse of his new condition did not in many cases lower him to something worse than what he had left, he should constantly bless the happy hour that lifted him for ever from the state of nature and from a stupid, limited animal made a creature of intelligence and a man.

To make sense of this tension, it needs to be plotted against two axes in Rousseau's thought that intersect in his critique of the liberal social contract as a device for maintaining inequitable social relations. One axis is ethical and teleological. At its retrospective pole, it postulates a state of nature from which a possessive and competitive society emerged, and so indicates the costs as well as the benefits of that transformation. At its prophetic pole, it imagines a future society in which free and equal individuals might create a political order based on self-assumed political obligation – and thus in tune with what is true and enduring in human nature. The axis defined by these poles of a reconstructed 'must-have-been' and a hypothetical 'could-be' make it possible to chart the weaknesses and duplicities of a corrupt present, as well as the dangers of changes in civil society that do not take account of man's nature. Rousseau's 'return to nature' does not signify regression to primitivism: 'when I want to train a natural man, I do not want to make him a savage and to send him back to the woods'. Rather, it offers a guide to surviving the present and creating a more democratic future. Similarly, the aspiration to freedom suggests not only an imaginable alternative to the experience of alienation, but a critical vantage point from which to deal with it.[5]

Whereas this first axis records social and historical transformations, the other charts the development and growth of the individual. Its poles are defined by Rousseau's contrast between 'the natural man' (or child) and 'the citizen'. 'The natural man lives for himself; he is the unit, the whole, dependent only on himself and his like. The citizen is but the numerator of a fraction, whose value depends on the community.' Rousseau recommends Plato's *Republic* as a guide to the education of citizens; children would have to be taken from their parents at birth and reared collectively.

> Good social institutions are those best fitted to make a man unnatural, to exchange his independence for dependence, to merge the unit in the group, so that he no longer regards himself as one but as part of the whole, and is only conscious of the common life.

Émile, by contrast, tells us how children should be educated in order to remain – or become – natural. Whereas citizens must be educated against nature, in accordance with the demands of society, boys and girls should be educated against society, in accordance with the innate pattern of their psychological development and their physical maturation.[6]

This is the *nature* of children that needs to be isolated from harmful social influences. 'Their defects of mind and body may all be traced to the same source, the desire to make men of them before their time.' But this nature cannot simply be allowed free rein: ' . . . there are so many contradictions between the rights of nature and the laws of society that to conciliate them we must continually contradict ourselves. Much art is required to prevent man in society from being altogether artificial.' Here the role of the Tutor becomes crucial in managing the child's environment in order to provide the spontaneous but desired changes.

> Let [your pupil] always think he is master while you are really master. There is no subjection so complete as that which preserves the forms of freedom; it is thus that the will itself is taken captive. Is not this poor child, without knowledge, strength, or wisdom, entirely at your mercy? Are you not master of his whole environment so far as it affects him? Cannot you make of him what you please? His work and play, his pleasure and pain, are they not, unknown to him, under your control? No doubt he ought only to do what he wants, but he ought to want to do nothing but what you want him to do.

The education Rousseau recommends thus involves the artifice and manipulation of 'well regulated liberty' rather than coercion or instruction. This regulation requires the definition of an external authority to which the child/citizen is subject, and yet which authorises him to act as a free agent. In *Émile*, this authority is that of nature; in *The Social Contract*, it is that of the general will. In both cases, the capacities and rules that enable the subject to know, to speak and to act are dramatised in a figure whose mastery and disinterested love are displayed through an incontrovertible competence; the Tutor and the Lawgiver. These then provide a point of symbolic identification; that is, 'identification with the very place *from where* we are being observed, *from where* we look at ourselves so that we appear to ourselves likeable, worthy of love'. It is thus as Émile identifies with the authoritative position from which he is observed by the Tutor that he is given a mandate to act as a free agent within the intersubjective symbolic network.[7]

In *Émile*, this agency appears as the interiorisation of a second nature that seeks to recreate the virtue embodied in the state of nature; a state deduced from man's potential for perfectibility within society. As Ernst Cassirer noted, Rousseau 'requires that Émile be educated *outside* society, because in this way alone can he be educated *for* society in the only true sense'. Thus the production of the good citizen comes to be understood as the supposed liberation of the natural child. If 'man was born free, and he is everywhere in chains', the future freedom to which Rousseau aspires is the transformation of these mind-forg'd manacles into equitable and reciprocal commitments between society and individual, into intersubjective bonds of union and love and respect. The virtuous citizen is the one who experiences these bonds as his or her own desires, aspirations and guilt, and thus evinces the capacity for self-policing. The well-ordered modern polity is one that depends less on coercion than on this self-policing of free citizens, and so can claim the authority of virtue and nature.[8]

YOUTH, NATURE AND VIRTUE

Rousseau's stories about the socialisation of youth and the formation of citizens did not just have a profound influence on educators like Pestalozzi in Europe and Horace Mann in the United States. They also set in place a definitive narrative of what it is to be, and to become, a social actor, which was to be widely elaborated, amended and contested in works of fiction and philosophy.

Émile, published in 1762, can thus be seen as paving the way for the *Bildungsroman* tradition in the European novel, with its tales of the moral formation of young men (or less often women) as they move from a restrictive provincial society to the dynamic but unsettling context of the city.[9] The founding text of this tradition, Goethe's *The Years of Apprenticeship of Wilhelm Meister* (1795–1806), takes from Rousseau not only his reconceptualised category of youth, but also the imagery of 'storm and stress' that fleshes out his view of the disjunction between the growth of individual capacities and desires and social codes of behaviour. What Wilhelm Meister learns in his biographical tribulations is to make choices that weigh the authenticity of the self against the demands of convention. This *Bildungsroman* narrative not only reflected a new experience of learning to live with uncertainty and vulnerability, but also learning to transform them into a capacity for self-creation and recreation. It also disseminated the categories of authenticity and convention, self and society, and creativity and compulsion that produced the terms for a new mode of conduct, a new relation of the self to the self.

It was primarily Romantic philosophers who took up the *Bildungsroman*'s categorical oppositions in their attempt to identify the capacities and competences necessary for self-formation. One of these was the practice of aesthetic reflection, and it was in this context that 'literature' and 'culture' were set in place as authoritative pedagogic categories. In *On the Aesthetic Education of Man*, for example – published, like Goethe's *Wilhelm Meister*, in 1795 – Schiller reconceptualised Rousseau's distinction between *l'homme naturel* and *l'homme artificiel* not in terms of fall and redemption, but more sociologically as a breach produced within man's ethical substance by the division of labour and the differentiation of spheres. But although 'it was civilisation [Kultur] itself which inflicted this wound upon modern man', it was nevertheless only culture that could heal the split between man's sensuous and rational drives. For Schiller, it is the task of culture 'to do justice to both drives equally: not simply to maintain the rational against the sensuous, but the sensuous against the rational too'. Works of art and literature could mediate and transcend the two drives through the impulse to play – a play regulated by the aesthetic tradition in much the same way as Émile's Tutor had managed the boy's physical environment. Thus the cultural authority of the Tutor was embodied in the works of art themselves. If studied properly, they demand, and so inculcate, perception, discrimination and self-correction. Although the development of such attributes does not represent a return to nature in Rousseau's sense, it too aspires to a state in which the dissociation of sensibility produced by the social is healed – here through the harmonising techniques of aesthetic response.[10]

At the same time as Goethe and Schiller were extending Rousseau's ideas about youth, education and self-formation, others were subjecting them to more radical readings. In her *Vindication of the Rights of Woman* (1792), for example, Mary Wollstonecraft had to recast his account of socialisation and citizenship in her attempt to rescue his republicanism for feminism. The scale and difficulty of the project are made evident by Rousseau's account of Sophy as the ideal companion for Émile. 'Sophy should be as truly a woman as Émile is a man, i.e., she must possess all those characters of her sex which are required to enable her to play her part in the physical and moral order.' That role, woman's nature, is a docile servility that disbars her from participation in the political life of the community. Her education should be guided by the fact that 'woman is made to please and to be in subjection to man'.

> To be pleasing in his sight, to win his respect and love, to train him in childhood, to tend him in manhood, to counsel and console, to make his life pleasant and happy, these are the duties of woman for all time, and this is what she should be taught while she is young.

Whereas Rousseau here invokes the brute fact of nature to justify women's exclusion from public participation, Wollstonecraft attributes sexual difference to the crippling conventions of socialisation. If women become little more than 'insignificant objects of desire', then blame their upbringing; if they become 'rakes at heart', then that is 'the inevitable consequence of their education'. 'Considering the length of time the women have been dependent,' asks Wollstonecraft, 'is it surprising that some of them hug their chains, and fawn like the spaniel?' For her, it was the unjustified and unjust 'divine right of husbands', not any natural deficiency, that disabled women. Women shared with men the God-given capacity to reason, even if this had atrophied through lack of use. If Rousseau's misrecognition of cultural attributes as innate characteristics were corrected, bourgeois women would become citizens as virtuous, effective and revolutionary as any man.[11]

Wollstonecraft goes beyond Rousseau by stressing that the exercise of liberty is contingent on having the means and opportunities to pursue self-chosen ends as well as to fulfil social obligations. Although she ascribes the degenerate state of women to culture rather than nature, however, she neither disputes Rousseau's assessment of the potential danger to social order of untrammelled female desire nor challenges his categories of nature and culture. The argument is once again that corruption should be ascribed to the effects of society and that (woman's) nature is inherently virtuous and rational. Wollstonecraft reproduces the Enlightenment view of liberty through socialisation; woman can only become woman by education.

A more spectacularly transgressive version of this argument appeared in the same post-Revolutionary moment as Wollstonecraft's *Vindication*. Whereas she tried to recuperate Rousseau's ideas, the Marquis de Sade's *Philosophy in the Bedroom* (1795) challenged their very foundations. Not only does Sade revel in the polymorphousness and irrationality of human desires, pleasures, perversions and cruelties, he also vigorously reviles the self-deception and hypocrisy of those virtuous citizens who disavow them. Here, then, is another tutor addressing his charge – this time Sade's Dolmancé.

> Ah, Eugénie, have done with virtues! Among the sacrifices that can be made to these counterfeit divinities is there one worth an instant of the pleasures one tastes in outraging them? Come, my sweet, virtue is but a chimera whose worship consists exclusively in perpetual immolations, in unnumbered rebellions against the temperament's inspirations. Can such impulses be natural? Does Nature recommend what offends her? Eugénie, be not the dupe of those women you hear called virtuous. Theirs are not, if you wish, the same passions as ours; but they hearken to others, and often more contemptible . . . There is ambition, there pride, there you find self-seeking . . .[12]

Eugénie, it has been suggested, is the double of the modest Sophy. Her transgressions are not only a deliberate affront to Sophy's virtues – as in the viciously ingenious vengeance she wreaks on her mother, the embodiment of long-suffering Rousseauian femininity – but also help to define their scope and limits. Virtue, proclaims Sade, cannot be rooted in nature because nature is radically amoral. This is the heresy that, as William Connolly observes, explodes Rousseau's moral universe.

> The Sadeian storm of passion and cruelty, raging within four walls of an imaginary bedroom, underlines the cosmic proportions of his opponents' narcissistic delusions; they demand that God inscribe guidelines and protections for the human comedy in the text of nature; they insist that the design of nature itself revolve around the fate of humanity.[13]

Sade thus de-deifies Nature, and by extension Reason too insofar as that is seen as an innate human capacity. He recasts the repression, self-deception and alienation imposed on the self by the demands of a socially prescribed virtue in terms more violently compelling than the *Bildungsroman* authors or the Romantic philosophers cared to consider. When he sketches his own version of the good society in the 'anonymous' pamphlet incorporated into *Philosophy in the Bedroom,* it is radically opposed to Rousseau's austere and strenuous republicanism. 'Yet Another Effort, Frenchmen, If You Would Become Republicans' envisages a minimal state that would set the stage for a libidinal anarchy.

GOVERNMENT AGENTS

Of course, Sade's account of nature, desire and agency, and the movement between them, is no more definitive than Rousseau's or Wollstonecraft's. By putting the normative categories and narratives of Enlightenment education so profoundly in question, however, Sade's pornographic pedagogy provides a useful contrast against which to set the techniques of public and mass schooling that emerged in the nineteenth and twentieth centuries. These have persistently attempted to shape children to their measure by means of disciplines that claim, like Rousseau's Tutor and Sade's Dolmancé, not only to understand the nature of the child, but to be able to emancipate it. They follow Rousseau rather than Sade, however, in suggesting that this will recover for civil society the virtues of its uncorrupted state. And, as Ian Hunter has argued persuasively in *Culture and Government,* they have followed the Romantic philosophers by proposing techniques of self-formation and self-monitoring based on self-expression within a morally managed environment.[14]

In this light, schooling can be seen as the paradigm of modern techniques of government. It works by deploying an intimate knowledge of the individuals who make up its target population, and an expertise in monitoring and guiding their conduct. Nikolas Rose explains this pastoral exercise of power in *Governing the Soul.*

> The conceptual systems devised within the 'human' sciences, the languages of analysis and explanation that they invented, the ways of speaking about human conduct that they constituted, have provided the means whereby human subjectivity and intersubjectivity could enter the calculations of the authorities. On the one hand, subjective features of human life can become elements within understandings of the economy, the organisation, the prison, the school, the factory and the labour market. On the other, the human psyche itself has become a possible domain for systematic

government in the pursuit of socio-political ends. Educate, cure, reform, punish – these are old imperatives no doubt. But the new vocabularies provided by the sciences of the psyche enable the aspirations of government to be articulated in terms of the knowledgeable management of the depths of the human soul.[15]

This sceptical attitude to the politics of expertise once again highlights the paradox that a degree of autonomous agency is both the target and the precondition of pastoral modes of power. Far from negating or denying freedom, argues Foucault, power requires freedom.

Power is exercised only over free subjects, and only insofar as they are free. By this we mean individual or collective subjects who are faced with a field of possibilities in which several ways of behaving, several reactions and diverse comportments may be realised. Where the determining factors saturate the whole there is no relationship of power . . .

This conception of power defines the conditions in which Foucault's 'governmentality' becomes a possibility. Here the subject is not only *subject to* the play of forces in the apparatuses of the social, but must also act as author and *subject of* its own conduct. Freedom is necessary because the machinery of government can only work on agency.

'Government' . . . designated the way in which the conduct of individuals or of groups might be directed; the government of children, of souls, of communities, of families, of the sick. It did not only cover the legitimately constituted forms of political or economic subjection, but also modes of action, more or less considered and calculated, which were destined to act upon the possibilities of action of other people. To govern, in this sense, is to structure the possible field of action of others.

Freedom thus appears not as the innate characteristic of a transcendent individual, but as the negotiation that produces individuation. Foucault calls it an *agonism*: 'a relationship which is at the same time reciprocal incitation and struggle; less of a face-to-face confrontation which paralyses both sides than a permanent provocation'.[16]

Whereas Rousseau believed that people's 'natural' character needed to be systematically 'mutilated' to shape it to the demands of citizenship, for Foucault the machinery of the social had become second nature. At its most effective, it operates as memory and as conscience. Donna Haraway captures this ambivalence in her image of the citizen as cyborg – a cybernetic organism, 'a fiction mapping our social and bodily reality'.

> Contemporary science fiction is full of cyborgs – creatures simultaneously animal and machine, who populate worlds ambiguously natural and crafted . . . By the late twentieth century, our time, a mythic time, we are all chimeras, theorised and fabricated hybrids of machine and organism; in short we are cyborgs. The cyborg is our ontology, it gives us our politics.

While cheerfully dismantling the distinction between pro-grammed information and human performance, Haraway goes even further than Foucault in suggesting that power relations can penetrate and inform the body without being mediated through the representations of consciousness. Foucault's insistence on the limits of consciousness lies behind his rejection of ideology as an explanation of agency. This does not imply, however, that there is nothing to be explained about how the programme is translated into subjective conduct and desire. That much is clear from his own questions about the finitude of the human: *What can I do? What do I know? What am I?* [17]

If structures of social authority are to appear in the form of such questions, that seems to me to presuppose the unconscious as a key mechanism in the formation of subjectivity. Only thus is it possible to grasp the relation of the self to itself that generates the indi-viduated conduct of pleasure, desire and intentionality. This is where my approach diverges not only from Bourdieu's notion of *habitus*, but also from post-Foucauldian analysts of cultural tech-niques like Ian Hunter and Nikolas Rose.

For them, it sometimes seems, individuals, automaton-like, simply act out the roles scripted for them. Thus Hunter, on the formation of trainee English teachers within a Kleinian English pedagogy: 'this is the form in which the student *internalises* the function of moral surveillance itself; finding in himself the onerous ethical antinomies and thereby beginning to shape a "balanced" self is the condition of shaping the selves of others'. Or, referring to an earlier form of progressive English teaching: 'Through adjustive techniques not unlike those which Donzelot has isolated in modern psychology, literary pedagogy *permits social norms to surface as personal desires* and personal desires to become the stake in social regulation'. Or Nikolas Rose on the family:

> The modern private family remains intensively governed, it is linked in so many ways with social, economic and political objectives. But government here acts not through mechanisms of social control and subordination of the will, but through the *promotion* of subjectivities, the *construction* of pleasures and ambitions, and the *activation* of guilt, anxiety, envy and disappointment. The new relational technologies of the family are *installed* within us, *establishing* a particular psychological way of viewing our family lives and speaking about them, *urging* a constant scrutiny of our inherently difficult interactions with our children and each other, a constant judgement of their consequences for health, adjustment, development, and the intellect. The tension generated by the gap between normality and actuality *bonds* our personal projects inseparably to expertise.

In this dance of language about what is going on in the transactions between the cybernetics and the organism – all this internalising, surfacing, promoting, constructing, activating, installing, establishing, urging and bonding – is it ever made clear exactly how social norms inform the texture of experience or how they are transformed in the process?[18]

For Hunter and Rose, this is a non-issue. In an article on representation, Hunter dismisses 'formal' modes of textual analysis because their conception of 'subjectivity' is limiting and reductionist: 'Social agency has no general form (subjectivity) whose structure can be read off from a theoretical analysis of meaning of the "subject-positions" made available by a linguistic system'. Nikolas Rose invokes Marcel Mauss to make the argument that 'the self' is a contingent social category. Quite correctly, he starts from the premise that, in the interplay between knowledge and power, historically variable definitions of the normal and the pathological act on, constrain and, in some sense, constitute populations and individuals.

'The self' does not pre-exist the forms of its social recognition; it is a heterogeneous and shifting resultant of the social expectations targeted upon it, the social duties accorded it, the norms according to which it is judged, the pleasures and pains that entice and coerce it, the forms of self-inspection inculcated in it, the language according to which it is spoken about and about which it learns to account for itself in thought and speech.

From this, however, he seems to infer that when social norms surface as personal desires, they will not have gone through the radical process of negotiation and transformation that Foucault referred to as *folding*. In Rose's account, the panoptic gaze of the apparatus sees all. Nothing is invisible or unknown; the subject should be no problem.[19]

And yet, as Rose admits in the comments on the family quoted above, the subject is always the problem. Even when 'the new relational technologies of the family are installed within us', there is still a 'gap between normality and actuality'. This makes family life 'inherently difficult'. The machinery never quite works.

The modern family . . . is a machine held together by the vectors of desire, and can only function through the desires that its members have for one another, and the operation of the family as a place where desires for the fulfilment of the self can be satisfied. Yet the incitement of 'social' desires required to fuel the familial mechanism is always threatened by the simultaneous incitement of desires out of bounds, anti-social desires, which can be satisfied only at the price of the destruction of that very socialisation the family is to achieve.[20]

If there is no self preceding the operations of the social machinery, however, where do these transgressive desires come from? What is there to make the machinery malfunction? Or does the problem only present itself in this way because Rose quietly reimports a pre-formed self as the necessary target on which the machinery works – 'the new technologies of the family are installed within us'?

One way out of this difficulty is to take his 'gap between normality and actuality' and rethink it as a splitting, a coding of different desires, conducts and destinies into the licit and the illicit, the normal and the marginal, the healthy and the pathological. This suggests that the production of the self does not work just through the incitement of desires. Rather, the norms and prohibitions instituted within social and cultural technologies are folded into the unconscious so that they 'surface' not just as 'personal desires' but in a complex and unpredictable dynamic of desire, guilt, anxiety and displacement. Subjects have desires that they do not want to have; they reject them at the cost of guilt and anxiety. Subjects are thus split from desires that remain incited but unrealised. It is only in the splitting that accompanies the interiorisation of norms and the repression of incited-but-prohibited wishes and fantasies that consciousness and the ego are formed. This creation of the unconscious through repression is thus also the moment of individuation that allows conscious, intentional, autonomous agency within the terms of identification established through the authority of the social machinery.

In this revised model, the *repression* of desires is as important to the formation of subjectivity as their incitement; it is a mechanism determining the form of expression of the repressed material and prompting its repetition. Ian Hunter and Nikolas Rose present desire not only as an *effect* of the machinery of the social, but also as its *realisation*. I am arguing that it is only through repression, the unconscious, and the splitting of the subject – all the guilty secrets of love, conscience and fantasy – that the authority of institutions and disciplines can be secured, however precariously. From this perspective, which can also claim lineage from Mauss, individual psychical responses are translations of a collective symbolic system but are not in an isomorphic relation to it.[21]

The splitting – rather than the gap – 'between normality and actuality' thus sets in train a movement or a series of transactions. The unconscious that is necessary to make sense of the negotiation of authority as agency and the translations of the pedagogic into the performative is not a kernel of hidden authenticity, the real me, human nature. It is not intimate but, in Lacan's coinage, extimate. In Lévi-Strauss's sense, the unconscious provides 'the common and specific character of social facts'.

> The unconscious would thus be the mediating term between self and others. Going down into the givens of the unconscious, the extension of our understanding, if I may put it thus, is not a movement towards ourselves; we reach a level

which seems strange to us, not because it harbours our most secret selves but (much more normally) because, without requiring us to move outside ourselves, it enables us to coincide with forms of activity which are both at once *ours* and *other*.

These forms of activity do not just 'surface' as individual desires and self-directed agency. Rather, they have to return transformed, as representations. They pass through a third space that is neither outside nor inside, but that psychic reality which Lacan located as 'the between perception and consciousness'. This is the scene of negotiation, of enunciation, of that active fantasy life which supports reality by giving it the appearance of consistency.[22]

Fantasy in this sense does not imply an escape from the process of subjectification. Rather, it refers to one of the most important moments in that process; the staging and imaging of the subject and its desire in relation to complex social-symbolic scenarios. The concept thus allows an account of subjective investment in the apparatus and its systems of signification which does not prejudge the particular paths the subject's desire will take, or its shifting and multiple identifications in relation to the social and cultural field. It also suggests the costs of this fantasmatic investment. The security achieved through the consistency of the fantasy construction entails a narcissism that is necessarily in conflict with the demands of social relations. In negotiating the self-images provided by (for example) education, the self never fully recognises itself. It remains suspicious that there must be something more than the norms and banal transgressions on display. 'What one loves in one's image is something more than the image', argues Joan Copjec. 'Thus is narcissism the source of the malevolence with which the subject regards its image, the aggressivity it unleashed on all its own representations. And thus does the subject come into being as a transgression of, rather than in conformity to, the law.'[23]

HABITUS

The underlying moral of my argument is simple enough. The dynamics of subjectification are more complicated and more painful than simply identifying with, or re-enacting, the attributes and behaviours prescribed by social and cultural technologies – or by the Tutor or by the habitus. Both Foucault and Bourdieu, it seems to me, attempt to get to grips with the ambivalent dynamics of authority and agency: the setting in place of social and symbolic structures, and the processes of subjectification generated as they are negotiated. They are both, in that sense, concerned with the techniques of government that characterise Western modernity. The strength of Bourdieu's work lies primarily in the meticulous detail in which he charts the classificatory systems that embody cultural authority (or distinction) and which authorise agency. What I find less convincing are his attempts to reduce that complexity to the crunching abstractions of *Reproduction* or to disavow the fantasmatic and libidinal dimensions of subject formation through the mystical category of *habitus.*

What difference would the model I have outlined make to an understanding of education and cultural reproduction? One practical example can be found in the account by Valerie Walkerdine and her colleagues of the ways in which girls negotiate the symbolic categories and connotations of mathematics in school. They insist that the perceived 'failure' of girls in mathematics at secondary school cannot be explained either by psychological notions of development (latterday Rousseau) or by a more sociological (Wollstonecraftian) emphasis on teacher expectations or pedagogic styles. The process involves a much more complex dynamic between the pedagogic and the performative. In the practices of the school and the family – and especially through the mother–daughter relationship – the authoritative categories of rationality and irrationality, masculinity and femininity, cleverness and stupidity, mastery and subservience, and compliance and resistance are instituted in relation to each other. So far, so Bordelian. The crucial difference is that Walkerdine goes on to argue that these systems of symbolic classification are remixed by the girls as fantasmatic scenarios of desire, denial and transgression. These then return not only as a self-identification, but as agency. It is in the formation and exercise of the girls' autonomy that, according to this evidence, the social and psychological injuries of sexual differentiation are systematically reproduced. This is not a formalist 'reading off' of a subject position from the *habitus* of the school – its institutional practices and its disposition of discourses. Rather, the focus is on the sexually differentiated subject always-to-be-produced, always-to-be-enacted through the fantastic improvisations of the girls within the school's play of disciplines, technologies and symbolic systems.[24]

It is in this sense that cultural reproduction is impossible. Pedagogic authority has to be both enacted and erased in the dramatic strategies of everyday life and in the fantasies of psychic reality. Bourdieu makes a compelling case for his account of reproduction, but he only tells us half the story.

NOTES

1 S. Freud, *The Standard Edition of the Complete Psychological Works*, vol. 23, J. Strachey (ed.), London, Hogarth Press, 1953–66, p. 248; I. Kant, *Education*, Ann Arbor, University of Michigan Press, 1960, p. 12.
2 Quoted in D. Robbins, *The Work of Pierre Bourdieu*, Milton Keynes, Open University Press, 1991, p. 83.
3 This formulation of the pedagogic and the performative I owe to Homi Bhabha. See his 'DissemiNation: time, narrative and the margins of the modern nation', in Bhabha (ed.), *Nation and Narration*, London, Routledge, 1990, pp. 297–9. On the formation of citizenship, see N. Rose, 'Governing the enterprising self', paper for the conference on The Values of the Enterprise Culture, University of Lancaster, September 1989, and *Governing the Soul: The Shaping of the Private Self*, London, Routledge, 1990.
4 Kant, op. cit., pp. 7, 28; and 'What is Enlightenment?', in E. Behler (ed.) *Philosophical Writings*, New York, Continuum, 1986, p. 269.
5 J.-J. Rousseau, *The Social Contract*, trans. M. Cranston, Harmondsworth, Penguin, 1968, pp. 64–5; C. Pateman, *The Problem of Political Obligation: A Critique of Liberal Theory*, Cambridge, Polity, 1985, p. 143; Rousseau, *Émile*, trans. B. Foxley, London, Everyman, 1911, p. 217.
6 Rousseau, 1911, op. cit., pp. 7, 40.
7 Ibid., pp. 9, 281–2, 84–5, 56. On this version of authority, see C. Lefort, *The Political Forms of Modern Society*, Cambridge, Polity, 1986, pp. 211–14. On symbolic identification, S. Žižek, *The Sublime Object of Ideology*, London, Verso, 1989, p. 105.
8 E. Cassirer, *Rousseau, Kant and Goethe*, New York, Dover, 1963, p. 9; W.E. Connolly, *Political Theory and Modernity*, Oxford, Blackwell, 1988, pp. 57–8.
9 My account of the *Bildungsroman* draws on F. Moretti, *The Way of the World: The Bildungsroman in European Culture*, London, Verso, 1987; see also the review by G. Murdock, 'Imagining Modernity: Moretti on the *Bildungsroman*', *New Formations*, 1988, no. 6, pp. 132–41.
10 Schiller's *On the Aesthetic Education of Man* cited in I. Hunter, *Culture and Government: The Emergence of Literary Education*, London, Macmillan, 1988, pp. 184–5, 79.
11 Rousseau, 1911, op. cit., pp. 321, 322, 328; M. Wollstonecraft, *Vindication of the Rights of Woman*, Harmondsworth, Penguin, 1982, pp. 81–3. My reading of Wollstonecraft draws on C. Kaplan, *Sea Changes: Culture and Feminism*, London, Verso, 1986, and D. Held, *Models of Democracy*, Cambridge, Polity, 1987, pp. 79–85.

12 Marquis de Sade, *Philosophy in the Bedroom*, in R. Seaver and A. Wainhouse (eds), *The Marquis de Sade*, New York, Grove Weidenfeld, 1965, p. 208. See also Connolly, op. cit., pp. 74–5. My account of Sade's relationship to Rousseau draws heavily on his 'First interlude: Hobbes, Rousseau and the Marquis de Sade', in *Political Theory and Modernity*.

13 Connolly, op. cit., p. 78.

14 Hunter, op. cit.

15 Rose, 1990, op. cit., p. 7.

16 M. Foucault, 'The subject and power', in H.L. Dreyfus and P. Rabinow, *Michel Foucault: Beyond Structuralism and Hermeneutics*, Brighton, Harvester, 1982, pp. 221–2.

17 Rousseau cited in A. Oldfield, 'Citizenship: an unnatural practice?', *Political Quarterly*, 1990, vol. 61, no. 2, p. 186; D. Haraway, 'A manifesto for cyborgs: science, technology, and socialist feminism in the 1980s', *Socialist Review*, 1985, vol. 80, pp. 65, 66; M. Foucault, *Power/Knowledge*, Brighton, Harvester, 1980, p. 186; G. Deleuze, *Foucault*, Minneapolis, University of Minnesota Press, 1988, p. 115.

18 Hunter, 1988, op. cit., pp. 150, 125; Rose, 1990, op. cit., p. 208 (all emphases added).

19 I. Hunter, 'After representation', *Economy and Society*, 1984, vol. 13, no. 4, p. 423; Rose, 1990, op. cit., p. 218.

20 Rose, 1990, op. cit., pp. 201–2.

21 The definition of repression is taken from M. Cousins and A. Hussain, *Michel Foucault*, London, Macmillan, 1984, p. 208. On the distinction between the subject as an effect of the law and the realisation of the law, see J. Copjec, 'The orthopsychic subject', *October*, 1989, no. 49, p. 61. (My general argument here also borrows from this article, as well as others by J. Copjec, see, for example, 'The delirium of clinical perfection', *Oxford Literary Review*, 1986, vol. 8, nos 1–2, and 'Cutting up' in T. Brennan (ed.), *Between Feminism and Psychoanalysis*, London, Routledge, 1989.) On the link to Mauss, see M. Cousins, 'In the midst of psychoanalysis', *New Formations*, 1989, no. 7, Spring, p. 79.

22 C. Lévi-Strauss, *Introduction to the Work of Marcel Mauss*, London, Routledge, 1987, p. 35; (see also Bhabha, 1990, op. cit., p. 313). J. Lacan, *The Four Fundamental Concepts of Psychoanalysis*, Harmondsworth, Penguin, 1977, p. 56.

23 Copjec, 1989, op. cit., p. 70.

24 See, for example, V. Walkerdine, *The Mastery of Reason: Cognitive Development and the Production of Rationality*, London, Routledge, 1988; V. Walkerdine and the Girls and Mathematics Unit, Institute of Education, *Counting Girls Out*, London, Virago, 1980; V. Walkerdine and H. Lucey, *Democracy in the Kitchen: Regulating Mothers and Socializing Daughters*, London, Virago, 1989.

4

YES–BUT LOGIC

The quasi-science of cultural reproduction

Stephen Featherstone

INTRODUCTION

This chapter makes a simple but very important point; namely, that whatever else is involved in some lay accounts of current affairs they have a quasi-scientific dimension, in particular they exhibit a YES–BUT logic.[1] Popular newspaper language involves, for example, analyses of empirical instances, adjudications between competing empirical accounts, the formulation of theories based on empirical accounts, adjudications between competing theories, the derivation of policies from empirical/theoretical accounts, and adjudications between policies.

These features combine with others to produce very powerful bodies of knowledge: cultural reproduction is complex and multi-faceted in ways underemphasised by influential analyses of media output.[2]

THE STRUCTURE OF YES–BUT ACCOUNTING

The *Daily Express,* the *Daily Mail* and the *Sun* are famous for their fierce support of Mrs Thatcher's government. The steel strike was the first significant challenge to the monetary policy and it is far from surprising to find accounts which place it in contexts like – a disastrous/crippling strike in support of an unearned/unrealistic wage claim which could but will not be settled by the government providing more taxpayers' money. On close inspection these contextualisations involve complex processes. Hence, for example, the structure of some of the *Sun*'s accounts is as follows:[3]

1 YES there are some reasons for being sympathetic towards the steelworkers, i.e. reason A,B. The notion of fairness can and has been used to understand their situation. (S1:2–S1:4)

2 BUT the fact of the matter is that the industry loses enormous sums of money, i.e. amount A. (S1:5) The main reason for this is the relatively low productivity of British steelworkers which is the result of union-inspired restrictive practices and over-manning. (S1:6–S1:10)

3 The steelworkers and those who are sympathetic towards them will have to accept the unrealism and impossibility of their case. (S1:11–S1:14)

4 YES – in the manner of the Labour Party the government could print more money (S2:2–S2:5, also S2:19), BUT this leads to lost jobs and higher taxes/inflation. (S2:6–S2:7)

5 The fact of the matter is that wages must be related to the economic value of the product, to the amount of money the industry earns and the productivity of the workforce. (S2:8–S2:10) Given advanced technology there is no real reason for the relatively low productivity of British steelworkers. (S2:11–S2:13) Raising productivity would improve wages, job prospects and overall performance. (S2:14–S2:15)

6 The unions and others who operate with the notion of fairness should be able to understand these fundamental principles and the crippling consequences of not applying them. If the country does not learn and implement these realistic lessons its fortunes and the fortunes of particular industries will never improve. (S2:15–S2:19)

One understanding of this kind of account is provided by Hall:[4]

Neither Keynesian nor monetarism . . . win votes . . . Thatcherism discovered a powerful means of translating economic doctrine into the language of experience, moral imperative and common sense . . . This translation of a theoretical IDEOLOGY into a populist IDIOM was a major political achievement . . . the conversion of hard-faced economics into the language of compulsive MORALISM was . . . the centrepiece of this transformation. 'Being British' became once again identified with the restoration of competition and profitability: with tight money and sound finance ('You can't pay yourself more than you earn . . . ') – the national economy debated on the model of the household budget. The colonization of the popular press was a critical victory in this struggle to define the common sense of the times. Here was undertaken the critical ideological work of constructing around 'Thatcherism' a popularist common sense.

In a sense it is not difficult to see the relevance of some of these arguments. Clearly, for example, one of the effects of the accounts seems to be to translate Thatcherism into a popularist form. On the other hand, it is equally clear that 'compulsive moralism', 'the language of experience', 'common sense' and 'moral imperative' are considerable glosses on both the form and contents of the accounts. They may be commonsensical and populist but are very sophisticated forms of common sense, and for that very reason all the more compelling forms of common sense. Readers are in a very clear sense invited to be objective analysts. They are not invited simply to believe or argue this or that, to be the unwitting recipients of slogans like 'You can't pay yourself more than you earn', or to moralise, berate and browbeat.

On the contrary, the author considers an argument which opposes the preferences of the *Sun* (i.e. sympathy for the steel-workers/fairness); states reasons why it is valid; switches to an alternative via a YES–BUT logic; provides empirical evidence to support preferences (i.e. productivity is low, unequivocally low); qualifies and thereby reinforces the validity and reasonableness of preferences (i.e. productivity is low *despite* investment and advance technology, YES there has been a recession BUT the main reason for low productivity is . . .); places facts and figures about low productivity into more general causal chains (i.e. productivity is low this is because . . . and leads to . . .); places reasoning about productivity into yet more general causal chains (i.e. the key to individual/collective success is to relate earnings to productivity/performance); adjudicates between different levels of competing account (i.e. YES sympathy is possible BUT . . ., YES fairness is a general criterion BUT economic value is sounder, YES fairness could be the basis for general policy and perspectives BUT it is *demonstrably* unrealistic/unreasonable and inferior to economic value).

Let us be clear about what is being suggested. The accounts may or may not have a truth value, they may be understandable via a variety of sociological perspectives, they may involve flawed or partial logics, and the form/content of the arguments may involve a variety of processes. They do, nevertheless, seem to have an internal complexity and logic which is a central element of the persuasive power of the texts. This can be elaborated by examining the *Mirror* which has similar forms/structures to the *Sun* but different contents.

MIRROR MIRROR – THE FAIREST OF THEM ALL

The notion of fairness rejected by the *Sun* plays a central role in the *Mirror*. In 'So why pick on steel?' (M1:1) the author notes the worsening situation (M1:2) and then accepts the central logic of the government's policy, i.e. that wages should be tied to productivity otherwise the result is higher prices/taxation (M1:3–M1:4). The author proceeds to challenge this policy with the question 'But why single out steel?' (M1:5). The rest of the text, amongst other things, provides various empirical examples of the ways in which the steelworkers have been treated unfairly and/or inconsistently (M1:6–M1:10). As in the *Sun* the central feature of this acceptance and challenge is a YES–BUT logic: YES it is possible – indeed perfectly logical – to relate wages to productivity and YES economic value/performance could be seen as a general criterion, BUT sympathy/fairness is a *demonstrably* better policy/perspective for the following reasons . . . ; 'The logic is undoubtedly right . . . But why single out steel?' (M1:4–M1:5). Again, readers are not asked simply to prefer this or that argument, or to unwittingly/ unreflexively support the steelworkers and castigate the Steel Corporation and the government. They are invited to be objective analysts: to acknowledge the validity of arguments which threaten their preferences and to maintain the latter via an adjudicative, reasoning process, to argue YES of course BUT on the other hand for the following reasons . . .

A similar process occurs in 'Men of steel' (M2:1), though in this case the author deals explicitly with some of the broader issues involved in notions like sympathy/fairness. The author notes that the pay offer amounts to a cut in living standards (M2:2) and then raises the issue of mass unemployment and devastated communities (M2:3–M2:4). The author proceeds by accepting the validity of an opposing argument – the chairman of the Steel Corporation has argued that 'It is not possible to protect trade unionists from reality' (M2:5) – and then challenges this YES with a BUT – 'Maybe not. But for 50,000 men whose jobs are going . . .' (M2:6). The rest of the text primarily fleshes out the BUT by asking readers to see what the steelworkers can see: BUT 'They see . . .' (M2:7); BUT 'They see . . .' (M2:8); BUT 'They see . . .' (M2:9); BUT 'They see . . .' (M2:10).

The immediate effect of this argumentative device is to generate a sense of sympathy for the steelworkers and to explain the threatened strike (M2:10–M2:11). Its more general effect is to develop preferences (i.e. sympathy for the steelworkers, criticism of the Steel Corporation and the government), and to complete an adjudicative chain of reasoning which validates preferences and invalidates threatening alternatives. The apparent objectivity of media language has, of course, been commented on. Hence, for example, in respect of TV language we have the arguments that accounts invoke legitimation 'based on direct perception of the world . . . a direct picture of "how things seem" . . .';[5] there '. . . is a sense of witnessing . . . a "reality" which is . . . made to seem "out there", separate from and independent of those positioned as witnesses'.[6] In the case in question the position seems to be not so much a passive witness of an external reality but rather an analyst of it, and an adjudicator between competing accounts.

FORMS OF ANALYSIS: A COMPLEMENTARY PERSPECTIVE

The texts in question could be analysed in a variety of ways. It might be argued that there is a limited 'inferential framework' common to all the newspapers, despite the opposition of the *Mirror* to government policy.[7] According to this argument, for example, the fact that all the newspapers accept the logic of the government's view about economic policy places a crucial limitation on debate and involves a very limited definition of the issues. Another 'inferential framework' or 'agenda' apparent from the research is the well-documented tendency from the media to define strikes predominantly in terms of the 'problem of damaging effects'.[8] The *Mirror* is a partial exception to this definition but in general the many proponents of framework/ agenda theorising could find plenty of evidence to support their case,[9] as would 'consensus' theorists. This kind of argument might take the general form of the suggestion that texts assume and reproduce fundamental assumptions about society, (i.e. the denial of 'any major structural discrepancies between different groups, or between the different maps of meaning in society'; the 'assumption that we . . . have roughly the same interests in society, and that we all have an equal share of power . . .'.[10] On the other hand, the consensus argument might take the form of the more specific suggestion that texts invoke and reproduce a 'WE' who have interests who are threatened by a 'THEY', 'THEY' are excluded from legitimacy because 'THEY' threaten 'OUR' interests.[11] We have already noted the possible relevance of the argument that the texts play a role in translating elite ideologies into populist forms. Hall and colleagues in their various works also stress the possibility that accounts obscure 'real social relations' and the necessity to relate accounts to broader social and cultural traditions. Hence, for example, the apparent inter-textual struggle between the *Mirror* and the *Sun* could be placed in the context of the struggle between Labourist and Monetarist traditions, as well as in the more specific context of the emergence of Thatcherism.

At the level of actual textual analysis/method Kress and Hodge[12] take us beyond quantitative content analysis[13] by pointing to the relationship between ideology and grammatical forms. Hence, for example, they suggest that groups denied legitimacy tend to be represented as the sole agents, the causers of adverse effects; versions of causality found in grammatical structures represent versions of the world, i.e. in the *Sun* the steelworkers are a primary agency responsible for adverse effects, while in the *Mirror* they are passive, adversely affected by other agents. Hall *et al.*[14] have related concepts like ideology and consensus to the way in which texts evaluatively identify the issues with the assumed lives, experience and interests of readers. This is a classic argumentative device[15] and much can be illuminated by considering the relationship between newspapers and the assumed interests of readerships.[16]

Still others deny that textual analysis in isolation is of any real value,[17] relate texts to audience reception and structure,[18] or emphasise the working practices and organisation of media professionals.[19] On the other hand contemporary and conventional wisdom underlines the trivial, sensational and often morally questionable content of popular newspapers.

THE SCIENCE OF PICKETING

From the point of view of this research the above and other possible ways of analysing media accounts are not so much flawed or inappropriate, but rather can be complemented and/or developed via a consideration of the possibility that the structure of some accounts has – amongst other things – an internal complexity which is persuasive partly because it has a rational or logical dimension, is in a very clear sense quasi-scientific.

Consider, for example, the account of picketing by the *Sun*. The author notes that 'AN OLD menace returns . . . bullying, threatening and sometimes violent secondary pickets' (S3:2). The author then gives two examples of this kind of behaviour during the steel strike (S3:3–S3:4), and suggests 'Such . . . scenes are all too familiar. They recall the "flying pickets" of the two coal strikes. Significantly, Arthur Scargill, who is supposed to have invented secondary picketing is said to be "advising" the strikers' (S3:5–S3:6). The rest of the text (S3:7–S3:14) emphasises picketing as a violent and intimidatory threat to the right to work and normal working/life, an unequivocal breach of the existing criminal law which diverse groups (i.e. Tory MPs, the Steel Union leader) are concerned about; a problem which can be responded to in various ways but which essentially requires the police and the government to ensure the enforcement of the existing law.

Part of the persuasive power of this text involves, as the literature alluded to in the previous section rightly suggests, strategies like:

1 The use of common sense/emotive images/language which emphasise the undesirable, anti-social, abnormal and extreme nature of activities, i.e. violence, bullying, intimidation.

2 Reproducing stocks of partial and sedimented cultural knowledge, which have diverse origins and interpretations, to understand or smother 'new' events which are an inherent threat to preferences because of their 'newness' and subsequent capacity to be understood in different ways, and thereby reaffirming the stock of knowledge and making it available for future use, i.e. 'AN OLD menace returns . . .' (S3:2), 'Such scenes are all too familiar' (S2:5).

3 Allocating legitimacy/illegitimacy by: (1) Criminalising activities, i.e. A is indisputably criminal and therefore cannot possibly be either X, Y or legitimate. (2) The suggestion that there is a THEY who threaten OUR specific civil/economic

interests and the more general civil/economic/public interest; and that THEY are led by a sinister unrepresentative, unreasoning, unreasonable, self-interested/politically motivated minority, i.e. the mythology of the 'folk-devil' Arthur Scargill played a major role in all the newspapers, e.g. in S3 the masterminder of picketing who is 'advising' (S3:6) the strikers and has the 'nominal leader' 'very worried' (S3:7). (3) Implied contrasts between reasonable/majority dissent and unreasonable/minority dissent. (4) References – implied or otherwise to the knowledge and disapproval of the majority and/or diverse groups/persons, i.e. picketing is a problem and is widely perceived as such, the only relevant question is how do we solve the problem?

However, readers are not just invited to make contrasts or to use labels and images; the latter appear in argumentative chains and reasoning structures, and the persuasive power of the text is to a significant extent the placement of, for example, evaluative and partial imagery in reasoning structures. The author does not just say the old menace/problem has returned but rather states a theory which has been affirmed in the past and gives empirical evidence which re-demonstrates the validity of the theory, i.e. the menace returns, for example at A, at B. It follows from this that perspectives and policies also have an objective dimension. Readers are not asked to simply label picketing as a problem and propose appropriate policies, rather they are asked to make relatively fine distinctions derived from and complementing their analytical skills. It is one thing to say that picketing is intimidatory and should be stopped or outlawed, it is another to say look the evidence about the nature of picketing is unequivocal, picketing is . . .; some argue that new legislation is required; they have a point but the issue of new legislation is separable from the fact that existing legislation can and should be used to solve what is self-evidently, and widely assumed to be, a problem.

The YES–BUT logic explicit in the editorials analysed earlier is less obviously evident in the case of S3. It might therefore be argued that it is best to count the explicit weighing of alternative arguments as a particular case of a more general phenomenon. On the other hand, readers are clearly in a position to meet the challenge of alternative arguments about picketing by proposing YES, BUT the fact of the matter is that picketing is indisputably intimidatory, a problem which is best resolved in the following manner . . . An alternative argument which the *Sun* touched on was the claim that picketing in particular and trade union action in general is a legitimate form of persuasion/dissent. The reply that readers are positioned to make is YES there are legitimate forms of dissent BUT this is not the reality; in the majority of cases we have seen . . .; we can unequivocally confirm that X not Y is involved in Z, that A and not B is the appropriate perspective, and that C not D is the soundest policy option; we are outraged but not senselessly so, we are outraged because of X, Y, Z and prefer particular policies for particular reasons.

CONCLUDING COMMENT

Of necessity this chapter has been brief; it has, however, made the essential point. Putting it a slightly different way: when we look at media accounts, and by extension ordinary language accounts in general, it may be fruitful to consider: (1) the way in which argumentative devices/strategies appear in argumentative forms/structures *defined at the text level*; (2) the possibility that there is a clear quasi-scientific dimension to accounting; (3) in particular a YES–BUT logic; (4) the possibility that the power of language is to a significant extent the result of the placement of, for example, images and evaluations, in text forms/structures which invite readers, in perhaps limited but nevertheless clear ways, to be objective analysts/moralists.

APPENDIX I: THE *SUN* SAYS

Sl:1   *Off the rails*

S1:2   *BRITAIN'S railmen threaten to black steel imports if our own steelmen go on strike.*

S1:3   OF COURSE, there is sympathy for the 50,000 steelworkers who are to lose their jobs.

S1:4   OF COURSE, it is understandable that a two per cent increase should be regarded as derisory when inflation is above 17 per cent.

S1:5   But the fact is that the steel industry cannot afford even one per cent. It is already £300 million in the red.

   Appalling

S1:6   This has happened partly because there is a world recession in steel.

S1:7   *But also for the far more important reason that the performance of the steelworkers is appalling.*

S1:8   Despite a massive programme of investment, each British steelworker produces only about half the output of a French or German worker.

Sl:9   Japanese workers produce THREE TIMES as much steel per man-hour as our own.

S1:10   And the blame falls chiefly on the steel unions, with their restrictive practices and their stubborn insistence on massive over-manning.

Realism

Sl:ll   Sooner or later, realism will have to dawn in our steel industry.

S1:12   It makes no sense at all for the railmen to help postpone the inevitable day of reckoning.

S1:13   In the past, the National Union of Railwaymen, under Mr Sidney Weighell, has often shown moderation and responsibility in its own demands.

S1:14   *Do these sensible, moderate men really want to go to the wall in defence of the indefensible?*

APPENDIX II: THE *SUN* SAYS

S2:1   *Stop this madness*

S2:2   *THE SUN has an urgent message to the steel unions before they plunge Britain into industrial chaos.*

S2:3   Stop this madness and start talking.

S2:4   THE LAST thing we want is government intervention, as Labour MPs demand.

S2:5   That really means printing money. An extravagant step for an industry approaching bankruptcy.

S2:6   And WE all know where THAT leads.

S2:7   To higher INFLATION, fewer JOBS, greater TAXATION.

S2:8   Instead the unions must start talking about how best to take the limited amount of cash the British Steel Corporation can offer.

S2:9   It isn't much.

S2:10   How could it be when the productivity of British steelworkers is so much worse than that of steelmen abroad?

S2:11   There is ample room for a dramatic improvement in the industry's performance.

S2:12   Its equipment is as technologically advanced as any in Europe.

S2:13   There is no valid reason why British steelworkers should not raise their output to the level of our overseas competitors.

S2:14   That way, they can boost their wage packets and save some of the thousands of jobs that would be lost in the wake of a prolonged strike.

S2:15   But if the strike does go ahead the unions must be clear about one thing.

Challenge

S2:16   While the country cannot afford this dispute, it can afford EVEN LESS to use taxpayers' money to meet their unrealistic demands.

S2:17   This will be the first big challenge to Mrs Thatcher's government from powerful trade unions in a state industry.

S2:18   Ministers must mean it when they say that it is up to the employers and the workforce to solve their own problems.

S2:19   *Let them show that the bad old days of buying off strikes with bags of unearned money have gone for ever.*

APPENDIX III: *MIRROR* COMMENT

M1:1   So why pick on steel?

M1.2   THE worst is happening in steel. The government won't do anything to end the strike and the management and unions are settling down to make it a long one.

M1:3   Sir Keith Joseph said yesterday that if the Steel Corporation offered more money without more productivity, 'workers in other industries would have to go on subsidising workers in steel'.

M1:4   The logic is undoubtedly right. Higher wages without higher productivity means higher prices or higher taxation.

M1:5   But why single out steel?

M1:6   Was the miners' 20 per cent rise paid for out of higher productivity? Or the local government workers' 13 per cent? Will the offer of 14 per cent to the civil servants be paid for by cutting costs?

M1:7   At the start of this dispute the steelworkers would have settled for any of those rises. Instead, they had an offer raised in dribs and drabs. Two per cent here, three per cent there, plus another one or two and then a further four. All on strict conditions.

M1:8   The government says it isn't intervening in the steel strike. But by cutting off the Corporation's money it prevented a settlement. That's intervening.

M1:9   It didn't do the same to the Coal Board or the local councils. It isn't doing the same for its own workers.

M1:10   Its policy can't always be right. Or even always wrong. But at least it ought to be consistent.

APPENDIX IV: *MIRROR* COMMENT

M2:1 Men of steel

M2.2 It's not just a two per cent wage rise the steelworkers are being offered. With today's price increases it's also a 15 per cent cut in their standard of living.

M2:3 And that's for those lucky enough to keep their jobs.

M2:4 Communities dependent upon steel are being devastated by closures. Corby, Shotton, Scunthorpe, Cleveland, Consett, Port Talbot and Llanwern fear mass unemployment.

M2:5 The Steel Corporation chairman, Sir Charles Villiers – who doesn't have a redundancy problem – says: 'It is not possible to protect trade unionists from reality.'

M2:6 Maybe not. But for 50,000 men whose jobs are going that sounds like the skipper saying: 'The ship's a sinking. Throw some more men overboard.'

M2:7 They see Sir Charles agreeing with the government to end a £300 million a year loss within a few months – and doing it at their expense.

M2:8 They see another loss-making industry, coal, offering miners 20 per cent more. They see derisory cuts in the Civil Service which mean that no one will actually lose a job.

M2:9 They see the Cabinet pursuing irrelevant changes in trade union law while production falls unhindered and unemployment rises unchecked.

M2:10 They see it and they think it unfair. Despite their fears about the future they regard a two per cent wage offer as a final insult.

M2:11 That's why we're faced with the threat of a national steel strike from January 2.

APPENDIX V: THE *SUN* SAYS

S3:1 *Rule of law*

S3:2 *AN OLD menace returns to the industrial scene: bullying, threatening and sometimes violent secondary pickets.*

S3:3 At Sheffield, lorries trying to get into a private steelworks find their way blocked by 100 angry men.

S3:4 At Corby, a woman office worker is punched in the mouth as she tries to cross a picket line.

Pathetic

S3:5 Such ugly, shameful scenes are all too familiar. They recall the 'flying pickets' of the two coal strikes.

S3:6 Significantly, Arthur Scargill, who is supposed to have invented secondary picketing is said to be 'advising' the strikers.

S3:7   *Their nominal leader, the pathetic Bill Sirs, wrings his hands and says he is 'very worried'.*

S3:8   Tory speakers declare that the events are demonstrating the need for tougher laws against picketing, which they promised at the last election.

S3:9   Of course, these are needed. And soon.

S3:10   But we do not have to wait for Acts of Parliament to appear like the Seventh Cavalry to save us.

S3:11   There are already laws against intimidation. Against violence.

S3:12   It is every bit as illegal to use force in an industrial dispute as it is in a robbery.

S3:13   No one has the right to stop workers who want to work. There is nothing sacred about a picket line.

S3:14   *The police should not hesitate to use their full powers. And the Government should back them with its full authority.*

NOTES

1 The paper is based on research carried out in the early 1980s; it summarises some of the results of a detailed qualitative content analysis of the editorial coverage of the steel strike (late 1979/early 1980) provided by the *Daily Express*, the *Daily Mail*, the *Daily Mirror* and the *Sun*.

   The research has been resurrected because I feel there is a point to make. Limitations of space forbid any detailed elaborations of the research or the particular issues raised; the paper has been written solely to make a simple but seemingly important point.

2 In line with 1) detailed elaborations of different analytical approaches has regrettably not been possible. I do, however, indicate in various places how my point can be seen in the context of some of the mainstream literature as it stood at the time of the research.

3 Copies of the relevant editorials are printed in the Appendices. It is essential for readers to read my analyses in conjunction with a close reading of the editorials. References in brackets – i.e. S1:2–S1:4 – refer to naturally occurring paragraphs.

4 S. Hall, 'The Great Moving Right Show', in S. Hall and M. Jacques (eds), *The Politics of Thatcherism*, London, Lawrence & Wishart, 1983, pp. 28–9.

5 C. Brunsdon and D. Morley, *Everyday Television: Nationwide*, BFI Television Monograph 18, 1978, p. 89.

6 I. Connell, 'Television News and the Social Contract', in, S. Hall *et al.* (eds), *Culture, Media, Language*, London, Hutchinson, 1980, pp. 154–5.

7 See J.D. Halloran *et al.*, *Demonstrations and Communications*, Harmondsworth, Penguin, 1970, for the classic 'inferential framework' analysis.

8 Glasgow University Media Group, *Bad News*, vol. 1, London, Routledge & Kegan Paul, 1976.

9 J.G. Blumler and M. Gurevitch, *The Political Effects of Mass Communication*, in, M. Gurevitch *et al.* (eds), *Culture, Society and the Media*, London, Methuen, 1982; S. Hall *et al.*, *Policing the Crisis*, London, Macmillan, 1978; P. Hartmann and C. Husband, 'The Mass Media and Racial Conflict', in D. McQuail (ed.), *The Sociology of Mass Communications*, Harmondsworth, Penguin, 1970.
10 Hall *et al.*, 1978, op. cit., p. 55.
11 S. Cohen, *Folk Devils and Moral Panics*, Herts, Paladin, 1973, for the classic 'folk-devil' version of this argument.
12 G. Kress and R. Hodge, *Language As Ideology*, London, Routledge & Kegan Paul, 1979; see also R. Hodge and G. Kress, 'Transformations, models and processes: towards a more usable linguistics', *Journal of Literacy, Semantics*, 1974, pp. 5–21; G. Kress and T. Trew, 'Ideological transformations of discourse: or, how the *Sunday Times* got its message across', *Sociological Review*, vol. 26, 1978, pp. 755–76; T. Trew, '"What the papers say": Linguistic variation and ideological difference', in R. Fowler *et al.* (eds), *Language and Control*, London, Routledge & Kegan Paul, 1979; T. Trew, 'Theory and ideology at work', ibid.
13 P. Hartmann, 'Industrial Relations in the News Media', *Industrial Relations Journal*, 1975/76, vol. 5, pp. 4–18; D. McQuail, *Analysis of Newspaper Content*, Royal Commission on the Press, Research Series No. 4, London, HMSO, 1976.
14 Ibid.
15 Aristotle, *Rhetoric*, in R. McKeon (ed.), *The Basic Works of Aristotle*, New York, Random House, 1941; H.D. Lasswell, *Propaganda Technique in World War I*, Massachusetts, MIT Press, 1927; C. Perelman and L. Olbrechts-Tyteca, *The New Rhetoric – A Treatise on Argumentation*, Notre Dame, University of Notre Dame Press, 1958.
16 A.C.H. Smith *et al.* (eds), *Paper Voices*, London, Chatto & Windus, 1975.
17 G. Murdock, 'Misrepresenting Media Sociology: A Reply to Anderson & Sharrock', *Sociology*, 1980, vol. 14, pp. 457–68.
18 D. Morley, *The Nationwide Audience: Structure and Decoding*, BFI Television Monograph 11, 1980; 'Texts, readers, subjects', in S. Hall *et al.* (eds), *Culture, Media, Language*, London, 1980b.
19 P. Schlesinger, *Putting 'Reality' Together*, London, Constable, 1978.

5

A REPORT ON THE WESTERN FRONT

Postmodernism and the 'politics' of style

Dick Hebdige

FOREWORD – BRAND NAME: DICK

*I am Ubik, before the universe was I am. I made the suns. I made the worlds.
I created the lives and the places they inhabit: I move them here, I put them
there. They go as I say, they do as I tell them. I am the brand name and my
name is never spoken, the name which no one knows. I am called Ubik but
that is not my name. I am. I shall always be.*
Philip K. Dick (the German edition in which the phrase 'I am the
word' is mistranslated as 'I am the brand name')

The nature of things is in the habit of concealing itself.
Heraclitus (Fragment 54)

*The problem is simply this: What does a science fiction writer know about?
On what topic is he an authority?*
Philip K. Dick

*When Dick was alive, he lived in Santa Ana, California just a few miles
from Disneyland. In fact he lived so close that when he was alive, he would
sometimes describe himself in lectures and interviews as a spokesperson for
Disneyland. One day he went there to meet his friend and fellow SF writer,
Norman Spinrad. The two men talked about Watergate on the deck of
Captain Hook's pirate ship. The same day Dick discussed the rise of fascism
with Spinrad as they were spun round inside a giant teacup. (Elizabeth
Entebi headed the crew that filmed these exchanges for Paris TV.) Dick used
to think a lot about simulation then. He could never forget the fact that he
knew how to get from his apartment to Disneyland and that Disneyland
was in some strange way the home of the obsessions that drove him on to
write. He used to worry a lot in those days about how to draw the line
between reality and fiction, copies and originals, the authentic and the
inauthentic:*

69

Well, I will tell you what interests me, what I consider important. (Dick once wrote) 'I can't claim to be an authority on anything, but I can honestly say that certain matters absolutely fascinate me, and that I write about them all the time. The two basic topics that fascinate me are 'What is reality?' and 'What constitutes the authentic human being?'

During his twenty-seven-year career as a science fiction writer, Dick explored these same two topics in over thirty novels and more than one hundred short stories. Towards the end of his life he addressed himself again – *and this time directly* – *to those questions in an essay entitled 'How to Build a Universe That Doesn't Fall Apart Two Days Later'. All the information about Dick you've just read came from that essay together with all the quotations (including Heraclitus and the blurring of the brand name and the Logos in the German edition of Ubik).*

In 'How to Build a Universe That Doesn't Fall Apart', Dick discusses his own work, the nature of 'coincidence', and the reversibility of time. He considers the viability of pre-Socratic thought, reflects on anamnesis, theology, the roots of his concern with simulation, his horror of the inauthentic. (When Dick was alive, this dread of the fake and the inauthentic formed at times his one stable point of orientation just as it did in the anti-authoritarian counterculture with which he was identified . . .) When dick was Dick's essay in October 1986, he found the correspondences between the arguments put forward by Dick and himself in this article simultaneously uncanny, unsettling and reassuring. Although Dick wrote the rest of this article before he read Dick's essay, and although Dick wrote his essay before dick even thought of writing his, the two arguments unfold along broadly parallel lines. There are the same limited obsessions. There is the same underlying structure of preference and aversion, the same general drift – the scarey, funny ride through 'Disneyland' and then the journey home.

When Dick died, he was in fact – metaphorically speaking – still in transit between what he called 'home' and Disneyland. (The last short story he ever wrote was called 'I hope I shall arrive soon' . . .) What Dick used to refer to as Disneyland is what Dick used to call the Western Front . . .
Ubik (October 1986)

Postmodernism – we are told – is neither a homogeneous entity nor a consciously directed 'movement'. It is instead a space, a 'condition', a 'predicament', an *aporia*, an 'unpassable path' – where competing intentions, definitions and effects, diverse social and intellectual tendencies, and lines of force converge and clash. The decor of a room, the design of a building, the diagesis of a film, the construction of a record, or a scratch video, a television commercial, or an arts documentary, or the intertextual relations between them, the layout of a page in a fashion magazine or critical journal, an anti-teleological tendency within epistemology, the attack on the metaphysics of presence, a general attenuation of feeling, the collective chagrin and morbid projections of a post-war generation of baby boomers confronting disillusioned middle age, the 'predicament' of reflexivity, a group of rhetorical tropes, a proliferation of surfaces, a new phase in commodity fetishism, a fascination for images, codes and styles, a process of cultural, political or existential fragmentation and/or crises, the 'decentring' of the subject, an 'incredulity towards meta-narratives', the replacement of unitary power axes by a plurality of power/discourse formations, the 'implosion of meaning', the collapse of cultural hierarchies, the dread engendered by the threat of nuclear self-destruction, the decline of the university, the functioning and effects of the new miniaturised technologies, broad societal and economic shifts into a 'media', 'consumer' or multinational phase, a sense (depending on who you read) of placelessness (Jameson on the Bonaventura Hotel), or the abandonment of placelessness (e.g. Kenneth Frampton's 'critical regionalism') or (even) a generalised substitution of spatial for temporal coordinates[1] – when it becomes possible to describe all these things as 'postmodern' (or more simply, using a current abbreviation, as 'post' or 'very post') then it's clear that we are in the presence of a buzzword.

That a single word should serve as the inflated focus for such a range of contradictory investments does not necessarily render it invalid or meaningless. An ambivalent response to what Barthes might have called the 'happy babel' of the Post seems on the whole more honest and in the long run more productive than a simple either/or. Viewed benignly, the degree of semantic complexity surrounding the term might be seen to signal the fact that a significant number of people with conflicting interests and opinions feel that there is something sufficiently important at stake here to be worth struggling and arguing over. The sub-stantive appeal of these debates consists in the degree to which within them a whole bunch of contemporary crises are being directly confronted, articulated, grappled with. In other moments, for me at least, an uneasiness concerning the rapidity and glee with which some intellectuals seem intent on abandoning earlier posi-

71

tions staked out in the pre-Post-erous ground of older critical debates predominates: an uneasiness which is no doubt under-pinned in this case by a squarer, more puritanical aversion to 'decadence', 'fatalism', 'fashion' . . .

For example, one influential mapping of the postmodern – fatally inflected through the work of Georges Batâille – revolves around the 'death of the subject'. In the (ob) scenario sketched out by Jean Baudrillard, the vagina and the egg – the images compulsively reiterated in Batâille – give way to the metaphor of television as nether-eye (never I): the 'empty' point of origin to which everything returns:

> It is well known how the simple presence of television changes the rest of the habitat into a kind of archaic envelope, a vestige of human relations whose very survival remains perplexing. As soon as this scene is no longer haunted by its actors and their fantasies, as soon as a large useless body . . . Thus the body, landscape, time all progressively disappear as scenes. And the same for public space: the theatre of the social and the theatre of politics are both reduced more and more to a large soft body with many heads . . .[2]

Sometimes this image of contemporary metropolitan existence as a kind of decentred 'hyperreal' or technicolour version of Hobbes's Leviathan seems more clearly applicable to the term 'post-modernism' itself than to any hypothetical 'postmodern' ontology. The claims made on behalf of the Post can appear grotesquely inflated. The putative signs and symptoms of a 'post-modern tradition' sometimes look too much like the morbid pro-jections of a cohort of marginalised, liberally educated critics trapped in declining institutions – the academy, the gallery, the 'world' of art criticism – for them to be taken seriously at face value. The Post becomes a monstrous phantasm: a shapeless body of ungrounded critique with countless tiny heads. We know from mythology that such a hideous apparition must be approached obliquely rather than directly. The monster must be read at an angle in the same way that the signal on a video tape is read diagonally by helical scan. It is this need for indirection that dictates the eccentric trajectory of the present report. What follows is an attempt to re-present my own ambivalence *vis-à-vis* the prospect(s) of the Post: to engage with some of the issues raised in debates on postmodernism, to cruise the text of postmodernism without forfeiting the possibility of another place, other positions, other scenarios, different languages. In what I take to be the postmodern spirit I shall try to reproduce on paper the flow and grain of television discourse switching back and forth between different channels. In this way what follows is likely to induce in the reader that distracted, drifting state of mind we associate with watching television. I shall address the problem of postmodernism then in the form in which I shall pose questions rather than in the argu- ments I shall incidentally invoke.

1 'Passing through Disneyland's turnstyles is like boarding a revolving restaurant. Disney's ambition to seamlessly graft the crowds onto an animated environment succeeds at the expense of immobilising them. The loony sidewalks turn into vicious circles and, though they are always shuffling round and round on maxi- mum rotation, the masses become as frozen and unchanging as the rings of Saturn. The parks are no kind of place for functioning flesh and blood bodies. The publicists proudly describe EPCOT (the new Disney theme park) as the best equipped city on earth for the handicapped, which only means, however, that it's as dynamically demanding as a hospital corridor. Taking its cue from the TV show, Disneyland mutates from the rugged to the precious, from Adventureland and Frontierland to Tomorrowland and Fantasyland, from Tom Sawyer's Island to Tinkerbell's Toy Shop . . . Freedom of movement is purely illusory; the visitor is trapped in the spectacle's theatricality. In Disneyland, critic Louis Marin claims, "the visitor is on stage; he performs the play and is alienated by the part without being aware of performing". But the French critic missed a crucial point during his American vacation. What he calls alienation is here called great fun.' Paul Taylor, 'The Disney State' in *Art and Text* (22) *and FILE* (25) joint issue, 1986.

2 Postmodernism resembles modernism in that it needs to be thought of in the plural.[3] Not only do different writers define it differently but a single writer can talk at different times about different Posts. Thus, for instance, Jean-François Lyotard has recently used the term to refer to three separate tendencies: (i) a trend within architecture away from the Modern Movement's project 'of a last rebuilding of the whole space occupied by hu- manity'; (ii) a decay of confidence in the idea of progress and modernisation ('there is a sort of sorrow in the Zeitgeist') and (iii) a recognition that it is no longer appropriate to employ the meta-

73

phor of the 'avant garde' as if modern artists were soldiers fighting on the borders of knowledge and the visible, prefiguring in their art some sort of collective global future.[4] To pick through some of these definitions, there is, first and most obviously, postmodernism in architecture though even here there are conservative, conservationist and critical regional conjugations. There is postmodernism as a descriptive category within literature and the visual arts where the term is used to refer to a tendency towards stylistic pluralism, the crises of the avant garde as idea and as institution, and the blurring on an allegedly unparalleled scale of the categories of 'high' and 'low' forms, idioms and contents. There have also been attempts to describe as postmodern the emergent cultures and sub-cultures associated with the new user-friendly communication technologies (VCRs, home computers, synthesisers, beat boxes, portable and 'personal' audio cassette machines, etc) and to place these emergent forms within the context of a general shift into a new 'consumer', or 'media', phase in capitalist development. Here there is much talk of bricolage, creative consumption, the decentring and de-professionalisation of knowledge and professional expertise, the production of meaning in use. There is talk, too, of a general breakdown of social and cultural distinctions: an end not only to the 'outmoded' fantasy of the (suffering) 'masses' and their corollary in the market (the 'mass' in 'mass culture', 'mass media' etc) but also of the historically grounded 'communities' of the industrial period: end of existing subjectivities, existing collectives. These fragmentations in their turn are sometimes linked to the erosion of the boundaries between production and consumption, between different media, and the incommensurable 'times' and unsynchronised rhythms of different processes, experiences, actions. It is sometimes suggested that together these blurrings and mergers have led to the collapse of the hierarchies which kept apart the competing definitions of culture – high culture, low culture, mass culture, popular culture, culture as a whole way of life – in such a way that these categories and their contents can no longer be regarded as separate, distinct and vertically ranked.

To introduce another though related nexus of concerns, Hal Foster in his Preface to *Postmodern Culture* distinguishes between neo-conservative, anti-modernist and critical postmodernisms and points out that whereas some critics and practitioners seek to extend and revitalise the modernist project(s), others condemn modernist objectives and set out to remedy the imputed effects of modernism on family life, moral values, etc; while still others, working in a spirit of ludic and/or critical pluralism, endeavour to open up new discursive spaces and subject positions outside the confines of established practices, the art market and the modernist orthodoxy. In this latter, critical alternative (the one favoured by Foster) postmodernism is defined as a positive critical advance which fractures through negation (1) the petrified hegemony of an earlier corpus of 'radical aesthetic' strategies and proscriptions, and/or (2) the pre-Freudian unitary subject which formed the hub of the 'progressive' wheel of modernisation and which functioned in the modern period as the regulated focus for a range of 'disciplinary' scientific, literary, legal, medical and bureaucratic discourses. In this positive 'anti-aesthetic', the critical postmodernists are said to challenge the validity of the kind of global, unilinear version of artistic and economic-technological development which a term like modernism implies, and to concentrate instead on what gets left out, marginalised, repressed or buried underneath that term. The selective tradition is here seen in terms of exclusion and violence. As an initial counter-move, modernism is discarded by some critical postmodernists as a eurocentric and phallocentric category which involves a systematic preference for certain forms and voices over others. What is recommended in its place is an inversion of the modernist hierarchy – a hierarchy which, since its inception in the eighteenth, nineteenth and early twentieth centuries (depending on your periodisation),[5] consistently places the metropolitan centre over the 'underdeveloped' periphery: Western art forms over Third World ones, men's art over women's art, or, alternatively, in less anatomical terms 'masculine' or 'masculinist' forms, institutions and practices over 'feminine', feminist or 'femineist' ones.[6] Here the word 'postmodernism' is used to cover all those strategies which set out to dismantle the power of the white, male author as privileged source of meaning and value.

'People are afraid to merge . . . '

Many of these diagnoses of the postmodern condition cluster round the threat or the promise of various kinds of merger. As we have seen, a number of immanent mergers have been identified: the coming together of different literary, televisual and musical styles and genres, the mergers of subjects and objects, originals

75

and copies, hosts and parasites, of 'critical' and 'creative' discourses, of criticism and paracriticism, fiction and metafiction. This tendency is signalled at one level in the much vaunted contemporary preference in art, literature, film, TV and popular music for parody, pastiche, simulation and allegory – the figures which have risen like ghosts from the grave of the fatally afflicted author. Epistemologically, the shift towards these tropes is rooted in deconstructionism, in the abandonment of the pursuit of origins and the post-structuralist attack on the metaphysics of presence. From the academy to Academy One, from Jacques Derrida to *Blade Runner*, there is the same blurring of the line(s) between shadows and substances, metaphors and substantive truths, the same questioning of the validity of all such binaries.

Somewhere in the middle, between the seminar and the cinema, sits the work of Jean Baudrillard (the rhyme seminar/ cinema/Baudrillard is an irritating if apposite coincidence . . .). Baudrillard has introduced Philip K. Dick into the body of 'serious' social and critical theory rather like a mad or malevolent scientist might assist the *Invasion of the Body Snatchers* by introducing a pod from outer space into a small, quiet mid-western town. Resorting to the hyperbaton – the rhetorical strategy favoured by the sophists – Baudrillard presents a heretical 'history' of the Simulacrum in which in a progression ('precession') leading from the religious icon to computational simulation, the model is seen gradually to precede and generate the real rather than vice versa. Through this radical in-turning or implosion of sense, Baudrillard attempts to evacuate not only Plato, the Western philosophical inheritance, and any untheorised belief in space-time oppositions, but also the Enlightenment achievement/ legacy, the dual drive towards universal liberation and social engineering which underpin that achievement/legacy and any notion of history, progressive or otherwise which might be used to clarify or valorise the experience of modernity.[7]

Behind this erosion of the twin epistemic faiths of the modern epoch – positivism and Marxism – a question is being posed. The question is: if the fictionalising prepositional copula 'as if' has been allowed into the 'hard' sciences along with the theory of relativity, catastrophe theory, recursive computational logics and a recognition of the limits of controls, then on what grounds is it to be excluded from social critique and critical theory, from the descriptive, interpretive and predictive discourses of the soft social sciences? The question is: if the Abraham Lincoln Simulacrum in Disneyland can give the Gettysburg address several times a day thanks to robotics and a computer program, then why not take simulation seriously, why not Disneyfy the sober body of 'serious' critique?

> People are afraid to merge on freeways in Los Angeles. This is the first thing I hear when I come back to the city. Blair picks me up from LAX and mutters this under her breath as her car drives up the onramp. She says, 'People are afraid to merge on freeways in Los Angeles'. Though that sentence shouldn't bother me, it stays in my mind for an uncomfortably long time . . . Nothing else seems to matter to me but those ten words. Not the warm winds, which seem to propel the car down the empty asphalt freeway, or the faded smell of marijuana which still faintly permeates Blair's car. All it comes down to is that I'm a boy coming home for a month and people are afraid to merge . . .
>
> Brett Easton Ellis, *Less Than Zero*

3 Postmodernism in architecture is identified with the end of the European modernist hegemony imposed with growing conviction and on a global scale from the 1920s onwards through what became known as the International Style. The reaction against International Style architecture was pioneered in Britain by people like Edwin Lutyens and has been taken up by a whole generation of British architects from the neo-classicists like Quinlan Terry to the bricolage builders like Terence Farrell and Piers Gough and community architects like Rod Hackney.

What this generation has renounced is the rationalist theology of High Modernism with its puritanical (some have called it 'totalitarian') insistence on clean, uncluttered lines – a theology framed by the programmatic utterances of Le Corbusier and Mies van der Rohe and realised throughout the world with varying degrees of finesse, varying degrees of brutalism in countless skyscrapers, office blocks and tower blocks from Brasilia to British council housing estates. Modernism in architecture is identified with the abolition of the particular, the irrational, the anachronistic and with the more or less intentional destruction of the coordinates through which communities orient themselves in space and time: the destruction, that is, of history-as-a-lived dimension and of neighbourhood as socially inhabited space.

In the 1980s, the Great British Tower Block collapsed along with the exhausted rhetoric of post-war optimism, welfarism, bureaucratic collectivism and the related cults of industrial expansion and mechanical progress – all of which it is uniquely seen to symbolise. Typically, modernist architecture and architects are linked (at least by their neo-conservative opponents) to the discredited ideals and objectives of Planning with a capital 'p' – that means – obviously in this context – town planning but also, by association, economic planning, and, by extension, social planning of any kind. The reaction is fuelled partly by the observation – which is, after all, pretty hard to refute – that the apocalypse when realised in concrete begins to look decidedly seedy twenty years on when covered in English drizzle, cracks, obscene graffiti and pigeon shit. For many opponents of architectural modernism, the decline of the tower block coincides with the decline of what it stands for in Britain. The tower block's collapse serves as a ghostly reminder of the weaknesses of that other larger edifice – the post-war corporate state with its mixed economy, its embattled health services, its strained, unlikely and ultimately illusory social and political consensus forged in the white heat of Harold Wilson's modernising techno-jargon. In architectural journals and books, the post-modernist *putsch* can be heard in the following keywords: 'value', 'classical proportion', or alternatively 'community', 'hetero-geneous', 'diverse', 'choice', 'conservation', 'neo-Georgian', and in the substitution of organic metaphors for the more mechanical analogies of Higher Modernism. No more futurist manifestos. No more spaceship earth. No more talk about houses being 'factories for living'. To borrow Alexei Sayle's words, 'No more living 200 feet up in the air in a thing that looks like an off-set lathe or a baked bean canner'.[8]

Instead, we get the reaffirmation of either or all of the following: the particular, the vernacular, the sanctity of regional or national materials, styles, methods and traditions; the desirability of maintaining continuity with the past. The architect-as-surgeon has been replaced by the architect-as-holistic-practitioner, the architect-as-homeopath and, in some cases, on some severely under-financed community housing schemes, by the architect-as-faith-healer.

Architecture is a relatively independent and isolable field but nonetheless there are definite links that can be made with other postmodernisms. There is the assertion, at least in the literature, of the legitimacy of ordinary people's desires and aspirations if not always an unqualified endorsement of their tastes. Here we find a theme common to all the radical postmodernisms: the articulation – in this case quite literally – of a horizontal rather than a vertical aesthetic: a flat-spread aesthetic rather than a triangular figure with the elite, the expert, at its apex and the masses at the base. An emphasis on difference and diversity replaces the stress on system, order, hierarchy (though this doesn't apply to Quinlan Terry who believes that the laws of both architecture and social structure were laid down in the time of Solomon).[9] But, more importantly, what links the architecture of the Post to its artistic, critical and more purely philosophical and speculative equivalents is the shrinkage in the aspirations of the intellectual practitioner him/herself. It is there in the questioning of the God-like role and absolute rights of the enlightened expert-as-engineer-of-the-future. It is there in the preference for structural, holistic or ecological models of the field over dynamic, teleological or modernising ones.

4 If the word 'postmodernism' signifies anything at all, it announces at the very least a certain degree of scepticism concerning the transformative and critical powers of art, aesthetics, knowledge. In its critical inflections, it announces the end of any simple faith in what have sometimes been called the 'grand meta-narratives' – the Great Stories which for thousands of years the cultures of the West have been telling themselves in order to keep the dread prospect of otherness at bay. The word 'postmodernism' marks the decline of the Great Stories the West has told itself in order to sustain itself as the West against the 'rest', in order to place itself as Master and as Hero at the centre of the stage of world history. Those great stories, those meta-narratives have many different titles, many different names. Here are just a few:

> divine revelation, the unfolding Word, the shadowing of History by the Logos, the Enlightenment project, the belief in Progress, the belief in Reason, the belief in Science, modernisation, development, salvation, redemption, the perfectibility of man, the transcendence of history through divine intervention, the transcendence of history through the class struggle, Utopia, subtitled End of History . . .

These stories – who knows? – may have functioned in the past as forms of reassurance like the first stories which John Berger talks about[10] – stories perhaps designed by men – for this is the gender which constitutes itself as the subject of history. Berger imagines the first men crouching round their fires at night telling stories – perhaps dreams, embellished or idealised biographies, perhaps boasts intended to amplify the storyteller's power or the power of the storyteller's tribe to keep the fear of ghosts and wolves at bay. Each story represents a ring of fire and light lit to pierce the ambient darkness. To chase it back forever . . . And we today crouching on our haunches centred round the dying embers of so many great stories, so many heroic, epic master-narratives – stories which have lost their light and lustre, their power and their plausibility. We, today, may have to learn to live without their solace and their comfort in a world where nothing – not even the survival of the world itself as something to wake up to in the morning – is any longer certain.

If postmodernism means anything at all, it means an end to a belief in coherence and continuity as given, an end to the meta-physic of narrative closure (and in this it goes no further than the modernism it claims to supersede). Postmodernism may mean what Paul Virilio calls (in a phrase that echoes Benjamin) the 'triumph of the art of the fragment':[11] a loss of totality, a necessary and therapeutic loss of wholeness.[12]

It may mean recognising in ways that were prefigured years ago in Einstein's physics that subjects can merge with objects, that discontinuities are as significant, as productive as continuities, that observer effects and random factors must be taken into account in understanding or re-presenting any process whatsoever, however material the process, however 'materialist' the account.[13] It may mean at worst substituting history as a game of chance for the older, positivist models of productive causality. Less fatalistically, it may mean substituting a history without guarantees for the older models of mechanical and 'necessary' progress. The choice is still there even in the nuclear age: history as a sound and fury signifying nothing or history as a desperate struggle to snatch back reason with a small 'r' from the jaws of desperation.

But if this still sounds too grandiose and pretentious and far too close to the modernist project it claims to displace, we can cut postmodernism down to size by reducing its terms of reference. There are plenty of signs of the Post on the frantic surfaces of style and 'lifestyle' in the mid to late 80s.

Postmodernism could certainly be used loosely to designate that range of symptoms which announce a break with traditional culture and aesthetic forms and experiences: the break, for instance, with traditional notions of authorship and originality. Postmodernism has been used as a shorthand term to reference certain qualities and tendencies which characterise the contemporary (Western) metropolitan milieu: a growing public familiarity with formal and representational codes, a profusion of consumption 'lifestyles', cultures, sub-cultures; a generalised sensitivity to style (as language, as option, as game) and to difference – ethnic, gender, regional and local difference: what Frederic Jameson has called 'heterogeneity without norms'.[14]

For it's not all dark Wagnerian brooding, this postmodern thing. In fact, it often gets depicted (in a spirit which can be hostile or approving) as quite the opposite – as a celebration of what is there and what is possible rather than what might be there, what might be hypothetically possible.

The switch from the austere and critical negations (of the sensuous, of the doxa) which marked the counter-cinema, 'anti-art' and the conceptualism of the late 60s and 70s into 80s eclecticism, bricolage and play, etc, indicates not so much a lowering of expectations as a shift in the register of aspirations: from the drive towards a total transformation in historical time (May 68 and all that) to the piecemeal habitation of finite space – the space in which we live. If we were to talk in terms of master-disciplines the shift would be from sociology to architecture.

While some artists and critics (e.g. Fuller) denounce postmodernism as a flatulent retreat from the sacred responsibility of the artist to bear critical witness for the times in which we live,[15] others (e.g. Owens and Kruger) stress the extent to which the sacerdotal postures and 'duties' of the artist must themselves be questioned and dismantled insofar as they serve to amplify and duplicate the voice of the father.[16]

5 Clearly, there are many good things to be grown in the autumn of the patriarch, many good things to be found in the ruins, in the collapse of the older explanatory systems. The unfreezing of the rigid postures of the past – the postures of the hero, the critic, the spokesman – may merely signal the long- awaited eclipse of many oppressive powers in our world – the power, for instance, of the white male middle-class pundit. It may open things up so that sense may begin to flow with less alarming gusto through more

varied and more winding channels. Such a dispersion of sense might lead to a loosening of the bonds that bind us to the single and the singular track, to a paranoid obsession with certitude and fixed and single destinations.

6 As if (i): Looney Tunes

'What's up doc?'   Bugs Bunny.

The drift of some postmodernist accounts implies that the modernist avant garde constituted itself through what amounted to an imaginary and paranoid projection of absolute Otherness on to an idealised, non-existent bourgeois 'norm'. The unitary subject which is incessantly attacked, dis-stressed, deconstructed in modernist art and literature and modernist criticism becomes the imaginary Subject of both economic/political and cultural/ symbolic power: the absolute Father. The avant garde – were it to exist today – could no longer feasibly counterpose itself against such a clearly phantasmagoric, literally fantastic projection. In the days of *Dallas* and Princess Di we find it hard to pin down the contemporary correlative of anything so coherent and stable as a unitary bourgeois 'norm'.

In some declensions of the Post, the unitary subject as the principal target of radical modernist avant garde practice has been revealed as a strawman in the late twentieth century because capitalism these days has absolutely no stake whatsoever in the idea of individuals being tied to fixed and stable identities. The ideal consumer of the late 80s is a bundle of contradictions: monstrous, brindled, hybrid. The ideal consumer as deduced from contemporary advertisements is not a 'he' or a 'she' but an 'it'. At the moment (November 1985) it is a young but powerful (i.e. solvent) Porsche-owning gender bender who wears Katherine Hamnet skirts and Gucci loafers, watches *Dallas* on air and *Eastenders* on video, drinks lager, white wine or Grolsch and Cointreau, uses tampons, smokes St Bruno pipe tobacco, uses Glintz hair colour, cooks nouvelle cuisine and eats out at McDonald's, is an international jetsetter who holidays in the Caribbean and lives in a mock-Georgian mansion in Milton Keynes with an MFI self-assembled kitchen unit, an Amstrad computer and a custom-built jacuzzi. The ideal consumer is not the ideal productive worker of an earlier epoch – a sexually repressed nobody, alienated from sensual pleasure, subjected to the turgid, life-denying disciplines of the working week and the nuclear family. Instead, the ideal consumer – It: enemy of the personal pronouns – is a complete social and psychological mess. The ideal consumer as extrapolated from the barrage of contradictory interpellations from advertising billboards to magazine spreads to TV commercials is a bundle of conflicting drives, desires, fantasies, appetites. What advertising conceived as a system offers is not a sanctuary from conflict and necessity, not a 'magical' refuge from the quotidian grind. It does not address or constitute a subject so much as promise an infinite series of potentially inhabitable (and just as easily relinquished) subject positions. What capitalism these days wants is a world full of loaded drunken boats – *bateaux ivres* loaded down with loot. The subject of advertising is not the rational sovereign subject of Descartes, the subject of 'consumer sovereignty'. Nor is it the manipulated dupe of some 'critical' analyses of advertising signs: the malleable wax to the thumbprint of either commerce or the law. Rather it is Deleuze and Guattari's 'body without organs'[17] – the absolute decentred subject, the irresponsible, unanchored subject: the psychotic consumer, the schizophrenic consumer.[18]

Donald Duck goes shopping!

This disruption of the relative certainties and stabilities of High Modernism takes place within the transfigured social/informational space opened up by electronic communications. In a world of instantaneous communication, multi-user systems, electronic polylogue, the artist and the critic pale even further than before into impotence and insignificance. The intellectual, the critic, the artist can no longer claim to have privileged access to the truth or even to knowledge, at least to the knowledge that counts. What artist can compete with advertising when it comes to visual impact, ubiquity, effect and general exposure? What use is a critical interpretation of a text or a semiotic reading of an image in a world where information never stays in place, where information, communication, images are instantly produced, transformed, discarded in a process of endless complexification, polyphony, supercession and flux?

But all is not lost. We may have lost the Big Theories, the Big Stories but postmodernism has helped us to rediscover the power that resides in little things, in disregarded details, in aphorism (miniaturised truths), in metaphor, allusion, in images and image-streams. It has led to a rediscovery of the ancient power of the parable and the allegory, for the 'allegorical impulse' is everywhere in evidence: –

7 As if (ii): Orbis Tertius

The Argentinian writer, Jorge Luis Borges, once wrote a story about an imaginary world called Tlön.[19] This world has its own science, its own languages, its own religions and philosophies – all based on premises totally alien to Western traditions of thought – premises most especially inimicable to the materialist tradition. Tlön is the invention of a satanic American millionaire who has secretly commissioned a group of experts to compile a multi-volume encyclopaedia detailing every aspect of life on this fictional planet. Thousands of pages are devoted to the geography, history, the social and cultural institutions of the imaginary world. As the years go by, the narrator, a specialist in esoteric literature, becomes intrigued by the mystery of Tlön and tracks down successive volumes of the encyclopaedia in obscure antiquarian bookshops dotted around the genteel suburbs and bohemian quarters of various European and South American cities.

The fine details of a highly complex but entirely imaginary order are thus gradually disclosed to him – the intricate details of an invented, invisible world parallel but totally alien to our own. The fantastic essence of this alternative world system is most clearly embodied in a special category of ideal objects called the hrön which are literally dreamt into being. The hrön are ideas in three dimensions and they don't obey the laws of normal matter: they have a palpable existence but proceed directly from consciousness and depend upon consciousness for their survival. Borges mentions hrön ruins sited in neglected landscapes which continue to exist solely because of an occasional visit from a few birds or a horse. They persist because they are seen to persist – they exist through the gaze of others.

The story ends with the discovery on a rainy night in a remote village in the heart of the Argentinian pampas of a small, impossibly heavy conical object – an object composed of matter of such density that it defies the laws of physics. The boy who finds this cursed object is driven mad by his discovery and the next morning the writer stumbles across the boy's corpse outside his bedroom door. The implication of Borges's story is that the fragile shell that separates the real world from the ideal world of Tlön has broken down. The shadow of Tlön may fall at any time across the face of our familiar primary universe and with the appearance of that shadow a kind of doom is pronounced upon us all, an end to the prospect of repose. The boy's death is the first sentence in a new parodic Bible: the beginning of a travesty of history. Humanity folds back upon itself condemned to endless repetition, endless simulation – life without substance, world without end. The imaginary is become the symbolic; the symbolic closes over the real: the hrön are upon us . . .

Borges's story plays on taboos deeply embedded in occidental mythology – taboos concerning the dangers of unrestrained hypothesis – the tragic consequences which flow from the exercise of an over-ambitious imagination. These fears have been embodied down the centuries in a succession of mythical types: in Lucifer who challenged God as author of the world, in Mary Shelley's Dr Frankenstein and Rabbi Loew who moulded the Golem, a human-like figure, in clay and brought it to life by breathing the secret name of God into its mouth, in Faust and Daedalus and Icarus who perished by flying too high, by seeking God-like mastery over natural mysteries. The diabolical nature of the conspiracy of Tlön masterminded by the shadowy millionaire who imposes one condition on his encyclopaedists – that they 'make no mention of that "false imposter" Jesus Christ'[20] – is signalled by the boy's death. The hrön are the embodiment in form of the tragically inflated aspirations of that doomed or doom-bringing lineage that leads from Lucifer to Oppenheimer – the lineage of those who have sought to snatch away the veil, to know everything, to exhaust the earth's resources, to manipulate and hence to obliterate the transcendental mysteries. The hrön come into this world like black holes engendering chaos and darkness around themselves. They arrive wrapped in an aura of dread . . .

Borges's story ends with a postscript in which the narrator explains how some seven years after the publication of his original article on the Tlön conspiracy, published initially in a small, specialist journal, a hideous international cult has grown up around the hermetic world which he described in its pages. This cult claims 'Borges' is threatening the entire world:

> Contact with Tlön and the ways of Tlön have disintegrated this world. Captivated by its discipline, humanity forgets and goes on forgetting that this is the discipline of chess, not of angels. Now the conjectural 'primitive language' of Tlön has

found its way into the schools . . . A scattered dynasty of solitaries has changed the face of the world. If our foresight is not mistaken, a hundred years from now . . . the world will be Tlön . . .[21]

8 As if (iii): The Encyclopaedia of Tlön: An I-D for the 80s

Today we have our own encyclopaedias of Tlön: perfect worlds untouched by time, grime and history. Our encyclopaedias of Tlön are science fiction, video games, computer programs, the popular press, advertisements, TV commercials, pop promo videos, first strike capabilities, the 4-minute warning and Star Wars laser defence systems. These are some of today's perfect (i.e. self-referential, self-generating: recursive) fictions. Internally consistent, entirely hypothetical, they remain hermetically sealed against contact with the brute fact of physical, material and human limitation. These are the encyclopaedias of Tlön and they flicker in the libraries which face out towards the enemy all along the disintegrating line of the Western Front like the neon signs in West Berlin blinking out towards the East across the Berlin Wall.

VOLUME ONE: STYLISH SIMULACRA

Two advertisements for Harrods' Way In Clothes boutique appeared in 1986 on the back covers of *I-D* and *The FACE*. The style of these ads was a pastiche of mid-60s modern graphics. There were nudging references to Op Art: the black and white, high contrast images, the self-consciously dated foregrounding of bold, black 60s type. The Way In – as the name suggests – opened up in the late 1960s but rather than play down the dated 'swinging 60s' connotations of the client's name, the agency which handled the Harrods account decided to camp it up, to cash in on the look. As the new becomes discarded as an outmoded category and the invention of the new is abandoned as an anachronistic presumption, the past becomes a repertoire of retrievable signifiers and style itself is defined as a reworking of the antecedent. Just as the Grey agency working for Brylcreem decided to re-run re-edited versions of 60s TV ads with an unobtrusively updated soundtrack, so these Way In ads invoke an only slightly skewed sense of the recent past. The putative appeal of both Brylcreem and the Way In ads is based on retro-chic – the paradox of the old-fashioned, smart young modern look. In the twenty years or so that separate the image and its echo, social and moral values may have changed along with the political mood, school-leavers' expectations, prospects, aspirations, but the look, the haircuts, the tailored profiles remain constant – transmitted down the line of the video generations as constant and invariable as a prayer or incantation.

However, in order to mark the product as up-market, the advertisers have contrived to signal to the sign-conscious constituency towards which these ads are targeted that the advertisers know that times have changed by using obscure quotations from esoteric texts. (After all, this is 80s narrowcasting: advertisers nowadays address a tightly defined demographic – a specific segment of the market, not the classless teenmass implied in 60s ads.) From *The FACE*, a caption beneath the silhouette of someone sitting on a chair reads: 'you are tired of provincial boutique Sundays, you want the mythical New York and the Champs Elysées'. A credit in fine print informs us that these words are taken from *Julie Christie* by Stephen Duffy. Not the real Julie Christie, icon to a generation of iconoclasts, the archetype of the British 'dolly bird' in the 60s, of the politically committed campaigner and protester in the 70s and 80s, but rather something called 'Julie Christie': Julie Christie in inverted commas.

The authenticity of the quote from the *I-D* ad is, if anything, even more uncertain. It is framed within a frame. In a two-page spread, below a heading 'Double Identity', a photo graphic of an eye and a fingerprint, we read the following words:

> The type of consciousness the photograph involves is indeed truly unprece- dented, since it establishes not a consciousness of the being-there of the thing (which any [copy] could provide) but an awareness of its have been there.

This quotation is attributed to 'Roland Brown' although it seems likely that Roland Barthes is intended here (the quote is from 'The Rhetoric of the Image'). Alternatively (and this would be appropriate) it may be that the quote is being attributed to a fictional blend of Barthes and James Brown, godfathers respectively of the sign and soul music. Such a condensation of black funk and Parisian intellectual chic would represent the perfect dream amalgam of the two elements that dominate the international high gloss style purveyed by *I-D* and *The FACE*: sex and text, somatic rhythm and continental theory – the point where the Sorbonne meets the South Bronx: an 'erotics' not of reading but of skimming.

What these ads represent is the coming out of what Barthes called the 'second degree' in a world where we are invited to live our whole lives out inside someone else's borrowed frames, in a world which becomes bounded by the body where the body becomes first and foremost an attractive setting for the eyes – something to be looked at and looked after. The social collective, the larger collective interest, the social body, the body politic, can no longer be either dressed or addressed within this discourse as it dissolves – this larger body – into a series of narrowly defined markets, targets, consumption, taste and status groups. No boundaries left within this discourse of the 'look', no far perimeter, no limits to consumption, no limits to the spirals of desire, no distinction between use value and exchange value, no distinction between truth and lies, structure and appearance, reality and the will. The banal consequence of all these collapses along the disintegrating line of the Western Front is this: there is nothing better anywhere: nothing but individual bodies bent on having a wild time until the lights go out.

Within such a discourse it is difficult if not structurally impossible to make plausible appeals to larger social unities and interests, to larger communities, to social and identity formations larger than those inscribed within consumption. Now in 1986 with the steady erosion of social, political and ideological alternatives, with the ascendancy of the stunted logic of the market, the implication is that there is nowhere else to go but to the shops even if all you have to go to the shops with is a bottle and a petrol bomb when you go shopping at midnight for the only things that lift you up and give you value: clothes, videos, records, tapes, consumption: high gloss i-d, high gloss identity . . .

9   VOLUME TWO: A MONETARIST IMAGINARY

Levis are aiming red tag 501's at the *Miami Vice* dole queue cowboys.

Kevin Foreman

This shrinkage of the imaginative horizons can be linked in part to wider cultural shifts associated with the consolidation of monetarist policies and agendas throughout much of North Western Europe and North America. During the 80s we have seen the establishment throughout much of the Western world of a

'New Realism' based around a primitive version of political economy and a Hobbesian view of society as an atomised mass of individual units (families) driven by self-interest and 'natural' appetites – which are regulated and satisfied by the free play of market forces and proscribed in the last instance by the law. This 'New Realism' in its turn has facilitated a number of cultural developments.

It could be said, for instance, to underwrite the formulation of a new consumption ethic – unconstrained by the puritanical residues of the dissenting tradition – and a corresponding consumer aesthetic which privileges the criterion of looking good, of style – a theology of appearances – over virtually everything else. On the one hand there are the *Miami Vice* cowboys of the dole queue and the black economy. But at the same time, the prioritisation of market criteria of value serves to naturalise entrenched status and income differentials so that existing social and economic inequalities are exacerbated. The consumption ethic/aesthetic is most clearly in play at the point where commodities are mediated to the public; at the point where future markets are invited to meet existing products, where the two converge in the dreamscapes of glossy magazines, commercials, mail-order catalogues.

Here on the boundaries of the real, the hrön of the late 80s are silently gathering.

Habitat catalogues provide a paradigm case. For 20 years, Habitat has pioneered the idea of pre-selected shopping in Great Britain. It has pioneered the notion of the totally designed or integrated package where the consumer buys a whole ensemble rather than a single item. The assumption is that one purchase will drag the rest of the (matching/complementary) ensemble behind it in a process we could call 'syntax selling'. In the last few years syntax selling has been directed at a much wider variety of social groups. Customers are now invited to buy their way into the particular package most suited to their aspirations, means and preferences instead of being subjected to one (stripped pine) house style. In this way Terence Conran's selection of designs for Habitat are being used to shape and frame what Pierre Bourdieu calls the 'habitus' – the internalised system of socially structured, class-specific gestures, tastes, aspirations, dispositions which can dictate everything from an individual's 'body hexis' to his/her educational performance, speech, dress and perception of life opportunities. [22] The Conran intervention in the habitus/Habitat aims to generate profits, to educate the public and to raise the general standard of design in Britain. It may also incidentally lead to the development of the '"cultivated habitus", a "semi-learned grammar" of good taste which would serve to perpetuate a hierarchy of taste by establishing a scale ranging from "excellence" (mastery of the code), the rule converted into a habitus capable of playing with the rule of the game, through the strict conformity of those condemned merely to execute, to the dispossession of the layman'.[23]

The syntax of the package offers the consumer the security and imaginary coherence of pre-scripted lifestyle sequences (institutionalised therapy for the psychotic consumer):

> This is the chair to sit in, the food to eat, the plates to eat it off, the table settings to place it in, the cutlery to eat it with. This is the wine to drink with it. These are the glasses to drink the wine in, the clothes to wear, the books to decorate the bookshelves with. Now that Conran has taken over Mothercare, you can colour co-ordinate your entire life from the cradle to the grave.

There is nothing unique to the 80s in syntax selling, the cultivated habitus, or the mail-order mode of address. What is perhaps new in Britain is the diversity of the packages on offer, the increased sensitivity on the part of manufacturers, and of retailers, to regional and temporal fluctuations in market taste, and the lack of local resistance to such strategies on the part of consumers. As resistance to market pressures, to market definitions of reality and worth are actively eroded with the spread and penetration of market values, so previously repressed or occluded social aspirations can emerge to find the appropriate cultural register and, too, the kind of legitimacy which has generally been withheld from such aspirations since at least World War Two. Here on the pages of the current Habitat catalogue, the service industries receive an unexpected boost in this happy gathering. The aspiring consumer of kitchenware is invited to dream of having servants: for what else can all these individuals be doing standing in this kitchen? Note the compliant smiles, the relaxed but servile postures. The poses, the lighting, the setting all invoke an echo of the code of those *Sunday Times* colour supplement profiles of up-and-coming restaurants. Here are the staff of El Pastos as open, warm and willing to be photographed as they are friendly, efficient and eager to please when you sit down to dine. The paradigm of service: one of the most significant looks this season.

Of course, *The Tatler* – the magazine which ran a campaign in which a photograph of the 'beautiful rich' sporting on a yacht was displayed beneath the line: '*The Tatler*: the magazine for the other boat people' – can go one better in the offensive stakes. The removal of the old restraints – conscience, compassion, a sense of fair play, of *noblesse oblige* – all the old aristocratic virtues which were the sentimental remnants of an older, more organic and feudal relation to 'the people' displaced by Thatcherism and the New (suburban) Right are here annulled in the name of the nouveau aristocracy. Recently, *The Tatler* urged its readers to think pink, to return not (it goes without saying) to the tiresome old dreary dogmas of the Left but back to riding pink. The blatant assertion of privilege is here disguised or euphemised by irony. It is, after all, just an image, just a joke because nobody really believes in much more than images and jokes these days.

In these ads we encounter the return of the milk-white English rose, of the beautiful blonde bully: a kind of proto-fascist narcissism in this obsession – increasingly marked in the fashion pages of so many magazines since 1979 – with aryan ideals of beauty: the unadulterated 'look', uncontaminated by the indigestible multi-cultural stew which – it's perhaps implied – 'they' are trying to serve us up from the sidelines . . .

The Miracle of the (English) Rose

Victoria likes the culture shock of East End shopping (Halal goats' heads, compasses to point you in the direction of Mecca, black light bulbs, Huguenot-style singing birds, and the best smoked salmon in London). 'Shopkeepers here are not smarmy the way they are to customers in gentrified parts of London, but refreshingly direct.' She has brought up three daughters in the East End, all with the proper English roseness you might find in Cheltenham. 'As the girls get older they become a bit impatient with Georgian authenticity. They would like Laura Ashley wallpaper in their rooms and fitted carpets, but you can't really stick wallpaper on top of panelling. The eldest girl's dream is to have a modern flat in the Barbican with mix 'n' match fabrics. Just as we reacted against our parents' taste, our children will react against us.' Victoria Cruickshank, from an article on the New Georgians,

'Home is where the art is', by Alexandra Artley, *The Sunday Times* colour magazine, 27 October 1985.

The terrain on which all these different but related imaginaries are built is the terrain of advertising, the imaginary of Tlön, a world which has surrendered to the simulacrum – the image which bears no relation to a pre-existent real but which nonetheless can have real effects, a world where reality is nothing more than an incessant staging of events to be framed, recorded, relayed, screened: a world where people's lives simply unravel in the blank, empty spaces of the Now. We are in danger of being rolled flat beneath the weight of all this imaging. People with real bodies and real minds have become within today's encyclopaedias of Tlön, the dreadful excess, the non-necessary, embarrassing surplus of the sign.

> The passive half of humanity (will be increasingly consigned) to a second hand world, a ghost world in which everyone lives a second hand and derivative life . . .
>
> Lewis Mumford

> So what's new, doc? Aaagh, quit beefin', will ya?
>
> Bugs Bunny

10 A New Conviction Politics

> 'Mirror, mirror on the wall
> Who's the fairest of them all?'
> Snow White's wicked step-mother.

Finally, we come to the *Mirror*, the comic book of Tlön.

At the climax of a mega-charity event organised by Jasper Conran, heir to the Habitat-Heals-and-Mothercare millions, a television personality called Selina Scott pretends to marry another television personality called Charles Villiers. And this is front page news in Mr Maxwell's new look *Mirror* in 1985. Selina Scott is a presenter. Charles Villiers is an actor but these fine distinctions are neither here nor there. They pale into insignificance in the luminosity of televisual fame – the condition these two share – a luminosity which unites this charmed duo and glows over their heads with all the radiance of D. H. Lawrence's rainbow. The marriage in inverted commas is consecrated in celebrity.

But of course this is just make-believe. It didn't really happen.

They aren't really getting married. The 'scandal'; or 'our Selina' marrying an already married man is just a counterfeit manufactured for the worthiest of causes: to help to feed the world. For this is Fashion Aid. The mock marriage ceremony is a fairy tale. Its fairy tale character is confirmed by the proximity of the adjacent item, on the withdrawal of Janet Street-Porter, yet another TV personality, from the event on the grounds that she wouldn't do it unless she got paid or received some material recompense (literally 'material' in this case: apparently she asked to keep the dress). We even have the Ugly Sister to Selina's Cinderella.

The fantasy appeal of a union between Charles and Selina was no doubt enhanced for the *Mirror* editor by the often remarked resemblance between Selina Scott and the Princess of Wales. The prospect of watching Selina, the image of Lady Di (the fantasy stand-in from the telly: more common than the original commoner), the Princess Diana simulacrum, sweeping up the aisle on the arm of another well-bred Charles in a reprise of the original performance – this was just too good to miss. In fact, there was no chance of its being missed. This was a marriage made not in heaven but on a PR person's desk. It was made to make a splash. It was literally designed to be front page news in 1985.

Any vague misgivings we may have about the 'status' or the 'meaning' of this 'mega-event' are ruled out of court by the proviso that, after all, this is . . . all for charity. After the phenomenal success of Band Aid and Live Aid, after the phenomenal impact of Bob Geldof on the popular imagination, how could we even think to question the value of the virtue of an event that calls itself 'Fashion Aid' and which manages to raise another much needed million for the starving people of Africa? This event might be make-believe but it is make-believe with a conscience; if it is vanity then it is vanity in the service of a higher ideal. The Royal Wedding is simply being playfully quoted in order to generate more cash and more interest in the stars who stood in at the Albert Hall for all of those who care about starvation in Africa and for the cameras which were present on the day to relay the event to the rest of the world.

And yet that quotation isn't innocent. The Royal Wedding isn't just any old event. It was a key event in the consolidation of the new mood of national pride and the new authoritarian populism which has characterised British popular culture in the 1980s. It was, after all, the Royal Wedding which – just days after the inner-city riots of

93

1981 – marked the magical renewal of the ideal of one nation welded together through its common history and pledged to uphold the time-honoured British traditions of Caste, the Christian Creed, the Family, Democracy and Due Ceremonial Process. The Royal Wedding – together with the electoral victory two years earlier of Mrs Thatcher – marked the real beginning of the 1980s. For what came in on Mrs Thatcher's train, what came swirling in on the silken hem of Princess Di's interminable wedding dress, was Romance, Resolve, Retrenchment: the three 'R's for the 1980s. Iron resolve from the Falklands to Orgreave, retrenchment of some pretty primitive ethical, social and economic context, romance – the word which must surely be the heading in italics over the decade – romance from the New Romantics to the New Georgians, from *Brideshead Revisited* to *Chariots of Fire*: romance – an alternative, softer synonym for that other 80s keyword – 'STYLE' ('style' would be etched out in hard-edged, hi-tec no-nonsense bold . . .).

So Selina and her beau act out a respectful and affectionate parody of the Royal Wedding for the cameras as part of a fashion show attended by similar media and fashion 'mega-personalities' in an event which took place in order to be recorded by the cameras so that funds could be generated for a campaign to 'Feed the World' – a campaign which to complete the circle was started when another media mega-personality, Bob Geldof, was moved one night by what he saw when watching a TV documentary about famine in Ethiopia.

To close the strange loops (the Disneyride) across the terrain of the postmodern sketched out in this report, we are back where we started with simulacra, hermetic systems, back beneath the shadow of Tlön. For sometimes the media's sole source of power, their entire fascination in the age of what Eco calls 'neo- (as opposed to 'paleo') TV', appears to consist in the relations which pertain between them, in the energy generated within their own field rather than in any putative links we might superstitiously or sentimentally believe they retain with a reality outside themselves, with what we might call the 'extra-textual' world. But in the case of the Aid phenomenon the postmodern 'explanation' seems barely adequate or plausible. A postmodern *langueur* is simply not appropriate in this case. For the image of hermetic systems shatters with the assertion of a categorical imperative that seems to be irrefutable, when the prospect of the real comes crashing in through the television screens in the shape of babies with distended stomachs demanding to be fed.

For the fact is that the chain of events that leads from Geldof watching TV in his living room to Selina, Charles and a line of Tina Turner lookalikes dressing up for a good cause was triggered off precisely because of just such a superstitious, sentimental conviction – precisely because enough people felt that something real and something terrible – the two ideas are related – was happening *somewhere else* and that we – all the rest of us – were directly connected to and in some ways responsible for that terrible though physically remote reality.

Whatever else we may feel about the Band Aid phenomenon, about what occurs around its edges in the *Mirror* piece for example, I don't think that anyone would deny the strength and the importance of that other conviction – in a sense, I think, everything hangs upon it, upon the survival of the capacity of ordinary people to identify, to bond together and to act constructively in concert to make things better; the capacity of ordinary people to discriminate when it really matters between what is real and what isn't, to decide what the real priorities are. I don't think anyone in his right mind would deny that real and vitally important moral resources were relocated and effectively deployed on a massive, international scale by Geldof and the people working with him. It may indeed be possible that what we are just glimpsing here in the Band Aid phenomenon is the formulation of a new set of moral imperatives, a new kind of eco-politics in which 'resolve' and 'conviction' – keywords in the Thatcherite discourse, terms which were given a definite authoritarian gloss as they were persistently invoked to counteract appeals from all sides for a U-turn away from monetarist policies – were themselves turned in a new and startlingly different way by 'Saint Bob' and his colleagues. After Geldof – the dishevelled, sometimes less than civil Irish man who spoke up on behalf of conscience – the real Enemy Within, the repressed term in the monetarist discourse – Thatcher could no longer claim to have a monopoly on either resolve or conviction.

The possibility of emerging eco-perspectives simultaneously developed through and bound into global communication networks is an important if problematic one and it goes directly against the dark, fatal grain of much postmodern prophecy. Such eco-perspectives will be articulated differently in different national-political contexts as they combine and are combined with, inform and are informed by, existing political, discursive formations. (Here in Britain Geldof mobilised an alternative 'decent' British common sense against Thatcher's 'little england-ism'.) There are of course no guarantees. There is no *telos* impelling humanity towards greater cooperation and mutual understanding in McLuhan's 'global village'. But there are vital lessons to be learned from Band Aid and the Geldof intervention concerning the mobilisation of affect, the as yet barely explored potentialities for organising and redirecting material and im-material resources through affective networks opened up within transnational communication systems.[24]

That is what I meant earlier when I referred to reason with a small 'r' snatched from the jaws of desperation. The potentialities sketched out around the edges of the Aid phenomenon can be glimpsed on the other side, as it were, of the morbid discourse of the Post . . .

11 Out of the Shadows

Photographs are the certificates of presence . . . From a phenomenological viewpoint, in the Photograph, the power of authentication exceeds the power of representation.

Roland Barthes, *Camera Lucida*, p. 77

The photograph as such and the object in itself share a common being, after the fashion of a fingerprint. Wherefore, photography actually contributes something to the order of natural creation instead of providing a substitute for it. The surrealists had an inkling of this when they looked to the photographic plate to provide them with their monstrosities and for this reason: the surrealists do not consider their aesthetic purpose and the mechanical effect of the image on our imaginations as things apart. For them, the logical dis-tinction between what is imaginary and what is real tends to disappear. Every image is to be seen as an object and every object as an image. Hence photography ranks high in the order of surrealist creativity because it produces an image that is a reality of nature namely, an hallucination that is also a fact.

Andre Bazin, 'The ontology of the photograph' in
What Is Cinema? Vol. 1

Roland Barthes was as convinced as Bazin that mechanically produced images retain an aura. For Barthes, they bear a direct relation to the real. In *Camera Lucida*, he defined the peculiar ontology of the photographic image – its doubleness (the photograph at once 'material' and 'immaterial'), its unique status as material testament to the undeniable facticity of history ('The name of Photography's *noeme* will therefore be: "That-has-been", or again: the Intractable').[25] He describes how, following his mother's death, he found among the family albums what was for him the *quintessential* photograph of his mother as a little girl of five caught in 1898 'at the end of a little wooden bridge in a glassed-in conservatory, what was called a Winter Garden in those days'.[26]

> My mother was five at the time, her brother seven. He was leaning against the bridge railing, along which he had extended on arm; she, shorter than he, was standing a little back, facing the camera; you could tell that the photographer had said, 'Step forward a little so we can see you'; she was holding one finger in the other hand, as children often do, in an awkward gesture. The brother and sister, united, as I knew by the discord of their parents, who were soon to divorce, had posed side by side, alone, under the palms of the Winter Garden (it was the house where my mother was born, in Chennevières-sur-Marne).

Despite his personal aversion to the fixity of image ('He is intolerant of any *image* of himself, he suffers at being named . . .'[27]), this photograph satisfies Barthes's yearning to encounter 'utopically' an image of his mother which would be 'both justice and accuracy – *justese:* just an image, but a just image'. The extreme *particularity* of the little girl's pose, the captured moment: this palpable *emanation* of his mother's presence in the world – the essential presence prior to, productive of his own appearance in time – together make this for Barthes 'one of the loveliest photographs in the world; a superogatory photograph which contained more than what the technical being of photography can reasonably offer'.[28]

When confronting the Winter Garden photograph, what mattered to Barthes was 'not the photograph's "life" (a purely ideological notion) but the certainty that the photographed body touches me with its own rays and not with a superadded light'.[29] According to Barthes, it was the intensity of this relation to the

97

beloved body (a need to protect it from the indifferent, curious, *impersonal* gaze of the reader) that prevented him from reproducing it in *Camera Lucida:*

> (I cannot reproduce the Winter Garden photograph. It exists only for me. For you, it would be nothing but an indifferent picture, one of the thousand manifestations of the 'ordinary'; it cannot in any way constitute the visible object of a science; it cannot establish an objectivity, in the positive sense of the term, at most it would interest your *studium*; period, clothes, photogeny; but in it, for you, no wound.)

Elsewhere in the same book Barthes meditates on genealogy and remarks on the extent to which the family album testifies to the reality of genetic inheritance ('the Photograph sometimes makes appear what we never see in real face . . . a genetic feature, the fragment of oneself or of a relative which comes from some ancestor'). Barthes accompanies these remarks with a photograph which appears above the enigmatic caption, 'The Stock'.

A little girl, five years old perhaps, 'holding one finger in the other hand, as children often do, in an awkward gesture' stands next to a boy aged perhaps seven. Here is the brother–sister snapshot of the classic family album. The boy leans against the 'monumental . . . Hugolian' figure of a bearded old man in a sun hat (the seated figure, pipe in hand, exudes paternity and lineage: is this the grandfather?). Barthes implies (it's never quite clear) that this is a photograph of his father as a child. The father is connected 'in a sense over his head' by facial lineaments to Barthes's paternal grandmother, even to Barthes himself. Yet in the next paragraph, the attribution of the image is switched. Barthes asks the question: 'what relation can there be between my mother and her ancestor, so formidable, so monumental, so Hugolian, so much the incarnation of the inhuman distance of the Stock?'

Who knows? Perhaps *this* is the Winter Garden photograph. Perhaps Barthes felt compelled for whatever obscure reason to reproduce the cherished portrait: to reproduce the image of his mother and yet to disavow/disguise the reproduction. Perhaps the old man is the 'bridge' in the 'Winter Garden' – the bridge that spans the 'inhuman distance' opened up for Barthes by the wound of his mother's absence: the /in Life/Death. Perhaps the old man is the bridge *and* the Garden: the soil in which the Stock is seeded has reached a barren point in Barthes: it is a 'winter' garden. The boy's arm is resting, extended along the old man's knee – the knee that functions like the ancient prohibition to separate the sister from the brother . . . 'He was leaning against the bridge railing, along which he had extended one arm . . . ' If such a fanciful hypothesis were correct it would appear likely that the Winter Garden is less a real location than a metaphorical state: an imaginary point of origin, a *fantasy* of origin not Edenic in Barthes's case, but thanatic: it is a *Winter* Garden, a literal ending of the line (the children secure beneath the swaying palms, the 'monumental' hands of history):

> If, as so many philosophers have said, Death is the harsh victory of the race, if the particular dies for the satisfaction of the universal, if after having been reproduced as other than himself, the individual dies, having thereby denied and transcended himself, I who had not procreated, I had, in her very illness, engendered my mother. Once she was dead I no longer had any reason to attune myself to the progress of the superior Life Force (the race, the species). My particularity could never again universalise itself (unless, utopically, by writing, whose project henceforth would become the unique goal of my life). From now on, I could do no more than await my total, undialectical death. This is what I read in the Winter Garden Photograph.[30]

When he was alive, Barthes's entire 'method' consisted in the scattering of sense, the dispersal of the code: a turning-in of language on itself. His most intimate confessions thus remained 'impersonal': once or twice Barthes's face would appear in a sentence or a phrase in the flickering of the 'I' at the edge between the enoncé and the enonciation. But for the most part Barthes preferred ellipsis, allusion, the flight of the signifier. In *Camera Lucida* Barthes plays again the game of hide-and-seek. How Barthes delights in the Janus code in this book: one hand clearing the water, the other swirling up the sand – merging 'confessions' with 'fantasies' and 'fictions', smudging the blood lines, blurring the mother and the father, the mother and her son, and then (in fulfilment of some promise to himself?) slipping in despite his own denials, 'one of the loveliest photographs in the world'! Of course, this is just a fanciful hypothesis – though one that's licensed by the liberties Barthes himself took with the 'truth' of texts . . . but what

if it were *really* true? What if Barthes felt compelled by the un-
bearable force – the agony – of his loss to 'break his word': to give
the game away in the closing chapter? What if he felt compelled in
a final, fatal gesture of profound resignation to give up the ghost,
to give her up to us: 'For what I have lost is not a Figure (the
Mother), but a being; and not a being, but a *quality* (a soul): not
the indispensable, but the irreplaceable.'[31] It would be, perhaps, a
just hypothesis because, for Barthes, photography was intimately
bound up with death and resurrection, and photographic images
were for him, as they had been for Bazin, material echoes, literal
traces of the real, signs and objects, documents of actual moments,
images of absent things and real things in themselves. As far as
Barthes is concerned we are being extraordinarily apposite when
we say that we find old photographs 'haunting'. In old photographs we meet the past in person ('cameras . . . were clocks for
seeing') and all photographs are old. On the one hand, they are
quotations from an irrecoverable text (the world of yesterday, of
the hour before last, of the second before this one) and on the
other they are ghostly emanations from the real (what Barthes
called the *spectrum* of the photograph – light radiating from an
object captured on light-sensitive emulsion through a combination of chemical and mechanical means). In the end, Barthes
was a romantic and a realist.

The agonised and excessive investments we make in personally
significant photographs, in photographs of people close to us, in
those images which glow for us, which we don't just steal from
others, glance at, throw away but rather which we take ourselves
(not 'take' in the literal sense of 'capture', 'press the shutter' but
in those images we choose and take into the body of our lives) . . .
those images are always literally impossible to bear – impossible to
possess those others caught at other times in other places.

When we choose such a photograph (or when such a
photograph chooses us) our 'choice' has little or nothing to do
with purely formal values involving as it does an attribution of
value which is always 'irrational', 'excessive', 'out of all proportion'
to the visible object. This attribution of value is always in another
sense *impossible* because it stems from a mysterious imperative (the
imperative of alchemy) to *transubstantiate*: to modify substance
through a transitive intervention, an act of will, perhaps, in this
case through an act of intense devotion: an absorption of the self
in the image of the Other. The auratic quality attached to such

photographs – the halo that surrounds and enshrines the particulars of the chosen image – is the trace of our desire to convert a precious 'hallucination' into a straightforward 'fact', to blur the loved one with the lived one and to install this super-imposition at the centre of one's life. To pull the shutter. To make time end.

And if it does (end), the rides at Disneyland are never going to be the same again. Because when time ends, the birds and hippos and lions and deer at Disneyland will no longer be simulations, and, for the first time, a real bird will sing.[32]

Philip K. Dick, *How To Build A Universe*

ACKNOWLEDGEMENT

This paper first appeared in BLOCK No.12 1986/87 and is repro-duced here with the kind permission of the Editor.

NOTES

1 See, for instance, H. Foster (ed.), *Postmodern Culture*, London, Pluto, 1985; L. Appignanensi and G. Bennington (eds), *Postmodernism*, ICA Documents 4, Institute of Contemporary Arts, 1986; J.-F. Lyotard, *The Postmodern Condition*, Manchester, University of Manchester Press, 1984; *New German Critique: Modernity and Postmodernism Debate*, No. 33, Fall, 1984; F. Jameson, 'Postmodernism or the cultural logic of late capitalism', *New Left Review*, July–August 1984, no. 146; L. Grossberg, *Rocking with Reagan* (forthcoming); H. Lawson, *Reflexivity: The Post-Modern Predicament*, London, Hutchinson, 1985. For a more developed and conventional critique of postmodernism than the one presented in this report, see D. Hebdige, *Hiding in the Light: On Images and Things*, London, Routledge, 1988.

2 J. Baudrillard, 'The ecstasy of communication', in Foster, 1985, op. cit., pp. 107–8.

3 See, for instance, M. Newman, 'Revising modernism, representing postmodernism', in Appignanensi and Bennington (eds), op. cit. Newman posits two distinct modernist traditions, one centring on an 'autonomous' fixation on 'honesty', 'purity' and 'reflexivity' (from Kant to Greenberg); the other focused round a 'heteronomous' aspir-ation to dissolve art into everyday life (from Hegel to the surrealists). Any simplistic model of a single modernist movement unfolding globally in time to the rhythm of 'development' is effectively dismantled by Perry Anderson in his response to Marshall Berman's book, *All That's Solid Melts Into Air*. See P. Anderson, 'Modernity and revolution', in *New Left Review*, 1984, no. 144, March–April.

4 J.-F. Lyotard, 'Defining the postmodern', in Appignanensi and Bennington (eds), op. cit.
5 For problems of periodisation, see Foster, 1985, op. cit., especially Foster, 'Postmodernism. A preface', J. Habermas, 'Modernity – an incomplete project', and F. Jameson, 'Postmodernism and consumer society'. Also Anderson, 1984, op. cit. and Newman, 1986, op. cit.
6 For a discussion of these categories see S. Ardener, *Perceiving Women*, London, Malaby Press, 1975; A. Kuhn, *Women's Pictures: Feminism and Cinema*, London, Routledge & Kegan Paul, 1982.
7 See J. Baudrillard, 'The precession of simulacra', in *Art & Test*, 1983, vol. 2, Spring. Also, *Simulations*, semiotext(e), 1983. P. Virilio explores similar themes in 'The overexposed city' in *Zone 1/2 The City*, 1986.
8 A. Sayle, *Train to Nowhere*, London, Methuen, 1983.
9 See P. Wright, 'Ideal homes', in *New Socialist*, 1985, no. 31, October.
10 John Berger in conversation with Susan Sontag on the TV discussion programme 'Voices'.
11 P. Virilio and S. Lotringer, *Pure War*, Semiotext(e), 1983.
12 The most extreme formulation of the 'postmodern ontology' thesis has been put forward by Baudrillard who argues that the 'space of the subject' (interiority, psychological 'depth', motivations, etc.) is being 'imploded' and destroyed by the new communication technologies. See Baudrillard, 1983 and 1985, op. cit.
13 See J.-F. Lyotard, 'Les Immateriaux', in *Art & Text*, 1985, vol. 17, Expressionism, April. This article is a translation of a document written by Lyotard as an accompanying gloss to the exhibition of the same name organised by Lyotard at the Pompidou Centre in Paris from 28 March to 15 July 1985. The mixed media installations which formed a series of nodal points through which the spectator/auditor was invited to 'drift' were designed to force modifications to existing models of aesthetics, knowledge and communications by exploring/exposing the epistemological implications of the new technologies. The installations were designed to stand as analogues of/catalysts for the new 'postmodern sensorium' – a sensorium constituted in part directly through exposure to the new technologies (understood first and foremost as the bearers of the next phase in human evolution: the era of the Simulacra). This new sensorium, it is argued, can only be properly understood/inaugurated if we 'move beyond' the post- Socratic distinctions between, for instance, mind and matter, body and spirit, subject and object which formed and go on forming the founding 'moment' of so much of what we call 'western' thought and culture.
14 F. Jameson, 1984, op. cit.
15 See for instance, P. Fuller, *Aesthetics After Modernism*, London, Writers and Readers, 1983; *Beyond the Crisis in Art*, London, Writers and Readers, 1980.
16 See B. Kruger, *We Won't Play Nature to Your Culture*, London, Institute of Contemporary Arts, 1983 and C. Owens, 'The Medusa effect or, The spectacular ruse', in Kruger, 1983. Also C. Owens, 'The discourse of others: feminists and postmodernism', in Foster, 1985, op. cit.

17 G. Deleuze and F. Guattari, *The Anti-Oedipus: Capitalism and Schizophrenia*, University of Minnesota Press, 1983.
18 Ibid. and F. Jameson, 1984, 1985, op. cit. Also Baudrillard in Foster, 1985, op. cit. For a more critical engagement with the postmodernist 'appropriation' of schizophrenia see D. Hebdige, 'Staking out the Posts', in *Hiding in the Light: On Images and Things*, London, Routledge, 1988 and 'Postmodernism and the other side', *Journal of Communication Inquiry*.
19 J.L. Borges, 'Tlön, Uqbar and Orbis Tertius', in *Labyrinths*, Harmondsworth, Penguin, 1969.
20 Ibid.
21 Ibid.
22 See P. Bourdieu, *Outline of a Theory of Practice*, Cambridge, Cambridge University Press, 1977, also *Distinction: A Social Critique of the Judgement of Taste*, London, Routledge & Kegan Paul, 1984.
23 P. Bourdieu, 1977, op. cit., p. 99.
24 For a more developed version of these arguments, see D. Hebdige, 'Vital strategies' in *Hiding in the Light: On Images and Things*, London, Routledge 1988.
25 R. Barthes, *Camera Lucida: Reflections on Photography*, New York, Hill & Wang, 1981.
26 Ibid., pp. 67–8.
27 R. Barthes, *Roland Barthes by Roland Barthes*, London, Macmillan, 1977.
28 R. Barthes, 1981, op. cit., p. 70.
29 Ibid., p. 73.
30 Ibid., p. 72.
31 Ibid., p. 75.
32 P.K. Dick, 'How to build a universe that doesn't fall apart two days later, in *I Hope I Shall Arrive Soon*, London, Victor Gollancz, 1985.

6

CULTURE MADE, FOUND AND LOST

The cases of climbing and art

Ian Heywood

What idea, what image do we have of society? What is the structure of society like? Does it have different elements, and if so how do they hang together? For a Durkheimian sociology there are two general answers to questions like these. The first is provided by sociology's developing corpus of knowledge; this is a *professional* answer. The second is rooted in and provided by the society to which the sociologist belongs; this is a directly social or *everyday* answer. The relationship between the two answers has rarely been explicitly addressed from within a Durkheimian framework. That is, the professional answer is scientific and detached, a view which tries to distance itself from the prevailing ideas, analogies, metaphors and classifications which play an important part in sustaining a particular form of social organisation. However, the Durkheimian sociologist also recognises the difficulty and partiality of the professional answer. The scientific account must be shaped by the prevailing stock of ideas, notions of possible mechanisms, patterns and so forth. In other words, this stock of ideas constrains the imagination of the theorist. Equally, the same set of images and metaphors will to some degree influence the public and professional reception of new theories. But for Durkheimian social science to be conceivable there must be the possibility of a distinction between professional and everyday answers.

We will consider in more detail later another feature of the relationship between professional and everyday ideas of social structure. Briefly, not only must there be a prevailing, everyday view of the nature of society, but this view must also be naturalised, it must appear to be either inevitable or reasonable. Its contingency, and the capacity of society to be other than it is, must be denied or even rendered inconceivable. Without this naturalisation, prevailing images and ideas will not command sufficient belief and respect to make possible a whole range of important but fragile social institutions.[1]

Again, the Durkheimian sociologist would have to recognise some difficulties implied by this view of his or her professional work. How deep, how pervasive is this limit to sociological awareness and imagination? Even when the sociologist believes that a theory has attained a critical distance from its host society, even when it is received by the public with incomprehension or hostility, even then may there not be a deep and hidden agreement between the demands of social structure and critical, social scientific thought? What, if any, are the reasonable limits of what Ricoeur has called the 'hermeneutics of suspicion'?

One way of describing culture is to suggest that it is what provides us with our ideas of social structure, through such things as art, politics, religion, ethics, law, history and social science itself. Culture encompasses both professional and everyday views of the nature of society. Thus, if there is trouble with the formation of compelling images of social structure, of the social whole, at either or both theoretical and everyday levels, then we might be justified in identifying a problem with culture. Is it being suggested that there is indeed such a problem?

Modernity has been usefully described as the autonomous development of different modes of representing and acting upon the world, the 'individuation' of the cultural field into discourses. With the Enlightenment, discourses – these systematic, public ways of showing and making – embark with a characteristic vigour upon a new phase of their development. This is the drive first towards *individuation,* in which each strives to realise in its full distinctiveness a particular vision and mode of action, and second towards *totalisation,* in which each attempts to reconstruct its relationships with other discourses. The import of modernity is, then, that there is no given, common culture which either reflects or reproduces social structures, or rather that any representation of a common culture or common cultural history can never escape the simultaneous visibility of its partiality, its fundamentally interested, limited and contingent character because of the particularity of the cultural 'region' from which the representation emanates. Cultural theory thus operates against a background of the lack or fragility of any common cultural context for such disparate discourses as art, science and politics; while these constructed

105

common cultures command the assent of discourse members, of the converted, there are always grounds for scepticism from the point of view of another discourse, another community. This, then, is not so much the emergence of sub-cultures understood with reference or in opposition to an overarching or dominant culture. It is rather an emergence through discourses of cultures offering different ways of showing and practising the social. In Durkheimian terms, this would be something like a decline or weakening of the *conscience collective* through the rise of individualised cultures; alternatively, it might also be described as the replacement of any general *conscience collective* by competing regional notions and practices of identity. Now if we treat sociology as forming either the whole or part of an individuating discourse – we might talk about the 'culture of sociology' – at one level this raises no serious social problem. At another level, however, it confronts the sociologist with severe problems. First, the situation is unproblematic in that the discipline continues to have an emergent body of knowledge, more or less professionally adequate ideas, models, methods, etc. Second, the position becomes more problematic when it is seen that sociology's account is just one way of representing society. Either explicitly or implicitly aware of modernity as the individuation of cultures, and in this sense operating with a view of the limits of modernity, professional and lay audiences can recognise both the validity but also the partiality of sociology's professional representations.

Turning to another tradition of enquiry, in *Culture and Society* Raymond Williams states that the very idea of culture is 'a general reaction to a general and major change in the conditions of our common life. Its basic element is its effort at total qualitative assessment.'[2] We can immediately see here one strand in a pre- valent and familiar way of understanding the nature of culture, that of a 're-action' in which culture – including both what we would conventionally understand as 'art' and what Williams calls 'a whole way of life' – culture in its more anthropological sense – somehow reflects or can function as an index of social structure; hence the possibility, through culture, of a qualitative assessment of the whole society.

Another strand, also to be found in Williams's work, emphasises culture as formative of social life itself. In *Culture and Society* the value of solidarity, associated by Williams with the working class, is vital to the realisation of community, an authentic society transcending the limitations of bourgeois *Gesellschaft*.

A third strand, which some of the modern and postmodern Left might find the most anachronistic, Romantic element in Williams's text, is represented by a specific trope: 'The idea of culture rests on a metaphor: the tending of natural growth. And indeed it is on growth, as metaphor and as fact, that the ultimate emphasis must be placed.'[3] Here the emphasis shifts from culture as symptomatic or as a field for rational social action to culture as the nurturing of creative possibilities inherent within human life, possibilities which call for a recognition of the limits of our self-understanding, and a curbing of our ingrained impulse to dominate and control.

The concerns of this chapter touch on two of the strands in Williams's classic work: the question of the qualitative assessment of our common life, and the necessarily metaphoric under-standing we have of culture. Is there a connection at this point with the Durkheimian approach outlined earlier? Does the question of culture, in particular its problematic modern character, connect with the question of the quality of our common life?

It is usual to say that Durkheim sought to explain various typical contemporary social problems with reference to a general weaken-ing of the social bond. It might be more accurate to say that he was concerned not with a structural weakening as with a certain for-getting or elision of the social in the thoughts and feelings of modern men and women, that is, in their representations, in their culture. In this way we might say that Durkheim offered a cultural criticism of modernity. However, if we transform the notion of an *individualistic* culture into that of an *individuated* culture then the objects of criticism are the false totality, and all who peddle the immediate, given availability of a common culture, either as national culture, popular culture, the culture of the oppressed, market culture, or whatever; it must also question all expansionist moves by cultures (or discourses) which disguise their interested, partial, cultural character – perhaps behind the universalism of science or rational critique or social justice – and which expand their domains by explaining or interpreting or criticising the cultures of others. One would obviously have to include sociology, or at least some sociological excursions, in this category, and at this point a problem emerges not wholly dissimilar to that discussed earlier of the relationship between professional and everyday accounts of society. What prevents sociology itself from promoting false totalities? How can sociology responsibly handle the paradox of having a view of modernity as the individuation of cultures but also a professional, that is, a constitutive commitment to a reasoned account of, and ultimately a judgement on, our common life?

Summarising, it has been suggested that whatever else it does culture supplies us with both everyday and professional ideas of the nature of society. If modernity involves the individuation of discourses, culture becomes cultures, and accompanying this change is a transformation of our given modes of theorising and living-out culture as a 'whole way of life', as a set of representations permitting an understanding and assessment of social processes, or as a set of naturalised symbols and categories reproducing particular social structures.

The change puts into question the ability of cultures to sustain a distinction between making and finding, yet this distinction is crucial to the possibility of culture insofar as culture relates to the ways in which human beings invest their existence with meaning. In this process of meaning-investment the practices constituting a culture are seen to deal with 'materials' provided for them by nature and human beings; we might think here of the response to the physical environment, to landscape, animal life, climate. On the human side we might think of the ways in which technological change, war, the rise and fall of civilisations, nations or social groups have formed the 'subject matter' of cultural works of different kinds. Equally, cultural work is seen to require a stock of images, metaphors, models, concepts and methods which usually go largely unnoticed or, when considered explicitly, are seen as unproblematic, necessary and reasonable. In describing, explaining, interpreting or justifying, culture does indeed *make* things into what they are. This establishes a certain ambivalence, to put it at its most benign, in our relationship with important aspects of contemporary cultural life.

Under the impact of modernity the capacity of cultures to make and find is imperilled by their depleted capacity to distinguish between these functions. That is, awareness of the significance of discursive individuation produces eventually the recognition that what members of a particular social world, members of a particular discourse community, believe to be unquestionable, necessary, ultimately reasonable or simply natural is revealed as eminently questionable, contingent, unreasonable and historical. To find is merely to forget, conveniently, what one has made. When even forgetting is a kind of making, the rule of *praxis*, of making in general, is universal. When a culture loses the distinction between what it makes and what it finds it also loses itself.[4]

What, then, of the possibility of culture? To practise or live-through a culture is to accept, to exist unreflectively within, certain fundamental assumptions, guiding metaphors and principles of classification; this is so even when the practice is that of under-standing, reflectively and critically, cultural practices. These ideas, metaphors and principles, possessed of a certain aura of reliability which it would be unreasonable to question, in this way resemble the found. Yet it is simultaneously felt or known that this aura is only an effect of the power of denial, specifically the repression of authorship and responsibility. The problems for the practice of living and the project of knowing are apparent, yet perhaps not often explored.

I propose to use two activities – rock climbing and visual art – to examine some of the dimensions of this problem. The question being asked is: How could we understand these activities culturally when the very possibility of a culture is problematic? We will search for an understanding of the ways climbing and art can provide a sense of culture, where culture is understood as a field of signifying practices providing and depending upon a distinction between making and finding.

In reading climbing and art for the ways in which they provide for a distinction between making and finding, there is of course a cir-cularity. All social worlds are sustained culturally. For a Durkheimian this would be equivalent to saying that they are sustained by a sense of the sacred. Routinely to produce problems with the distinction between the made and the found is to jeopardise the sacred, and therefore to put at risk the possibility of culture. Yet is it not the case that to read activities for the ways in which they provide for their own cultural possibility is merely to restore arbitrarily what had previously been declared problematic or unavailable?

Modernity engenders the inherently contestable character of cultures. To identify a practice as cultural is to expose it to questions of all kinds, and even to render it fundamentally questionable. The reading offered here might be described as a hermeneutic dialogue with a practice in which one tries to show, to discover, how the practice finds and what it makes. In this way hermeneutics might be described as a practice of cultural under-standing and restoration.

What I want to consider are different ways in which climbing and visual art might be understood as cultural. What is it to understand art and climbing as cultural practices within the context of an individuated cultural field? It would follow from this notion of modernity that to understand a cultural phenomenon is not simply to reveal the connections between a specific practice and a given common culture. The global questions become rather how the practice makes its own social world, how it tends to make other worlds in its image, and how this might be moderated by its own resources? The local questions become how the practice provides for and preserves a distinction between making and finding; without the distinction between making and finding, between self and other, its reconstruction of culture will amount only to an exercise in totalisation, not a relationship between social worlds. To understand visual art and climbing as cultural practices is to recognise not the ways in which they *reproduce* culture, something which exists securely prior to their action, but rather the ways in which they might be capable of invoking it, of calling it forth, of discerning its vitality and validity.

At first sight rock climbing might seem an almost wholly physical, material, concrete activity only distantly, if at all, touched and shaped by culture or society. The climber's hands and feet, the cracks, rugosities, ledges of the rock face, gravity impeding upward movement are the raw ingredients of this supremely physical activity. Mentally the climber is often totally engaged in the move being made or yet to be made. Indeed, for many, part of the attraction of climbing is the way that its immediate mental and physical demands expel all other thoughts, concerns, worries and projects; it is almost as though the activity of climbing negates culture, or at least the culture of everyday life.

Yet a second look quickly reveals the importance within climbing of wider cultural phenomena. To become a climber, as opposed to someone who simply decides to ascend a piece of rock, is to acquire skills, expertise with equipment, attitudes, histories, values, symbols and ideas; in other words, it is to belong to a specific province of the humanly made world of representations and things, it is to behave culturally.

It would not be difficult to provide a lengthy description of the more salient features of climbing culture, an ethnography of climbing, but a few examples will have to suffice. First, we might consider the notion of the 'route'. Climbers do not just climb anywhere or anything. To climb is to follow or initiate a route, a particular line of movement often keeping to natural features of the cliff, like cracks, slabs, grooves or corners. In most countries where climbing is popular, routes are described in climbing guide books in terms of their location, major features, length and difficulty.

Sometimes a potential route will have been identified by climbers long before someone comes along capable of getting up it. However, many historic new routes, routes which change the attitudes of climbers as to what is possible, which inaugurate a new era of difficulty or danger, are not generally identified as possible lines before their first ascent. In other words, the same physical features of a rock face are *seen* differently as standards, equipment and attitudes change; one might say that the changing culture of climbing modifies what climbers perceive.

My second example relates to how the climbing world determines what counts as the ascent of a route. One normally assumes that the climber, armed only with a guide book description or what can be seen from the ground, ascends from the bottom to the top in a more or less continuous process. However, what if the climber first inspects and prepares the route from a rope? What if the hardest moves are practised with the protection of a rope from above, or protection equipment is placed before an actual ascent? What if the climber falls, either accidentally or deliberately, on to his or her protection devices and then gets lowered to the ground for a rest before completing the climb? All these cases have arisen in recent years and provoked considerable discussion and controversy about first and even subsequent ascents of difficult routes. As with the notion of the route, climbing in this case seems not to be the simple physical activity it initially appears. They reveal that climbing is a social activity in which cultural notions are embedded and which, through direct transmission or argument, give rise to particular and changing views about the nature of the activity held by the climbing world; they also suggest that in some areas even perception and cognition are shaped by culture.

Art has for a long time been recognised as a cultural phenomenon, as belonging unproblematically to that part of the man-made world which has to do with representations and evaluations. Unlike climbing we do not have to establish that art in general, and visual art in particular, belong to culture.

There is an obvious difference between art and climbing, or

111

sport generally, given that both are cultural activities in that the former is centrally concerned with representing and evaluating while the latter, although necessarily employing representations, values and judgements, does so only secondarily or peripherally. This might suggest that climbing, or sport generally, does not construct its social world in the same way as art, and that it is less likely to be driven by totalising impulses. This may well be the familiar everyday experience of sport; sport usually seems to be less reflective than art, and to recognise its limited character. On the other hand, sport does provide a stock of metaphors which have been employed to make sense of aspects of life beyond its confines. One thinks for example of the late nineteenth-century emphasis in public school education on games like rugby and cricket. They justified their place in the curriculum on the grounds that their demands resembled those made by life itself, and that the qualities of character required for sporting success were identical with those characteristic of a gentleman. At a more philosophical level, Lyotard's version of postmodern theorising as 'general agonistics' (or gaming) comes to mind, and in relation to sports involving self-imposed hardship or danger, Heidegger's interest in 'reso-lution' (*Entschluss*), a kind of existential courage, is also relevant.

We can now pose three questions: first, what do climbing and art make?; second, how might they be imperilled by unlimited forms of making?; third, what do climbing and art find?

Artistic creation is a making process, bringing into being through ideas, skills and materials, new objects with aesthetic properties. This is both true and yet perhaps banal. What then would an unlimited making be in the case of art? It would occur when art loses a sense of its own limits, when the way in which art makes things is seen to lie behind all other ways of making. Some would trace this aestheticising process back to the Romantics or Nietzsche. Most of us are also aware of its more popular and vulgar forms: 'If art can be anything, then everything is art, and everybody is an artist.' It would thus incorporate not only politics (Benjamin) but all other cultural practice or discourses too. Art loses itself through this universalisation because it becomes an imitation of an idea of practice, the practice of the idea of practice. It loses contact with what shapes its shaping, the specific and singular quality of its materials. Art becomes a metaphor for *praxis*, the exercise of man's power to shape and control nature and society in accordance with his desires.

112

There is of course a traditional range of materials and their uses for each of the visual arts, although it would be foolish, given the innovative drive of contemporary art, to attempt to provide a definitive list. Here, however, it is not a listing of permissible materials and techniques that is important but the recognition of a particular relationship in which objects or substances become the materials of art. In becoming the materials of art something of the integrity and quality of these substances is perceptually revealed. The relationship acknowledges their resistance and independence. They are not consumed in their use.

One might note here that these independent perceptual qualities paradoxically depend upon the ways in which an art work positions the material within a general discursive or cultural framework. In order for the perceptual qualities of what has been achieved with some everyday substance to become apparent it is necessary to present that substance in particular ways, perhaps by making an unexpected, dislocating juxtaposition with some other substance or object, by depriving the material of its familiar everyday uses, or by placing it within an unusual semantic context.

My argument is, then, that a certain relationship with its materials is a limit condition for art as a cultural practice. Art is not just a making process with materials as its means and aesthetically defined objects as its results. Art treats its materials as already possessing intrinsic qualities which need to be revealed and demonstrated in and by the work, whatever the work might be about. It is not enough, however, just to use paint, for example, in an obvious or 'painterly' way; it is necessary that the painted quality of the image is appropriate to what the picture is meant to convey. Neither is the right use of paint specified completely in the artist's initial conception. The painter regards his or her materials almost as having the potential to specify their appropriate use. Part of their use, then, becomes a sensitivity to their demands, to what, perhaps despite the intentions of the artist, they are trying to declare. The artist needs to have faith in what materials can reveal, and in this sense in what the processes of art can find in and through them. This might bring to mind Michelangelo's theory of sculpture famously expressed at the start of one of his sonnets, translated by Blunt as follows: 'The greatest artist has no conception which a single block of marble does not potentially contain within its mass, but only a hand obedient to the mind can penetrate to this image.'[5]

One might note here that this kind of attitude to materials is invariably learned, and might thus be considered directly cultural.

While it seems obvious what art makes it is less so with climbing. Climbers make routes, friendships and enmities, experiences, memories and so forth through climbing, but what does climbing make?

Climbing makes climbs. Climbing 'conquers' previously un-climbed mountains, it overcomes apparently impregnable rock faces, it litters the globe with routes, it transforms a hostile, alien environment into an aspect of the human world. Yet in this relentless transforming process is a threat to the very existence of climbing as an activity. If climbing is too successful in its appropri-ation and securing it will lose something which lies close to its core. This point has been acknowledged by many climbers. For example, the enormous, heavily equipped Himalayan expeditions of the 1960s which virtually sieged mountains into submission provoked a new movement of smaller parties with much less equipment and back-up resources. The current 'bolt controversy' in British climbing – which is concerned with where and when pre-placed protection with expansions bolts may be permissible – clearly touches on issues which are vital to the identity of the sport. In principle the unlimited use of bolt protection could make every climb in Britain almost completely safe; on the other hand, bolts could open up new areas of unclimbed rock, and enable those climbing at the highest levels of difficulty to improve their technical competence, thus keeping in touch with developments in Europe. The issue is the same in both cases. The activity of climbing both depends upon and threatens a difference between the natural and the human worlds. Climbing requires the limited use of human power, it must curb its capacity, through its very uncertainties and risk-taking, to secure physical nature for climbing.

What then does climbing find? Another way of posing this question might be to ask after the impact of climbing on those involved in it. In an essay called 'The effects of mountaineering on men' the climber and writer W. H. Murray makes two arguments. He suggests that climbing enables greater self-knowledge, parti-cularly of inner resources and resilience one may not realise one possesses until challenged:

Life on earth gives to a man the chance for full development of his powers and potentialities. Their need of fulfilment arouses the spirit of exploratory adventure in all planes of his life, according to the degree of his soul's unfolding. The mountaineer, as such, is distinguished from other men only in finding some of the help that he needs more readily among mountains.[6]

The mountains are a stage upon which inner potentialities may be revealed.[7]

The Romantic effusions aside, arguments of this kind, popular with educationalists, the Outward Bound Movement and even with management training agencies, would be rejected by sceptics who hold that climbing does not make climbers either better or worse as human beings, that someone might be a hero in the hills but an untrustworthy wimp at work.

While many would have doubts about the moral effects of climbing, the notion that it has the capacity to reveal personal qualities and limitations – climbing for self-knowledge – runs deep through much climbing talk and literature. On this model of climbing discourse the removal of danger is seen to transform the activity into a primarily technical undertaking characterised by the acquisition and rational use of appropriate resources: strength, agility, stamina, knowledge of the terrain, specialised equipment, etc. This is not to say, however, that danger in climbing is always actively sought for. Most climbers do not climb in order to place them- selves in danger; rather, risk is a consequence of what they choose to do. The particular level of danger under normal conditions and for most of the time is probably not very high. But on occasions or under unexpectedly adverse conditions climbers do encounter significant degrees of physical danger and fear, and it is then, facing the uncertainties of the environment and of their own likely reactions, that climbers encounter a layer of truth which is funda- mental to climbing culture. At a profounder level than the exploration of new cliffs and mountain ranges we might say that through its self-imposed hardships and dangers climbing uncovers for participants aspects of character.

Summarising, I have suggested that art's making can be moderated by its faith in a particular kind of relationship with materials; this amounts to a belief that materials and material processes are capable of revealing the form appropriate to what the artist is trying to convey, that those items which become the materials of art are almost co-producers alongside the artist. The confidence of sculptors that the right form is 'already there' in the block is a belief of this kind. I have also suggested that climbing is imperilled by the success, through its risk-taking, of its drive to humanise an aspect of the natural, physical world intrinsically inhospitable and threatening to human beings. It can preserve itself only by curbing its power to grasp and domesticate the physical world, and will desire to do so insofar as it values the capacity of dangerous uncertainties to reveal character.

I have suggested an approach to the cultural productivity of climbing and art. Both are threatened by unlimited or immoderate forms of productivity, but they also have the resources to resist the propensity to create in this way.

None of this may take us very far to answering the questions, posed at the beginning of this chapter, about the possibility of a common culture or its assessment. It may, however, indicate a way in which reductive appropriations characteristic of the social relationships between modern totalising discourses could be offset by another kind of engagement. A hermeneutics of culture tries to understand both the way in which a culture makes a social world, but also how, from its own resources, it might be capable of restraining this production through a sense of what it reveals as the basis of its own possibility. That is, cultural hermeneutics tries to show both the power of cultural processes to form social worlds, but also their capacity to restrain this power in order to preserve the identity and validity of the social world through change.

The relationship between the everyday and the professional dimensions of enquiry raises what might be called the cultural problem of Durkheimian social science. The argument above implies that there can be no social or methodological solution to the possibility that the distance upon which objectivity is based may be revealed to be another form of intimacy. There will always be a discrepancy between the confidence the sociologist has in the results of professional work, of what Rorty calls 'the usual empirical-cum-hermeneutic methods', and the confidence he or she can have about its deeper social character. No discourse is safe from suspicion, including hermeneutics itself. How this ambivalence, and strategies and devices to deny it, will affect sociological consciousness, practice and writing remains to be seen.

116

We understand culture through the languages it provides, through images, metaphors, principles of classification. If we wish to say that the play of language does not stop at a transcendental signified, a 'ground' beyond words, then we might see speculative theory as a deconstructive return to this play. Applied to social worlds and their cultures we would be listening for or, less innocently, suggesting ways in which discourses may become dissatisfied or uneasy with ruling metaphors. The theorising itself *rests* upon images of dis-solution, play, flux, negating movement. And here we may discern another moment of cultural life: the need to complement the movement of speculation with the ways in which cultures form around the right metaphor, the appropriate image, the correct principle of classification. In this moment of cultural hermeneutics the stress is not on change, movement, deconstruction but on formation, collection, identity. The concern for metaphor, for language in general, is not just an attraction to the erotics of change but also a sober interest in rest, stability and identity.

NOTES

1 As Mary Douglas writes: 'To acquire legitimacy, every kind of institution needs a formula that founds its rightness in reason and nature.' (M. Douglas, *How Institutions Think*, London, Routledge & Kegan Paul, 1987, p.45) Later, thinking specifically about the formation of latent groups, she argues:

> Before it can perform its entropy-reducing work, the incipient institution needs some stabilizing principle to stop its premature demise. The stabilization is the naturalization of social classifications. There needs to be an analogy by which the formal structure of a crucial set of social relations is found in the physical world, or in eternity, anywhere, so long as it is not seen as a socially contrived arrangement. When the analogy is applied back and forth to nature, its recurring formal structure becomes easily recognized and endowed with self-validating truth.
>
> (Ibid., p.48)

2 R. Williams, *Culture and Society*, Harmondsworth, Penguin, 1958, p. 295.
3 Ibid., p. 335.
4 At a more philosophical level Stanley Rosen makes the following characteristically trenchant argument. The proliferation of elaborate theories of reading or interpretation indicates a contemporary malaise: 'for the Greeks, the distinction between theory and interpretation is rooted in the distinction between seeing and making.

117

Whereas we must state what we have seen, it is equally necessary to see what one is talking about' (S. Rosen, *Hermeneutics as Politics*, Oxford, Oxford University Press, 1987, p. 150). The modern loss of this possibility entails the loss of the rationality of two central contemporary projects: the project to master nature through science and technology, and the project of social justice. Without the opportunity to distinguish between what is found or seen, and what is made by human activity (at the level of representation, or simply physically), the project to know and control nature is indistinguishable from creative fantasy. Equally, the effort to install social justice will be vulnerable because of the instability and partiality of the identities of the oppressed and the oppressors; historically and culturally who is master and who slave is subject to constant redefinition.

In Plato and Aristotle, Rosen finds the making associated with the discursive intellect (*dianoia*) presupposes and supplements a seeing of things, sensuous or theoretical (*parousia*). Without a found nature, including of course human nature, knowing, speaking and writing are indistinguishable from creation *ex nihilo*. The subsequent history of philosophy initially places the active, constructive human subject at the centre and meaning of things, but eventually the subject is historicised (Marx, Nietzsche, Freud) and then displaced (Kojeve, Foucault, Derrida). The result is the loss of any sustainable sense of an abiding and accessible human nature, and the triumph of interpretation. 'We now see that at a decisive level, theory has been transformed into interpretation. *Doxa* is the successor to *episteme*, and poetry has triumphed in its ancient quarrel with philosophy' (ibid., p.153). This implies that a general theory of interpretation – what Rosen calls 'hermeneutics' – which would securely distinguish between legitimately and illegitimately found meaning, and legitimately and illegitimately made meaning is impossible. It is impossible because contemporary thinkers typically reject common sense (or what Rosen calls the 'pretheoretical talent of natural reason') and its domain of practical reason on the one hand, and the idea of a completable project of theory, which would therefore be saved from the flux of perspectival struggle or history, on the other.

5 A. Blunt, *Artistic Theory in Italy 1450–1600*, Oxford, Oxford University Press, 1962, p. 73.

6 W.H. Murray, *Undiscovered Scotland*, London, J.M. Dent, 1951, pp. 215–16.

7 Murray also suggests that the experience of climbing can produce a truer, a more balanced view of the world. After a near miss in the Alps he reports feeling that:

> if any bearer of ill-tidings had come to me reporting the total loss of everything I possessed in this world I should not have thought the news too serious. I had health and life and the ability to support myself by work. . . Life was seen very much in its proper perspective.

> (Ibid., p.215)

118

The difficult conditions, the hardships and dangers of climbing (particularly winter mountaineering) lend everyday problems their true proportions. This kind of argument is again not uncommon in climbing circles.

BIBLIOGRAPHY

Durkheim, E. (1915) *The Elementary Forms of Religious Life*, trans. J.W. Swain, London, George Allen & Unwin.

Lacoue-Labarthe, P. (1990) *Heidegger, Art and Politics*, trans. C. Turner, Oxford, Basil Blackwell.

Nietzsche, F. (1983) *Untimely Meditations*, trans. R.J. Hollingdale, Cambridge, Cambridge University Press.

Ricoeur, P. (1970) *Freud and Philosophy*, trans. D. Savage, New Haven, Yale University Press.

Rorty, R. (1982) *Consequences of Pragmatism*, Brighton, The Harvester Press.

Summers, D. (1987) *The Judgement of Sense: Renaissance Naturalism and the Rise of Aesthetics*, Cambridge, Cambridge University Press.

7

THE NECESSITY OF TRADITION

Sociology or the postmodern?

Chris Jenks

My objection to the whole of sociology . . . is that it knows
from experience only the decaying forms of society and takes
its own decaying instincts with perfect innocence as the norm
of sociological value judgement. Declining life, the diminu-
tion of all organising power, that is to say the power of
separating, of opening up chasms, of ranking above and
below, formulates itself in the sociology of today as ideal . . .
The unconscious influence of decadence has gained
ascendency even over the ideals of the sciences.

Friedrich Nietzsche

If we are ignorant of the past, we will be obliged to declare
that everything durable in our societies was constructed by
ghosts; and consequently we ourselves are nothing more
than the souls of the departed. Without the culture of tradition we would not have the tradition of culture. We would be
orphans of the imagination.

Carlos Fuentes

In less than a decade postmodernism has moved from the status of
a mood to that of a reality. Its nebulous empire has expanded, in
step with this elevation, from occupying a limited concern (or
perhaps a dull ache) in relation to the limits of Modern Art to
ranging broadly in terms of a critique of modern life and, more
particularly, the forms of knowledge that support and sustain such
living.

The critique offers not alternative ways of knowing from whence
to confront the 'new' but rather a continuous scything at the knees
of existing epistemologies, a reduction and depotentiation of explanations that is premised on the wholly unprivileged quality of

all discourses. Deriving from the deconstruction of post-structuralism Baudrillard has mobilised the wasteland between the signifier and the signified and justified it in the manner of a diagnosis of our time. For Lyotard the difference between moral or political positions is as significant as the play of language games and the theorist, the self, derives from the intersection between these games through which the various messages flow.

The battle for the sign is on, with no prior claims holding any justification. Within this postmodern swath social theory stands or falls, which brings me to the debate. This chapter is about tradition, its necessity and the necessity of its reproduction. It is a reaction but it is not reactionary, it is an affirmation of a belief in the collective life. It is also 'agonistic' or contesting in a manner that Lyotard might recommend. Callinicos[1] has already generated a fine and sustained attack on what he sees as the pretensions and excessive claims of this neologistic movement which I would wish to support, albeit from a different perspective. I write as a sociologist and thus with particular attention to the sociological tradition. This tradition I shall formulate as the moral philosophy of modernity. The origins of such thinking are to be found in the Renaissance issuing out of the darkness of medieval times. A grand humanism emerged, a caring for others but in the sight of God. This humanism, still essential today, was rendered secular and scientific through the Enlightenment and through the logistical demands of the density and complexity of a social life that accompanied the rapid division of labour, the move to mass urbanisation and the shift of the productive base over to industrialisation during the nineteenth century. The humanism properly retains in the tradition through its pluralist image of the human relation and its commitment to a vision of a 'good' society.

This is not to suggest that modern sociology is without its problems; in fact, a major section of this chapter will be concerned with an elucidation of such problems, but the contemporary weakening of sociology's resolve is in large part due to the compromises made by its practitioners; compromises aimed at gaining acceptance, gaining respectability and thus gaining funding. The aspirations of the tradition have been betrayed – this is not due to the historically inappropriate character of our knowledge (a postmodern condition) but rather to its cultural unacceptability (its proper condition). Sociology's ideal has become corrupted through the incorporation of its practice, through the technicisation of its method and through the pragmatism of its professional practitioners. It is, however, still not sufficiently disabled to succumb to the random slights and vagaries that stem from the malaise of the postmodern. This chapter may well be contesting in its nature but it recognises its opposition as wholly internal and not constituted through the tangle of variously enlightened self-interest that presents, or is presented, as postmodernism.

The noise of postmodernism may instance a warning of complacency, if any such warning were necessary; it does not, however, justify the designation of a threat. Practically it has come to provide a categorical repository within the academy that assembles, at its weakest, discontent and, at its strongest, challenges to reason, which it then renders political. The timid style of liberalism that has infected much modern intellectual discourse responds defensively. Thus also social theory, historically the gadfly, the articulation of different interests, the defiler of graven images erected in the name of avarice or sovereignty, the conduit for the voice of the oppressed . . . social theory responds defensively. No longer the cultural critic now the appeaser; the harasser becomes harassed – it is a topical image from which to begin.

From the obvious fatigue displayed in the explanatory power of some of the categories transposed from social theory at the turn of the century to an analysis of phenomena in the present has arisen a vociferous disparity of counter claims addressing, within my realm of concerns, the efficacy of sociology as a persuasive voice of today. In the face of much of sociology's intransigence in failing to regenerate and reinvigorate its tradition through a dialectical and synthetic method a voluable polysemy has emerged. So, for example, it is argued that 'social class' no longer articulates a viable sense of community or a course of action; that 'masculine' dominated rhetoric provides little space for the female experience or the polysexuality of identity in modern life; that 'capitalism' is an exhausted metaphor to handle the politics and psychology of relations in the contemporary market place; that 'race' and 'ethnicity' are absent or rather negative categories in the explanation of human difference; that the 'family' is no longer an adequate realisation of socialisation or the private and so on. All of these discourses are true as is the discourse of history. However, all of these changes, though not predicted, are nevertheless anticipated in the sociological tradition. Marx' imperative is clear, that we should generate categories of analysis that are apposite to our time, that is, ideas which are historically grounded; his own critique of traditional political economy is an exemplar of this point. Durkheim's method revolves around the systematic generation of classificatory schemes, that is, the production of taxonomies of social types, through comparison, that will expand to incorporate the phenomenon at hand at that time. Weber never deviates from his insistence that the construction of an ideal type is the unique outcome of the confluence of the particular theorist's value orientations, the values of his time and the particular phenomenon as intended.

What is novel about the latest stage of Western history is, then, containable and intelligible within the existing, traditional epistemologies – such is the richness of historicism. Through these devices of methodic renewal recent sociology has developed the powerful concepts of the 'post-capitalist' and the 'post-industrial' society, concepts which, Bauman tells us, '. . . have served the purpose well: they sharpened our attention to what is new and discontinuous, and offered a reference point for counter arguments in favour of continuity'.[2]

What is disturbing beyond this, however, is the crude assumption that postmodernism is, in some sense, the direct efflux of these altered structural conditions, that it is a superstructural realisation of shifts in the material base. '. . . it (postmodernism) designates the state of our culture following the transformations which, since the end of the nineteenth century, have altered the game rules for science, literature and the arts.'[3] This provides postmodernism with the status of object, albeit ideational, rather than object-in-thought, mood or fashion. In the wake of this new politic of fact follows the malcontentions of an infinity of factional interests which 'must now be heard' and the reason that informs (or previously informed) social theory shrinks or dissembles or acts defensively rather than reaffirming its topic and purpose.

In this way postmodernism assumes what T. S. Eliot, writing in another context, described as '. . . simply a way of controlling, of ordering, of giving a shape and a significance to the immense panorama of futility and anarchy that is contemporary history'.[4] It is as if 'anything goes' in the manner of a true nihilism. The tragedy of this injunction, as also recommended for scientific method in Feyerabend's methodological anarchism, is that whereas some 'things' should be heard with a voice loud enough

123

to silence common sense, *all* things 'go' with a competitive equiva-
lence and are thus diffused under the banner of the postmodern.
The rights of women, child abusers, the unemployed, racial
minorities, the unborn, the serial killer, the drugdealer, the poor
– postmodernism fragments them and ghettoises them and
renders it impossible if not inconceivable to distinguish between
them. As modern differences they must resist the 'totalising'
effects of social theory. They cannot be assembled under a body of
work seeking to explain the character of human community and
social action, they are already predicated upon their unsharability,
their very emergence as difference, it would seem, has already
been oppressed within the conditions of global explanations – like
social theory.

McHale[5] indicates that every theorist and commentator 'constructs' postmodernism in different ways and in relation to
different ends, as have I; he also notes, as if in a phenomenology
of the object, that all accounts are 'finally fictitious', as, I would
suggest, is the phenomenon itself. His further point, which is of
some import, is that postmodernism displays an ontological
'dominant' in opposition and reaction to the epistemological
'dominant' of modernism. This is an interesting idea and an
intriguing device but one that both stems from and gives rise to a
weak version of ontology.

When writing about Nietzsche, now much vaunted as the source
of postmodern thinking, Heidegger[6] tells us 'That period we call
modern is defined by the fact that man becomes the centre and
the measure of all things'. Leading off from this motif Levin[7] offers
us an archaeology of modernity beginning with the Renaissance
and the origins of science and technology, accompanied by a
vision of humanism in the form of a self-validating rationality that
provided an overwhelming assault upon the authority of faith that
supported the Middle Ages. The point of this tale, mediated
through the 'cogito' of Descartes, is that thought grew not to
worship but to empower and impose. Reason provided a priority of
human kind before God and the independence, self-determina-
tion and self-affirmation that ensued posited the self – in fact, the
ego (a weak version of ontology) – as the hub of the modern. All
of this predates and signals the potential collapse and fragmentation of postmodernism. Again this was amply anticipated within
the sociological tradition through what one may refer to as the
'pain' clauses of classical theory, that is, through such metaphors

as 'alienation', 'anomie' and the 'routinisation of charisma' (with the later addition of Freud's 'neurosis'). But prior to this such entropic tendencies were envisaged and adequately restrained by the moral philosophical systems of Kant, Hegel and Saint-Simon, all of whom provided the grounds of sociological knowledge.

Both Baudrillard and Lyotard, in their different ways, expunge the influence of antecedent theorising by positing an unprecedented fracture between the past and the present. A leap into the postmodern which is an extrapolation from a huge conceit, one which Kellner[8] points to, ironically, as a theory of an 'epistemological break' resting itself upon a 'meta-narrative' of the nature of recent history. Baudrillard has prepared us for this failure of continuity and in a Thatcher-like pronouncement has declared the end of society. The social bond has, it would seem, dispersed into a proliferation of signs and the reality of our being together is fabricated through a series of infinitely reproducible similarities; the simulations of simulacra. History becomes no longer ordained through human desire and purpose but through an apparently semi-autonomous cybernetic technology. Different but uniform models or codes (transposed from the 'texts' of post-structuralism) come to structure life through social organisation. Modernity exploded through 'growth' and 'production' into differences; postmodernity espouses de-differentiation through the implosion into simulations. The consumptive but non-generative 'black hole' becomes a central, and suitably science fictional, metaphor. We contemplate the swirling pit of despair to the sound of hands being washed, violins playing and flames roaring in the background. Callinicos[9] suspects this analysis of the postmodern condition, what others have referred to as 'intellectual bile', to be, at one level, the sound of regret and political defeatism emitting from the generation of the '68 Revolution.

Lyotard's postmodernism is a far more cognitive condition than that of Baudrillard. It is primarily a commentary on knowledge and not a description of social structures, though in many instances it implicitly depends upon a Baudrillardian formulation of the latter. He seems concerned to develop an epistemology appropriate to the emergent conditions of knowledge: but this is too optimistic a claim on my part. He reveals himself as resistant to epistemology, he rejects its meta-narratives, its totalising thought such as the humanist vision of an altruistic moral commitment inherent in the sociological tradition, and he recommends the play of 'language games at a local level'. At one point he cites as desirable the replacement of the 'expert's homology' with the 'inventor's parology'. Is this an attempt to democratise knowledge claims or perhaps a contemporary invocation of the principle of 'falsification'? It is neither, this is Cartesian radical doubt gone schizoid, this resonates with Kroker and Cook's[10] hyperreal darkness within postmodernism. Faulty logic, mistakes and accident are now the methodological imperatives!

Let us view the sociology of late-modernity in another way. It was Polanyi[11] who first suggested that in the days when an idea could be silenced by showing that it was contrary to religion, it was theology that provided the greatest single source of fallacies in our understanding of the world. Today, when any human thought can be discredited by branding it as unscientific, the power exercised previously by theology has now passed over to science – hence science has become, in its turn, the greatest single source of error, of constraint, of dogmatism and of resistance to interpretation. It would appear, nevertheless, that sociology's relatively brief history has been marked by a continuous, vigorous, unhappy and one-sided relationship with the body of science. It is a relationship that has never been properly consummated, one that has certainly not been celebrated by any marriage and one that appears perpetually unlikely to produce any healthy offspring. What, then, could be the nature of this unrequited passion and why is it so ill-conceived?

We can perhaps begin by looking at the nature of sociological practice within our modern culture. Contemporary society is built around certain major dominant structural forms and belief systems and all of these have serious implications for our conceptions of sociological method. The modern world is first of all *industrial* – it is committed to the dominance of human kind over nature, as opposed to the primitive who worships the natural and obediently succumbs to its dictate, vagaries and benevolence or violence. Modern humanity seeks to be the architect of its world and its destiny and thus labours to transform what is other than itself into a tangible and useful objective form. Industry, then, is the systematic conversion of the natural into the cultural, the wild into the tame, the wilful and the random into the conventional and the useful. An industrial society produces, indeed it mass produces, objects for our consumption – objects which bear little resemblance to their original form.

Secondly, the modern world is *expansionist*; it is committed to 'growth', an idea which since Darwin has become confused with progress. So through the transition of the division of labour from a stable, contained, simple society to a heterogeneous, diffuse organic solidarity which continuously threatens to fragment we clearly need more – but we simultaneously create more needs. Our contemporary capacity to consume and possess is cumulative, more begets more and within a liberal democracy we express this insatiable desire as a right.

Thirdly, the modern world is *capitalistic*. Through its industrial expansion it seeks not simply to fulfil human needs on a caring, egalitarian basis, but rather it seeks to accrue profit. Modernity's productivity is organised not on the basis that we create things because people might want them, but because they want them enough to pay for them. Objects are produced on the basis that they will generate more value than was invested in their original production, or they will not be produced. Thus at every level within our society from commodities, through ideas, to people themselves, all things are judged and related to in accord with their potential profit or 'surplus value'. This, in turn, emphasises the necessity to count. All forms of human expression have to be quantified. Quality is hard to assess and different qualities are difficult to judge in relation to one another, so they must therefore be reduced to a single standard, that of number. In this way quality becomes quantified and value must be transformed into fact.

Finally, the modern world is *bureaucratic*; it attempts to handle and control all aspects of being through rational process. The value at the heart of this 'rational process' is at the same time capitalistic, expansionist and industrial in character. People or ideas cannot be properly understood unless they have been appropriately processed; in fact, their truth, validity or very intelligibility may depend upon it. In order to process people or ideas in this way they have to be produced in a tangible, object form – this form is what we call 'information'.

In the widest sense science is responsible for all of these elements that comprise contemporary culture, but this is far too simple. Science is not powerful because of its intrinsic truth but instead it is true because of the social power that it carries. Science is both a cause and effect of these developments within the culture because it is part of the context of that culture. Oddly, at another level, science as a practice claims to be free of its social context through the principle of bias-freedom. Part of this confusion derives from the contemporary use of the term 'science' as a blanket description to cover not only the disciplined specialist practices of 'scientists' but also to include the ideas that sustain and reproduce the infrastructure of our society and finally the beliefs that bind us together 'instrumentally' and 'rationally' as members, e.g. 'scientists say . . .', 'it has been scientifically tested . . .', 'it has been proved . . .'. This is what I take to be the ideology of science, and this ideology I shall refer to as *scientism*. Further I shall assert that most manifestations of contemporary culture are themselves scientistic or at least they are standing in a relation to scientism.

There is a major irony here. In many ways we might view the origins of sociology as being the dramatic confluence of human, intellectual and material forces that generated industrialisation, urbanisation and the division of labour towards the end of the nineteenth century. In essence sociology took on a polemical role of cultural critic and a reparative role of social engineer. Thus Marx, Durkheim and Weber were all concerned to describe and analyse the rapidly transforming social conditions that engulfed them, but they were all also concerned to recognise and argue for the potential 'good' in a new order of society. Modern sociology, however, seems to have given way to its topic, the division of labour; it specialises and compartmentalises and as such falls under the ideological constraints of *scientism* – it wishes to be prolific, cumulative, profitable and rational, all of which are elements that echo the structural constraints of industrialism, expansionism, capitalism and bureaucratisation.

This is partly due to the historical legacy of sociology's mistaken, yet wholly understandable, dalliance with positivism – that way of knowing that Nietzsche described as 'the doctrine of immaculate perception'. Even if one might wish to argue for the relevance of sociology modelling itself on the scientific method it would appear singularly inappropriate for it to model itself on a particular view of science that is now a century out of date. Sociology has simply failed to keep up with the imaginative leaps that facilitate modern science. While contemporary physicists are contemplating the metaphoric relationships between unobservable and perhaps fictional phenomena, sociologists are still arguing about how best to measure the observable characteristics of, essentially, social facts. Sociology has been kept in this time-warp because of its adherence to a 'positive' relation with knowledge and the accompanying dominant 'empiricist' approach to the social world – the concrete relation of the senses. Empiricism provides no adequate basis for any theoretical science, natural or social; it is merely concerned with grasping and collecting. Whereas sociology is essentially the dialectical union between theory and method, through the division of labour, through the empiricist adherence to scientism an alien- ation, or split, has occurred and method, or indeed imagination, has become a distinct activity. Method has become methodology, that is, a language or knowledge about methods. Concretely, methodology is little more than the systematic substitution of techniques in the place of theorising; rules of constraint replace interpretation and freedom. Through the development of the dis- cipline of sociology, I want to suggest that in certain ways there has always been a potential crisis in social theory in its relation to method. The most recent revelation of this crisis is what the 'voices' of postmodernity are seeking to exploit. The crisis, or its conditions, are the result of two arrogant assumptions that derive from the varieties of positivism. These assumptions are that sociology should necessarily be a science and the claim that sociology could prescribe the conditions for and the ultimate nature of a new society. These assumptions function in two contradictory ways. On the one hand, they are instrumental in attracting new members to the discipline and on the other hand they persistently create and reinforce the professional paranoia of existing practitioners. The young are fired by the prospect of positively understanding and actively re- constructing the world, and the sociologically mature are haunted by the very problem of adequately understanding the social world and by their ensuing impotence in the face of social change. This negative and introverted self-image of the old order is reflected in the funding of sociology.

In an attempt to gain some emotional and collective security when contemplating this problem, this failure to live up to positiv- ism's demands, we tend to relate to the sociological tradition through an apostolic stance, that is, we invite our students to engage in ancestor worship. So sociology can easily become a catalogue of its past achievements rather than an active in- vestigation of its potential. This is not the sense of the living tradition that this chapter has been recommending.

If we insist on 'looking backwards' in this way then our sociological training or socialisation is the constitution of an identity in relation to the 'greats'. This identity consists in displaying one's membership to a museum – it is all revisiting. Such deifying of the tradition depotentiates the young; it is their identity as supplicants that is socialised. Their abilities to present accounts of the world and their powers of conceptualisation become reproductive; we inhibit creative artists. There are basic differences between the natural and the social sciences but these are to do with what it is that we come to know rather than with how we come to know them. The differences do not arise out of the methodological problems of verification, but rather out of issues of conceptualisation. The differences might be seen to arise precisely out of the formal constraints that are placed upon our powers of conceptualisation during our training as sociologists; thus the problem lies in the construction of our identity not in our abilities to construct accounts.

The differences between the natural and the social sciences are differences not of degree but of quality and texture. Sociology's unit of study is human kind, not animals or objects, yet positivism does not make this clear; in fact, it attempts to demonstrate the continuity. The relations between human beings have a distinctive feature which is realised through their form of communication. Since de Saussure human language has been characterised at a formal level as an arbitrary but finite rule system capable of generating any number of other rule systems. The system has no biological necessity, though this may be involved in its acquisition (Chomsky takes a different position on this issue). A further significant feature of the system is that it is arbitrary in terms of symbols also. The potential built into this communication system is its power in realising an infinite range of realities. Relations in consciousness and relations between people can be reordered as a direct consequence of the formal properties of this communication system. Thus the fact of human language creates the potential for instability in the structure of communication. We have bound and unbound choices; we are syntactically bound in terms of the options taken up through our lexical choices, yet we are unbound in terms of the infinite number of available substitutions. Thus our language system is open; it makes possible structural instabilities in the realities people construct, and at the interactional level it allows for ambiguities. Because of this fragility people have constructed devices like methodologies and logics to provide stability at all levels, but these in turn provide a restrictive choice – positivism is just such a constraint. When we confront the sociological problem despite the instability of the system, how is it that there appears to be constancy? How is order possible? The answer lies in conventional constraint, wilful in origin but unconscious in its reproduction. Common sense and everyday language systematically resist the instability of the system; it embraces platitude and linguistic cliché in a continuous attempt to avoid choice and commitment. Sociology is bound to common sense as both topic and resource, thus the vast potential of the linguistic system cannot be realised in the social sciences.

The natural scientist is less bound, less restricted by the common sense orderings of everyday existence. The relations that the natural scientist imputes to his data are separate from the common sense orderings of his daily encounters, except in metaphor, e.g. wave, particle, organism, etc. The modern natural sciences are populated by the multi-realities of fictional worlds – like relativity, anti-matter, quarks and charm. Natural scientists are able to anticipate and infer realities before they are discovered. Sociologists conventionally shy away from such thought, they tend to remain rooted in the thing-like character of their phenomena. Even the variety of perspectives in sociology seems not to generate alternative realities but rather politicised versions of common sense – to this extent they are ideologies.

Social scientists are not properly socialised in the disciplined yet disruptive way of their tradition. We do not try hard enough to disrupt, invert, subvert and destabilise their everyday consciousness – a clear feature of the thinking of Marx, Durkheim and Weber. In this sense they experience a heavy implicit form of socialisation which is through the common sense classification of the world. They find it difficult to overcome this impulsion of the mundane and thus impute the same common sense motives to their actors. The practice becomes conservative and unable to theorise alternative realities; it becomes susceptible to the destabilising complaints of, for example, the postmodern.

Social anthropology does offer examples of the collective imagination of people at work in simple societies but there is no suggestion that the anthropologist might theorise the cosmology prior to having produced his ethnography of the people.

I am suggesting, then, that these constraints on the sociological imagination arise out of the inevitably blurred boundary between

131

the structure of common sense meanings and the structure of meanings in sociological theory. Beyond this, the vice-like grip of positivism, through common sense, on sociology has given rise to certain elements within the language of sociology. Sociology's form of speech about the world, through methodology, stands, once again, in an ideological rather than a critical relation to the world. Thus as methodologists we seek 'data', 'information', 'validation', 'truth', 'measurement', 'testability', 'objectivity' and 'prediction' and on and on . . . Our sociological speech begins to stand in an intimate relation with the interests of other groups in the society; most significantly the group who control and manipulate – that is the nature of valuable 'information', it is marketable. The dominant metaphor for the sociologist in relation to the world becomes the 'watcher', the 'observer', the pure empiricist being uncluttered by social engagement (in appearance at least).

Such an approach produces a set of terms in which the most important distinctions are eliminated. It replaces morality with conformity; if action falls short of conformity it is a 'deviance' or a 'maladjustment'. Sociology becomes unable to distinguish between the good and the evil. The scientistic culture has overwhelmed sociology's endeavour and produced it in its modern empirical form – it has come to follow in the wake of two centuries of industrialisation, technology and the mechanical transformation of nature. In this way sociology does not construct its own problems, it has them provided, it gets drawn into the mundane problems of everyday life, e.g. 'why do working class children fail?', 'why do some people riot?', 'why do unemployed people commit suicide?', 'why do women suffer from depression?', and 'why do some people take heroin?' . . . it is no longer directing its questions at the social structure.

To return to my earlier remarks about religion and science, we can witness this movement as a transition from religious assurance to a scientific and secular attempt at demystification. However, when religion is replaced by the ideology of scientism we still seek answers to global questions. Thus the deity is replaced by a rational assurance of future progress. Scientism, then, becomes a myth, not a lie, but a story based on certain values and not others and the selected values support the existing system.

This, then, is the beginning of an explanation of the state of enfeeblement that characterises much of sociology today. A condition brought on not so much by a monumental historical leap into an era of the postmodern than by a non-reflexive relation to our tradition inflated through the influence of positivism and reproduced by the mentality of the estate agent that seems to have possessed many modern practitioners in their scramble to gain funding and a high profile.

Such a state of complacency may well be deserving of its own disruption, an address through the carnivalesque, now itself an analytic device in cultural studies much recommended by such as Bakhtin for its powers of deflation: 'No dogma, no authoritarianism, no narrow-mindedness can coexist with Rabelaisian images; these images are opposed to all that is finished and polished, to all pomposity, to every ready-made solution in the sphere of thought and world outlook.'[12]

However, sociology's state of being lies in a tense and fertile relation with its 'living' tradition; it is not yet ready for or deserving of our abandonment to the woeful lamenting of postmodernism. Even postmodernism itself risks the invitation of incorporation: 'Postmodernism paradoxically manages to legitimize culture (high and low) even as it subverts it.'[13]

We might remember C. Wright Mills's injunction that 'the sociological imagination enables us to grasp history and biography and the relations between the two within society. This is its task and promise.' Later he tells us that 'to the individual social scientist who feels himself part of the classic tradition, social science is the practice of a craft'.[14] I agree.

> . . . I think the ultimate argument against his philosophy, as against any unpleasant but internally self-consistent ethic, lies not in an appeal to facts, but in an appeal to the emotions. Nietzsche despises universal love, I feel it the motive power to all that I desire as regards the world. His followers have had their innings, but we may hope that it is rapidly coming to an end.
>
> Bertrand Russell

NOTES

1 A. Callinicos, *Against Postmodernism*, Cambridge, Polity, 1989.
2 Z. Bauman, 'Is there a postmodern sociology?', *Theory, Culture and Society*, 1988, vol. 5, no. 2–3, pp. 217–96.
3 J.-F. Lyotard, *The Postmodern Condition*, Manchester, Manchester University Press, 1984, p. 23.

4 Quoted in Callinicos, op. cit., p. 11.
5 B. McHale, *Postmodernist Fiction*, London, Methuen, 1987.
6 M. Heidegger, *Nietzsche*, vol. 1, New York, Harper & Row, 1979, p. 27.
7 D. Levin, *The Opening of Vision*, London, Routledge, 1988.
8 D. Kellner, 'Postmodernism as social theory: some challenges and problems', *Theory, Culture and Society*, 1988, vol. 5, no. 2–3, pp. 239–69.
9 Callinicos, op. cit.
10 A. Kroker and D. Cook, *The Postmodern Scene: Excremental Culture and Hyper-aesthetics*, New York, New World Perspectives, 1986.
11 M. Polanyi, *Personal Knowledge*, London, Routledge & Kegan Paul, 1958.
12 M. Bakhtin, *Rabelais and His World*, Massachusetts, MIT Press, 1968, p. 3.
13 L. Hutcheon, *The Politics of Postmodernism*, London, Routledge, 1989, p. 15.
14 C.W. Mills, *The Sociological Imagination*, Oxford, Oxford University Press, 1959, pp. 6, 195.

BIBLIOGRAPHY

Baudrillard, J. (1983) *Simulations*, Semiotext(e).
Connor, S. (1988) *Postmodernist Culture*, Oxford, Blackwell.
Feyerabend, P. (1975) *Against Method*, London, New Left Books.

8

SNAPSHOTS: NOTES ON MYTH, MEMORY AND TECHNOLOGY

Short fictions concerning the camera

Justin Lorentzen

I don't really go to the cinema that much (I have always felt a sense of unease in that dark place) though there are certain films that I know in great detail (*Citizen Kane*, *Blade Runner*, *Performance*). I don't have a camera although I secretly enjoy having my picture 'taken', and I am something of a collector of photographs that 'catch' the eye. My interest is therefore both amateur and academic; I'm familiar with the technologies of analysis that are taught in the academy. These languages have enabled me to engage in a great deal of talk about film and photography. However, when all is said and done there is something missing . . .

1963: THE ASSASSINATION OF PRESIDENT KENNEDY

Sure everybody remembers what they were doing when . . . but a more important memory is the recollection of Zapruder's grainy Super 8 that has become part of a collective mnemosyne. As J. G. Ballard has pointed out, there is poetry in disaster and the death of popular icons that remains profoundly unspoken in our culture.

YOU CAN'T TAKE A PICTURE OF A DREAM

I was in Chinatown. Jack and Roman were there, as were Faye and MM; we were wearing raincoats and hats. Some guy started shooting reels of film and there were flash bulbs and things. The only problem was that this guy was shooting me. Jack and his pals were laughing. I lunged at the lenseman and in the struggle a stream of film poured from the back of the box and dissolved slowly (like the memory of a dream) on the wet pavement. I heard voices . . . 'As little as possible' . . . 'Forget it, it's only Chinatown' . . . I was going down . . . I was in over my head.

STRANGE THINGS BEGIN TO HAPPEN . . .

If the postmodern image is a field of immaterial perceptions then new forms of visual language are required to engage the mislocation of time and space. From Bazin to Barthes via a myriad of contemporary discourses on the visual, the spoken and unspoken presense of memory and death in relation to technological reproduction of images has been a constant source of analytical fascination. For Barthes in particular this seemed to suggest a way of escaping the doxa of classic semiological analysis which proposed a rigorous codification of film/photography.

> Society is concerned to tame the photograph, to tamper the madness which keeps threatening to explode in the face of whoever looks at it.[1]

Barthes's book begins to find a space where Theory dissolves. Where the language of contemporary visual knowledge ceases to have a purchase (in this way Barthes is a theorist of theory) either in apprehending the 'object' or in constructing meaning. It is perhaps commonplace in the postmodern to describe 'reality' as arbitrary and therefore 'meaning' as a byproduct of 'slippage'. But I think that Barthes is proposing something a little more radical. Like his erstwhile compatriot Georges Bataille, Barthes is concerned to articulate EXCESS . . . a DEPENSE in culture where language fractures and communication congeals into a wound of silence. Here in this twilight zone (geographically comparable to the edge of an abandoned city) we find new forms of experience and perception where the poetic, myth and ecstasy mix in equal measures, to produce the possibility of creative intoxication.

THE EXCESS OF VISION?

> The poetic word probably was invented as the medium for speaking with the dead.[2]

> . . . communication techniques are not necessarily of the present day but can be quite ancient and turned to the past.[3]

The dead can speak and look straight at you. They are the phantoms of the screen and the light-sensitive paper. You can hear them chattering across time and space via celluloid and tape. They are frozen on walls and fixed in albums. Everywhere there are traces. They live in parallel yet adjacent worlds; we know that they are there but we continue to ignore them because we are too busy embalming and fixing with the cameras' darkroom fluids. For too long we have neglected the gaze of the dead.

This 'unthought' of film and photography discourse is troubling. The implications, both theoretical and political, are difficult to address and think through in a realm where the processes of mechanical reproduction are inspired by myth and fantasy. However, as Alice Jardine pointed out, it is precisely via mythical narrative that we gain access to the phantasms of perception.

> . . . technology has always been about the maternal body and it does seem to be about some kind of male phantasm.[4]

DARKNESS AND LIGHT 'CAPTURED' ON FILM

> In the story You: Coma: Marilyn Monroe . . . I directly equate the physical aspect of Marilyn Monroe's body with the landscape of dunes around her . . . The suicide of Marilyn Monroe is in fact a disaster, through which of course, she committed suicide as an individual woman, but a disaster for a whole complex of relationships involving the screen actress, who is presented to us in an endless series of advertisements on thousands of magazine covers and so on, whose body becomes part of the external landscape of our environment.[5]

There is alchemy at work at here, what Winifred Woodhull in an essay on Michel Tournier's novel *The Erl-King* calls '. . . technologically sophisticated means to the primitive, magical end of controlling others through the manipulation of images'.[6] This 'bad magic' is the unspoken desire of the photographer, a desire for enslavement that via the technology of the camera is displaced by the 'fixing' of the image of 'others'. There is something that the camera wants to get close to, an impulse that can't be resisted; something that escapes the 'eyes' of discourses that structure our ways of seeing. Think of the resonances and connotations involved when we 'take' a photograph or 'capture' on film. The motives remain unclear but perhaps as Jacqueline Rose has pointed out, by using psychoanalysis to engage the visual image and its relation to desire we ignore the processes by which desire is mobilised through erotic/political configurations.[7]

A MEMORY OF HADES

It is through the media that we maintain connections to the dead. We shall not forget this side of Orpheus' productions: returning as a living body from the regions of Hades . . .[8]

The myth of Orpheus and Eurydice is a rich and suggestive story linking death, memory and the gaze. As such it provides a powerful metaphor by which to engage the phantasms of modern media technologies. Klaus Theweleit has used this mythical coupling to explore the complex relationship between creative practice (artistic production/reproduction) and collective (male) fantasies that surround real and 'imaginary' women. Crucial to the understanding of Theweleit's device is the role played by recording technologies from the written word to the cinema and beyond. Theweleit argues that Orpheus's journey down into Hades in search of his lost love is a journey made possible by the power of words which enable him, as a poet, to speak with the dead. In case you have 'forgotten' the story goes something like this:

Orpheus enters the 'realm of shadows'. He sings to Pluto asking for the return of his Eurydice to the living world. Overcome by the beauty of his song, the King concedes and Eurydice is brought from the shadows. Orpheus is allowed to take her on the condition that he does not turn back to 'look' at his wife until they have left the underworld. Through the darkness Orpheus leads Eurydice until tragedy strikes on Hades' border, where through love or anguish he turns . . . with a single glance Eurydice slips away for eternity.

Alas, in the last instance, Orpheus cannot believe in the 'real' Eurydice. It is her existence in image that Orpheus loves; the real Eurydice is a threat to the fantasy that is his own poetic creation, and so Orpheus dissolves her back into memory, which is the source and keeper of his desire.

138

WINDOWS ON HADES

The point of this story is not to turn myth into an epistemological category but to show how writers like Theweleit and Jardine, in albeit different ways, are posing questions regarding myth, fantasy and memory that are not simply reducible to existing theoretical discourses, psychoanalytic or otherwise. For Theweleit the power of modern media technologies to maintain 'contact with the dead' is a replayed affect or excess of contemporary film and photo-graphy theory, continually present but strangely absent from dis-cussion. Likewise for Jardine techno-myths represent one avenue of analysis by which access to 'male phantasms' regarding women's bodies and technology can be achieved. Essentially these questions are about metaphors of reproduction (technological/biological) and the strange invisible process (the Dark Room) that make it possible. One can begin to glimpse why Ballard laments the tragedy of Monroe's suicide by equating her body with a physical landscape, a mythical realm, that lies 'behind' the technology that reproduces her image in the present. Like Kennedy the repetition of her death is the source of the collective memory we can only remember through the screen.

NOTES

1 R. Barthes, *Camera Lucida*, London, Fontana, 1984, p. 117.
2 K. Theweleit, 'The politics of Orpheus', *New German Critique*, 1986, Winter, p. 154.
3 P. Virilio, *War and Cinema*, London, Verso, 1989, p. 34.
4 A. Jardine, 'Of bodies and technologies', in H. Foster (ed.), *Discussions in Contemporary Culture*, Seattle, Bay Press, 1987, p. 156.
5 J.G. Ballard, 'Re/Search', Nos 8 and 9, San Francisco, Research Publications, 1984, p. 155.
6 W. Woodhull, 'Fascist bonding and euphoria in Michel Tournier's *The Ogre* (The Erl King)', *New German Critique*, 1987, Fall, p. 86.
7 J. Rose, 'Sexuality and vision: some questions', in H. Foster (ed.), *Vision and Visuality*, Din Art Foundation, Seattle, Bay Press, 1988.
8 Theweleit, op. cit., p. 154.

9

EVERYDAY LIFE, TECHNOSCIENCE AND CULTURAL ANALYSIS

A one-sided conversation

Michael Phillipson

'Da-ad, what is it about us?'

'That sounds more like the kind of ontological question your mother should answer.'

'Come off it, Dad! You know she's not with us at the moment. So, tell me, what do you think's taking place out there now? See, I've heard that the US Navy recruits dolphins and trains them to locate floating mines. And biotechnologists are producing human haemoglobin in genetically altered pigs in order to provide a human blood substitute. Then there are research groups which are concentrating on altering the genetic structure of certain animals to make their organs more acceptable to the human body.'

'Well, it seems that that's life now.'

'Not always. What about the research biochemist who died from cancer after twelve years of injecting cancer-inducing chemicals into rats? Apparently the drug used is also used as rocket fuel. And speaking of rockets, what about the missile whose warhead camera transmits pictures of its target right up to the moment of impact?'

'So what's new?'

'EuroDisneyland is! Did you know that, after the chunnel, it's the biggest investment project in Europe? Then there's that data "superhighway" just made possible by fibre optics technology; it'll have a capacity of 3000 million bits of data per second – about the same as transmitting 500 novels every second.'

'Well, I'm afraid all that's just everyday life now.'

'What do you mean, "everyday life"? Isn't that a bit too general?'

'That's exactly what it is!'

'I don't get it.'

'On the contrary, you've already got it. It's got you, gets

everywhere, permeates everything – the tea bag in the cup of being.'

'Forget the appalling metaphors you gnomic old fool. Just tell me what you think it is.'

'Well I can only tell you what it is *in theory* now, and that's a long and dense story. Obscurium per obscurius!'

'Go on then. I've got all the time in the world, but just leave out the dead Latin.'

'Right, here goes: everyday life is the place where techno-science rules, OK? Science – the construction of knowledges – has, under the sway of technocapitalism, become technoscience and this writes itself into the fabric of our being.'

'So *you* are something of an ontologist too?'

'Condemned to ontologise! Abandoning all empiricisms that's the fate and only hope of cultural analysis under technocapitalism. I'll try to show you, *in theory*, some of the terms and conditions of that fate. Are you with me?'

'I'll only be able to answer that when I know where, *in theory*, you are.'

'OK! Right. You're asking about "place" – my place – and "place" is the crucial metaphor in what follows. The very point of analysis is to constitute itself as a "place" which is other to that which is all about it and us – the everyday life of technocapitalism. Here it is *in theory* . . .

Everyday life has become the "place" where technoscience "takes place". It takes over and reconstitutes the "quality" of life (the terms on which it is lived) every day. "Every" is totalitarian – there can be no exception; "every" names that which is repeated, reproduced, represented, in its sameness for us – the unnoticed background terms for quotidian living.'

'But surely cultural analysis can escape, isn't that its very po . . .'

'No! That's precisely its and our problem! Try not to interrupt again, space is short. To continue: "day" is a metaphor for the way time is made to pass, is reconstituted under technocapitalism. There are now only days for technoscience which, in bathing everything in its own blank light, abolishes night (darkness, the other). Note that we don't talk about "everynight life". Our en-lightened days speed past in no (earthly) time at all. "Every" "day" hints at, but cannot name or site, the space, the "place", which "life" takes. For, in the aftermath of modernity, time (the ubiquity of the all-encompassing day) takes over, invests and controls space.

In this displacement (the undoing of "place") it is no longer (even if it ever was) a question of an equality, a balance, between the ontological terms of space and time in the way life is "held together", but rather of time's taking over space on its own terms. "Life" becomes that which the dominance of "every" "day" allows. Under technoscience "every" "day" is defined as a recurring time for the possibility of a generalised experiment whose subject is "life" itself. "Life" is what is subject routinely (every day) to an infinite experimentation (measurement, tests, trials, predictions, plans). Within experimentation all boundaries between "nature" and "culture" are shattered and dissolved. For technoscience "life" is a calculable appropriateable process that "takes place" "every" "day" without distinction between species or realms of being. For the experiment all are sources of nothing but the calculable whose concrete form is constituted in and as information.

And with this abolition of boundaries and limits, "structure", as a concept that is crucially dependent on space, becomes increasingly anachronistic. The search for "structures" (of "nature", "culture", "life", "language", "society") was borne of the desire for fixity, for theory to establish its identity through the relative fixedness, givenness (datum/data) of its constructed findings. "Structure" enabled the construction of "fields", "areas" (and hence discourses), "spatialising" themselves within "boundaries" and with some sense of "centre" and "coherence". "Structure" became the metaphor which made the proliferation of technoscientific disciplines and their emergent "identities" (coherence) possible. They themselves sought to exemplify and mirror what they attributed to their topics – rules of a coherent "structure".

But the time of technoscience, time-as-speed (the desire of technoscience to abolish distance, to go from here to there in no time at all – now, thanks to superconductors, already a virtual accomplishment as information passes through "every" "day" "life" in nanoseconds) bypasses, passes through and beyond, the net of "structure". If analytical practices are to engage the consequences of "life" becoming the time of the experiment, of speed, they will have to untie and dissolve their dependence on "structure" as the conceptual means to identity and work. For the concept of "structure", as the originating and orienting term for analytical practices across knowledge specialisms, seems tied inextricably in its reference to an analytical realism, a rhetoric dependent upon the assumption of an essential relation between *theory*'s constructions of "presence" and "place" and the "present" places to which they refer.

What is, could be, the (analytical) point of constructing "structures" which were not "really there" (beyond the analysis in the precise present "place" named by the theory)? Time, represented as infinitely measurable speed, deprives the language of analysis of this long privileged aesthetic and requires alternative strategies of practice, of analytical writing. If space (place) seemed to offer us a certain fixity (continuity, sameness) that appeared amenable to the literalisms and correspondences of realist theoretical practices, time affords no such securities. It cannot be placed. It will not be had. Rather it recoils on theory itself by "placing" its writings unequivocally in the past. They are left far behind, scriptural monuments to the now dead time of structuring things, of putting them in their "real" places (the still strong echoes of the positivist demand). On the other hand, if the point of analysis, the timelines of its theories, is to show its difference to its referents (the rushing away of everyday life under technoscience), then theory's task is to enact another time in its representing practices (writing – a process marked in the present participle). To be timely, theoretical practice has to bear us along in a time(s), the time(s) of its writing-reading, that is (are) other to the calculated time of everyday life. But, for this other time to be a possibility, analysis has to think itself out of its old ties and obligations and write itself into a different relation with language, "every" "day" "life", and its readers. Its relation to knowledge is at stake, for it is precisely what knowledge may have become under the culture of technoscience that provokes analysis to redefine its project.

Critical analysis in all its forms has always wanted to be true to its topic (experience, practices, everyday life), to represent the truths of concrete practices through its analytical constructions. But it cannot. It can only represent *analytical* truths – constructions that are true to its vision of itself, its "place" in everyday life, and its way of representing these in its relation to language. As a practice of writing it constructs its own truths that are not the truths of everyday life, of practice, precisely in order to display the value of its difference to the truths of everyday life.

"Every" "day" "life" names the "place(s)" and "time(s)" which are both the topic, the horizon, and the conditions within which cultural analysis seeks to "take (its) place". "Every" "day" "life", being beyond even the "last analysis", names analysis's limit and its other – that which, despite all reflexive turns, the language of analysis can never grasp because analysis is itself contained and permeated by "every" "day" "life". Where does a recognition of the consequences of this otherness leave analysis? It projects it into a practice whose unavoidable first and last question is always the question of what it is to "take place" (analytically) "here" and "now" in a culture where time abolishes "place". And analysis can only do this through conceptualising (representing in its writing) its "vision" of what "every" "day" "life" (the horizon of the concept of "culture") "is", whilst knowing all along that this "object" ("every" "day" "life") "is not" (is the other to) how it is represented analytically. Analysis has to assert what "every" "day" "life" "is" (analytically) knowing full well that this "is" is an ungroundable metaphor, that it doesn't have a real origin to which it can be traced back and which accounts for it (in the last analysis). Analysis can thus be true to its metaphoric representations of "what is" (its vision) but knows that these are its constructions, concrete fictions: analytic truths are concrete fictions. They reproduce the truth of the analytic vision (the deep reason for offering its difference) through constructed stories about the concrete ("every" "day" "life"). And analysis's constant reproductions of itself – its everyday life, its difference – draws us into the play of production– reproduction, of presentation–represesentation, draws us in short towards the difference that the prefix "re-" makes to the practice of cultural analysis.

In the displacement of "production" by "reproduction", the "re-" marks the ways cultural analysis (its representing practices) is itself permeated and compromised (undone) by its referents (the transformations in everyday life and its analysis figured by such concepts as "post-capitalism", "post-industrial society", "postculture", "postmodernity", "post-structuralism"). In reconstituting its referent (everyday life) around the sign of the "post", analytical practice transforms not only its object of knowledge but also its own possibilities. Itself caught up in the tow of these post-al(l) processes, analysis has reflexively to address their consequences for its own work of representation. And in its displacement of "production" by "re-production" cultural analysis reveals its own complicity with the processes and the problematic legacy of that complicity. For analysis's founding concepts (concepts that allowed the production of analysis to emerge in its "presence" –

the "industrial", the "capitalist", the "modern", the "cultural", the "structural") named/referred to that which originated, founded, its topic.

What generated "society" and "culture" for analysis, what made it the specific "society"/"culture" it was (in theory), what provided for its origin, was that which generated the absolutely specific qualities of its "presence". Analysis has named this originary process "production".

"Production" in its ontological primacy (most obviously in Marxist analysis) was the processual "means" that guaranteed origin-as-presence. There was nothing before (social) "production" and "production" named the practices/processes in and as which "things" (human beings and their constructions) originated in their presence, came to be present to and for themselves and others. "Production" was the process (socially organised labouring practices) in which "things"/"beings" originated, always anew in their difference, in the uniqueness of their originality. "Things" and "beings" could only be present (for us and for analysis) if they had been "produced". "Production" was both constitution and origination, the beginning and frame of "social"/ "cultural" possibility. To be "present" was to have had an origin and to be maintained (in one's "presence") within (a) specific process(es) of "production". For analysis there was nothing outside of "production'; it was itself a moment(s) in the history of "production", a history whose inner coherence it sought to "re-produce" ("re-present").

And this founding production-dependence held (still holds?) analytical sway in spite of the early recognition that modern "production" (the structuring and culturing of industrial capitalism) had become "re-production", that "production" (in "producing" many of the same) was repeating, "producing" itself as "re-production". Industrial capitalism's rule of dynamic innovation kept analytical attention focused on the supposed primacy (for analysis, in theory) of the socially organised productive forces (technology) as generators of the new (the "production" of endless successive, supposedly original, presences ("products")); to "produce" the new was to "re-produce" newness as the meaning of "production". Each new "product" "re-produced" the rule of "production's" movement. And analysis (as the text of critical "productive" science – the knowledge of that which made (in analysis's view) a critical difference to everyday life) was itself

145

bound to the rule of the privileging of "production", with its necessary displacement of "re-production" to a secondary or derivative status.

As a science in search of origins ("productive" causality) analysis "reproduced" itself through its constitutions of the (endlessly new) effects of "production" on social being (that which was present to and in everyday life). Its constitutions were, at the same time (the movement of theory) of course, themselves "re-productions" of the rules for good analysis (adequate analytic writing) which founded and (almost) held together practitioners of analysis as on-the-way-to-community (a pre-community). Analysis sought to stand apart from the ceaseless flow of innovative "production" (concrete differences) by re-presenting itself as a text on behalf of sameness; the principled grounds of knowledge (its commitment) had to be "re-produced" (readable) on every occasion of its textual practice ("production"). It had to re-present itself as the same controlled, masterful, assured voice of knowledge in the face of the plethora of innovation (the hysterical chaos of "products", of beings in the difference of their concrete presences under "re-productive" capitalism). But in this commitment to its own identity, to its self-"re-production", it ironises its project – the project of offering its "production" of knowledge as an exemplary display of otherness to the everyday life of industrial capitalism. For knowledge-"production" suffers the same fate as all the creative practices of modernity in the face of the all-absorptive drive of self-transforming capitalism.

Institutionalisation eliminates the possibility of practising and displaying otherness – the difference that knowledge could make to everyday life. No longer occupying an extra-liminal site in the culture and co-opted to the technoscientific task of reconstituting everyday life, knowledge-"production" loses the grounds of its claim to be working on behalf of real difference (the generation of an "other" community, the achievement of a first "real" community). As its institutionalisation reminds us, its "taking place" now defines where the "centre" is, and, indeed, what "place" itself has come to mean for us. "Centre" occurs everywhere, that is, that socially legitimated (guaranteed by the representations of institutionalised technoscience) knowledge is "produced". And "place", as the some-where that practices take, take over, in securing their legitimacy, is dependent upon the speed and flow of knowledge for any contingent and temporary identity which it seeks to claim.

146

Caught fast within the everyday life of (pre-post-)industrial capitalism, but invested by an almost unavoidable technoscience, analysis mimes its topic (the "re-production" of "production" as the everyday life of capitalism) by "producing" endlessly different analyses that "re-produce" its contingent identity as analysis. Thus technoscience effects the ruination of cultural analysis. Infiltrating and surrounding the body of analysis it sets the terms, provides the form of and the institutional settings within which analysis seeks to "take place", its place. By virtue of the inescapable binds of its institutionalisation, and aside from all personal commitments, visions and hopes, analysis is entrammelled by technoscience. The textualised knowledge(s) of analysis, through which it both represents and represents itself to the embracing culture, is permeated by the forms, properties and interests of technoscience, for analysis can only "take its place" *within* the everyday life that technoscience sets up as the site of its instrumental experimentations. In this transformative movement technoscience has appropriated and re-formed science. Science is no longer what we thought it was, no longer what the social "sciences" have taken it to be when it was regarded as the standard and ideal model for knowledge "productive" practices.

For declining subverted science is gathered, co-opted and led back to everyday life by the technical, most manifestly in the common sense form of technology. The idealising conception of science as a site of autonomous (pure) knowledge "production" is no longer (if it ever was) sustainable, for the sciences have been subject to intense institutionalisation, a process which itself marks the internal transformations of twentieth-century capitalism into technocapitalism. The dynamic of the process is dependent upon and traceable in the ascending dominance of the technical-calculative knowledges in which the other (world, person, collectivity, phenomenon) is constituted as a "thing-to-be-used-up" within a calculus of measurable means directed towards applications whose ends are unquestionable within the technical-calculative frame. Science is co-opted for uses that then invest the very practices of (techno)science itself. Science becomes a front, a cover, an alibi, for the technical-calculative.

The institutionalising of knowledge-constituting practices inevitably sites knowledge under the constraints of institutional interests (and the powers they invest) so that knowledge is of "interest" only insofar as it lends itself to calculation in a context of application (use). Under technoscience the only "interesting" destiny of knowledge is the possibility of its instrumental relevance for the development of projects whose ends are represented as wholly external to the knowledge-"producing" practices themselves (everyday science). Yet these projects necessarily invade and reform everyday science which comes to live as the provision of means under the sway of institutionalised technical control. And this institutionalised technoscience, as the producer of knowledges which can be transformed precisely by technology into empirical categories relevant to any institution's problems of application, becomes the model (the criterion) for all sites of knowledge-constitution. Under these conditions a knowledge's truth claims are only of interest (and thus in the longer term their survival is dependent upon their ability to show this) if they can be transformed into empirical terms relevant to some project of application (use). However esoteric (and cultural analysis in its vanguard forms may seek to epitomise such esotericism) knowledge-constituting practices may be or seek to be they can only ensure their long-term survival by carrying out their work under institutional auspices whose controlling interests unerringly penetrate every cell of their analytic bodies. Knowledge-"production", in the conditions of its self-"re-production" (institutionalised), is undone, ironised, from within.

Technoscience thus reinvests the everyday life of capitalism through its elaboration of the practical possibilities of technical-calculative practices; it is, of course, most explicit and recognisable in its compromising and gathering of the sciences (whose supporting myth represents science as a practice committed to the constitution of knowledges in and for themselves) to interests "outside" themselves. These institutional interests (themselves responsible for making technoscience explicit) treat the sciences (all sites of knowledge-"production") solely as a source of means for the accomplishment of other non-knowledge ends. Under the rule of instrumental calculation scientific work is directed and redirected by interests which are radically dissociated from the search for all knowledges, all truths, except the empiricist. This emergent centralised, multiplied, institutionalised, internationalised, manipulated, "science" erases the classical distinction between knowledge and interest. It becomes the prime site on and through which the terms of everyday life of very late (pre-) post-industrial capitalism are endlessly re-constituted and reconfirmed. The days when modern science, like modern art, worked out its concerns in relative (but never absolute) independence at "the margin", almost lost in the pockets, hollows and folds of an adolescent and ignorant capitalism, are over. Technocapitalism's hyper-intelligence (information systems) enables it to float with the most extraordinary skill over the biggest black hole of all, the "nothing" on which it is "founded".

Co-optation, investment and penetration by means-thought, means-practices, suborn and seduce science and represent it as the technically necessary place where the re-formulation of all value(s), as subject to the means test, must begin. Its "value" (as potential means) displaces and defers any value as end (analytical knowledge as ontological revelation) because it is the condition through which other values (ends) are to be achieved. As knowledge-as-means it undercuts and permeates all other values-as-ends, even those which seem radically antithetical to it (artistic, religious, communal, sexual, ethnic, emotional, relational and so on).

Technoscience, as the control and penetration of all knowledge-constitution by means-thought in the service of application, orders the terms of and becomes the model for the everyday life of an endless ateleological culture, a culture without ends (and therefore without politics). For none of the constituents of everyday life remain untouched by it. Everyday life is not some dissociated unchanging background condition or fixed "structure" on the surface of which technoscientific practices are worked out; rather it is itself incessantly re-constituted in and around means practices (the calculative). For the latter represent the "quality" (a "quality" without qualities) of everyday life as process, how it "moves" in and as calculation.

But this is no longer the "instrumental rationality" of classical and modern sociological analysis where the instrumental was one, albeit privileged, rationality among others. For technoscience as model is not an option, appropriate to a restricted range of action contexts. Rather it transforms everyday life into an applied experiment whose terms and content are the raw "materials" for institutional interests and their developing experimental practices. Everyday life becomes a testing "place", a testing ground, somewhere where "things" (displacing beings) are put to the test. In every institutionally managed and manipulated process within everyday life (and few remain insulated from appropriation) we are put to the test, measured and held accountable for our

149

performances. It is how we perform that counts and performance is constituted as that which can be counted or measured (against a criterion or (statistical) norm). In this way criticism is an essential accompaniment of experimentation and testing, for norms represent standards of test performance, departure from which provides grounds for evaluation – criticism about the means constituting the performance. The critic (the institution's technically accredited representative) calculates the gaps between performances and norms which, as statistical constructs, are always "abstract", "pure", without concrete reference, and therefore subject to the critic's technical power of legitimation (through the claim to authority of the institutional text which he/she articulates – an authority that seeks to secure itself through its displays of technical expertise, the possession and application of an esoteric collection of technical knowledge practices, recipes, for the displays of textual control of a "field").

Everyday life, then, is the "place" where we are required to measure up and may be called to account at any time under the terms of applied knowledges which subdivide its terrain and mark out its boundaries; all practices are increasingly subject to a technical calculus both in the guides/rules for their constitution and in the criteria for judging them as performances. Wherever work "takes place" it does so violently, for "reproduction" under technoscience cannot avoid the appropriating means of calculation. Thus technoscientific work itself, represented in its narrowest form by institutionally based technician-scientists, treats culturalised (technoscientised) "nature" as a resource-full "thing", supposedly independent of the technical practice, whose energies (where "energy" is a metonym for all the "properties" in and as which technoscience reconstitutes "nature" in its own image) are to be appropriated, extracted and stored as the means in turn of subsequent domination. Re-ordering the terms of "life" technoscience gathers up those practices (typically collected in common sense under "medicine" and the construction of "health") that take and re-construct the "body" and its "life" as their objects of applied knowledge. Under technoscience it is precisely the "life" in "every" "day" "life", the (human) "life" (whose limiting ontological dimensions we (moderns-as-existentialists) always thought we knew) that is actively (technically) de-stabilised, equivocated and displaced – a dis-placement that doesn't "re-place" "life" with some other "positive" but, by dissolving its boundaries, endlessly differs and defers it (the life-support machine, the organ transplant, the prosthesis, *in vitro* fertilisation, artificial insemination by donor, surrogate pregnancy, blood from other species reconstituted for "human" transfusion and so on). Technoscience represents the becoming-inhuman of human "life"; the death of the "author" (as a controlling existential subject) is perhaps given a more literal sense than Barthes intended. As for other species (non-human life) technoscience's clones, designed bacteria, reconstituted agricultural animals and fall-out mutants, give new meanings to the saw that "life is what you make it". Under such technically managed conditions, "origin" and "disappearance", "beginning" and "ending" (birth and death), lose their boundaried certainty. Life/death is no longer what it was.

Likewise, the technoscientific alliance with institutionalised military interests ignores the distinction between organic and inorganic "nature" in treating the earth and its surrounding space as a site of generalised testing for the development and "production" of both the means of violent destruction and their intertwined "controlling" communication technologies. Dissolving the boundaries between war and peace this enterprising alliance between the machines of war and communications makes explicit and unavoidable their common essential defining concern – delivering "the thing" at the highest possible speed: to get "it" (the laser beam, the message, the missile) "there" pre-emptively (where "there" – the target, the audience – is always supposedly a "somewhere else" rather than a "somewhere-that-we-share"). And this technoscientific construction and management of contemporary communications under the auspices of war (the world as a zone for limitless transmission through superconductors of least resistance) sets the terms of representation itself.

Representation (in its double sense of representation of (the picture, the text, the code), and representation on behalf of (the delegate, the representative)) is re-constituted now as a technical problem (speed, accuracy of delivery, effectiveness of manipulation (persuasion/destruction)) and no longer as the essential question of value in politics, aesthetics, science and culture. Or, at least, the question of value is always framed and penetrated by the technically constituted conditions within which that which has to be represented and transmitted (weapon/text/other person) is

151

sent on its way – the perennial displacement of ends by means, a displacement that here works ontologically to re-define what it is to be (represented).

If war is the general global form of world ("place") destruction through the managed confluence of speed and transfer, modern "industry" has always worked this out locally under discrete, segmented and particular conditions. If, in its nascent period, this controlling interest was worked out in an essentially *ad hoc* way through the occasional quality of "inventions", now, in the after-life of "production", post-industry's taken-for-granted represent-ation and practical grasp (appropriation) of nature is dependent upon the unquestioned assumption that (culturalised) "nature" is an infinite and infinitely calculable and gatherable resource for (in)human "re-productive-re-consumptive" practice. Essentially reliant upon its research and development programmes post-industry blasts, fragments, cuts up, reduces, re-synthesises, "nature" under the rule of the calculative plan. The violence is subject to planned control which represents "nature" through the abstraction of information. In its representation as this calculus "nature" has been transformed, re-presented, as that information-without-qualities (values) that planning requires as the immaterial material for its means-projects. When human interests get in the way (the local protest, the displaced culture) they are simply re-presented as one more element of information to be added into the abstract calculus of control. Post-industry can only re-present – recognise – science as technoscience.

Thus the violent everyday life of the multiple sites of work is organised around the calculus of "re-productivity"/output and the technical ordering (planning) of energy expenditure (ergo-nomics). And everything that we gather as non-work ("leisure", free-time) is framed for us by the calculative requirements of work. The terms on which our "leisure" is to be worked out are institu-tionalised and represented as matters of performance – we are endlessly exhorted to measure ourselves against standards, norms, ideals, to become self-assessors of our own performances in the tests of leisure consumption. Non-work, as the end of work, has to be worked at and assessed (right down to seemingly the most "trivial" of entertainments such as the TV "sit-com" where we are forced to "measure" our own response against the technically planned response of the dubbed "audience" laughter). Our performances across the multiple sites of "non-work" become the

152

materials out of which our "lifestyles" are re-presented. Transformed into measurable "opinion" and "taste" they enter as information profiles into marketing, advertising, product design – all those work practices whose object is the calculative "reproduction" and re-generation of "taste".

Under the technicising of being the unrepresentable dimensions of desire and the "self" are reconstructed as measurable needs and sociopsychobiological attributes. Politics follows suit, constructing a parodic version of representation through its reliance on opinion sampling. Incorporated into the everyday life of media institutions (exemplified by TV) politics becomes one media "production" among many in which politicians, themselves put to the test, have to learn to play and display the role of politician in someone else's "production". The media reassemble politics for us as the aestheticisation of (political) representation; we are offered only the *appearance* of politics – representation of representation. Representational politics is thus only possible on the terms within which politics itself is represented according to other technical-calculative interests (the management of desire).

Thus technoscience in its informational mode works itself out most explicitly in everyday life through re-constituting representation, with disastrous consequences for politics. Representing itself through technical "neutrality" as "outside" politics, technoscience comes to define the space within which politics "takes place". Questions of "end" (values) are evacuated and displaced by "means": politics is represented through means-discourse, an instrumental project whose "goal" is the endless manipulation of the means of organisational control (of the means of representation, of the means of violence, of the economy, of other cultures, of values, of norms, of bodies, of social relations). Politics, in its re-definition of public space as subject to technical control and in its own representation within that space by the media, becomes the "place" where representation itself is actively de-constituted into a calculative manipulation of meaning as informational "means". Political representation finds itself represented in turn by technical-calculative practices. Held fast within the vice of technoscientific experiment it represents its (human) subjects as discrete collections of abstract manipulable information which are endlessly cut up and re-placed within the disseminating flows of information. Within these flows politics can no longer maintain itself as the master metaphor for sociocultural praxis, underpinning all other practices. It becomes just one discrete category of "production" among others.

The only life politics comes to have is within the framework of its representing technical calculus; politics is available and recognisable only on the terms which this framework allows. Political practice becomes a space whose borders and margins are constructed according to the "production" "values" of the information-spectacle, so that the space of political practice (what is possible within it) is defined (and therefore limited) by these "values". We no longer have representational politics (a politics defined by the struggle for the right to be represented and to participate in the ordering terms of our representation) but the representation of politics by other means for other ends. If war, as Clausewitz proposed, is the pursuit of politics by other means, then, under the rule of technoscientific experimentation, these other means are appropriated to re-define the possible places and inter-relations of both war and politics. Both are constituents of a wider field of technoscientific operations. And practice within this field has nothing to do with representative politics but everything to do with the construction of representation (some thing/person standing (in) for some other thing/person) as a problem of technical calculation. Politics and war "take place" as the calculative turning of representation against itself. Politics comes to "live" only in and as its "re-production"; we are left with nothing, but the "re-production" (copy/simulation) of politics.

Wherever work or practice is subject to an attempted control and manipulation by a technically specific knowledge, the being of the practice (work) is transformed into a neutral calculus. This applies indifferently to even those areas we regard as other to the technical (the self/identity, sport, sex, religion, art). "Relations" between human beings (or between human beings and "objects") themselves become calculable processes, performance within which can be measured (put to the test) and improved (via therapies, sexology, art criticism, sports science and so on). Such knowledges intertwine desire (for qualities of being) and fantasy through myths that form such qualities into supposedly concrete possibilities (e.g. myths about the relation between specific appearances and sexual attraction). The possibilities of (self-) transformation are represented as functions of the acquisition and application of technically specific knowledges as information resources. Before it is anything else, then, the object-of-technical-

154

knowledge must be represented as a detached "thing". The techno-scientific underwriting of being guarantees the thing-status of its objects – their separation from interests, values and commitments, and their calculability. Re-forming (the self and its "relations") becomes a matter of manipulation and performance enhancement, rather than a qualitative transformation of the conditions of being and relating. Everyday life becomes a problem-solving exercise defined and guided by the resources of technical knowledge.

Even art (whether modern, pre-modern or post-modern makes no difference) under the framing conditions of its institutional-isation is made available to us under the auspices of non-art interests (bureaucratic/economic/political/academic) which use art in these interests. As text/object/performance the work of art becomes something the terms of whose "appreciation" are produced through technically specialist discourses. Appreciation and response are managed organisationally through the provision of the means for technical discrimination (the formation of taste). Analysis, criticism, history, comment, education – all set up in advance the terms for appropriate (technically normative) response to the works; we learn to feel and appreciate under expert guidance. And these terms are guaranteed by their organi-sational power – as technically specific knowledge, they share many of the same interests as the organisations within which they are sited and practised (bureaucracies).

Similarly wherever the body is in performance the tendency is for it to become some "thing" whose performance is to be monitored and adjusted either individually or collectively. Eating, gaming, sexing, exercising bodies are becoming-measurable bodies the conditions of whose performance-as-work ensures that what may have been represented in celebratory terms now "takes place" under the rule and critical inspection of the technical. And typically the yardstick for the measurement of the "event" is the organisationally constructed media produced "professional" spectacle in which the represented performance is underwritten by technical competence and training. The technical demands of staging the information-spectacle set the ground terms for relating to and assessing one's own and others' performances. The generalisation of testing (the monitoring, checking, measuring and modification of performance through information feedback) thus sets the terms within which the "life" within "everyday life" is some "thing" (test) to be worked at under the rule of calculation.

It also sets the terms for the paradoxical project of cultural analysis. Caught within and supported by the institutional machinery of technoscience (most explicitly the contemporary university) it "takes its place" as a technically specific sub-discourse. It participates in the programmes of training, research, publication and discursive exchange whose "ends" (the endlessness of means-politics) it may not share but which indelibly frame and mark its practices. The pursuit of the good of representing critical difference (analysis's otherness to all that "is" in everyday life) is subverted by analysis's institutional setting. It is steadily eroded and ruined.

Terms and practices that seemed to suffice the day before yesterday are reconstituted as monuments to a lost past; they cannot cope with the appropriations of the technical-calculative machineries that sweep them along. The consequences of this plight are radical, for to resuscitate the project of critical difference requires a de-institutionalising of analytical practice, a strategic dissociation. Cultural analysis gathers itself now as a practice marked by loss, and hence engaged in a process of mourning, mourning for its lost object of knowledge, for its lost presence (its belief in its ability to present us with the "presence" of its object of knowledge), and for its lost commitments and attachments (to science and its supposed methods as model for the constitution of its object of knowledge). Where the mourning takes the form of a continuing attachment to the old models (worship of the dead – construction of memorials, monuments) it founds itself on a nostalgia that is blind to its own irony, for it hopes to "re-produce" (and to represent the virtue of) the past in the present: a perfect cultural "re-production" of that frame of analysis which projects it as primary "production", as "origination".

For the analysis of culture within the social, linguistic, aesthetic and critical sciences has always represented itself as "production": "production" of origins, of primary causes, of causal narratives, of objects-of-knowledge-as-information about the "world as it is", of conceptual structures as the ground of (generators of) cultures, "production" of itself as work (not play), and so on. Treating the social world, "everyday life", as subject to (the object of) the analyst's model meant "producing" that world (the world of praxis) through analysis as an object of theoretical knowledge in which praxis was transformed into a directly corresponding theoretical "product". And to confirm the good, worth, value, validity (however these are understood) of this "productive" work necessitated the endless "re-production" of the analytical model (whichever it may be). To become analysis, to represent it (again and again and . . .), analytical practice had (has) to reveal, to display, itself (this is the "self" of analysis, that which gives it a centre, an identity) as a perfect "re-production" of its own commitment; this "re-production" is a double project – to produce itself as the perfect exemplar of analysis and also as the perfect "re-production-as-representation" of its object of knowledge – its object of knowledge had (has) to be the perfect "reproduction" (representation) *in theory* of the phenomenon in the world (praxis).

This double task represents the paradoxical "re-productive" struggle of analysis as "productive" work. It confirms that, as far as analysis goes, there is only "re-production" (of itself as the same) but that this "reproduction" only "works" through representing its object of knowledge as concretely different on each and every analytic occasion: object of knowledge equals concrete difference and analytic identity. This is accomplished in analysis's mundane work through "typicality". For, as part of its constitutive work, analysis is always searching for what is typical, recurring, common, the same, in its focus on specific phenomena. But this constructive search always "takes place" in a specific "place" and at a particular time so that the specificity of its object of knowledge is defined by the relation between what it "discovers" (constructs) as typical and what is unique to this "place" and time. Analysis seems then to be condemned to "re-production"; every phenomenon in the world becomes an occasion to "re-produce" itself, to "re-produce" analytical work (and its upshot – writing) in order to reveal the necessity (the value) of its own means of representation (as having the measure of culture). And this is done in the belief (or, better, as the overriding commitment) that this is how the world has to be represented, that there is no alternative (analytically) to this "productive" work of self-"re-production" as the means to theoretical praxis (and this holds irrespective of what might be called paradigm differences between analysts). For analysis's sustaining commitment is always that it must seek to display itself as other to the discourses of everyday life through the work of self-"re-production". It is offered, returned, to everyday life only in order to show itself as this difference. But under realism and naturalism (correspondence) the analytic text is offered as a corrective to common sense, as a more accurate and rational object of knowledge than that constituted mundanely within common sense practices.

By re-enacting the existing model for good practice (constituting again the good (scientistic) object of knowledge) as a transcendental "moment" and space within tradition (something that defined the significance of the "tradition" itself) analysis seeks to remind us of why it "takes place". But it can only show us this "why" (the reason for doing analytical work in the culture) in the way that it is written out; the "why" is invested in, represented by, the "how" of the writing – how the writing represents its relation to the culture(s) which is (are) its referent(s). And under techno-science the "how" of traditional analytical writing practices loses its critical difference. For analytical writing is still grounded on a vision and permeated by the forms of scientism that treat the relation between (analytical) language and the world of everyday life (reality/praxis) as essentially non-problematic. Analytical writing still assumes in its practices that its concepts are technical, scientific and correspondential. That is, they use the means of technoscientism through a writing that seeks to generate technical concepts (specific to and instrumental for the needs of a particular knowledge discourse). Such "technical" discourses (the social sciences, cultural studies, aesthetic criticism and so on) have to prioritise their boundary maintaining rules (for appropriate writing) in order to ensure identity and survival. And this is accomplished through the construction of discourse-specific objects of knowledge that claim both a separation from but also a direct relation (realist/naturalist) to the world of everyday life – the practices of common sense. To solicit recognition and response by other practitioners in the specific discourses that construct (hopefully) shared objects of knowledge entails the "re-production" of legitimate forms (the technical concept) of analytical writing. The representation of analytic knowledge (contributing to and participating in debates about "the way things are" in the world) works within a technical division of labour that is precisely "about" the generation and sustenance of technically differentiable tasks.

Even under the late-modern conditions of shifting disciplinary boundaries, imploding paradigms and exploration of interdisciplinary collaborations, new forms of analytic practices can only survive by asserting their critical difference. This always entails the representation of the technical specificity of their objects of knowledge and thus the construction of an analytic identity which differentiates them from other (earlier, competing) discourses. The conditions of analytical practice require this formal-technical differentiation as the means of both analytic innovation and continuity. The issue is always that of how a specific text "places" itself in relation to a tradition of writing.

Thus the emerging (or established) identity of a discourse is necessarily reliant on and constituted through terms and conditions for practice that are "outside" itself, prime among which is the demand for a formal-technical double differentiation – from common sense and from other specific knowledge discourses. And the one thing that identity-constitution, in establishing the oneness of its difference, must, by definition, seek to eliminate, marginalise and repress is the possibility that it is not "one". Analytic and double (multiple) meanings appear irreconcilable, for analysis's life is dependent upon its ability to show *in* its writing the claims to its unicity (the critical difference which its own unique "vision" makes to knowledge). The formal-technical (or ontologicoepistemological – where "being" is some "thing" that can be known) conditions of analytic practice require that it seek to represent in its writing singular, unequivocal (the rule of non-contradiction) truths, irrespective of the "theory of truth" to which it subscribes. And, of course, the singular, unique, discrete, unambiguous "object" is essential to measurement, to the technical-calculative practice to which, at the deepest level, analysis still allies itself.

But what if the "object" which is to be transformed into the "object of knowledge", together with the "means" for this transformation (language/writing) are recalcitrant, stubbornly resistant, to this requirement? What if the immense baroque architecture of the analytical enterprise is dedicated to achieving the unachievable – locating, "placing", the (singular) meaning of being (culture, practice, the world of everyday life)? What if the identities of the "objects" of analytic interest (phenomena named by terms like "nature", the "material world", "capitalism", "class structure", "human subjects", the "self", "cultural re-production" and so on) are constructs of practices that always recede, efface themselves, in the face of analysis's singularising violations? In other words (and this may be analysis's problem for there may always be other words), what if analysis's tacit ontological assertion and assumption that everything has an underlying identity independent of but available for analysis's representing work remains a hypothesis necessary for the continuation of analytical (and every other knowledge-constituting) practice?

It is precisely these questions about identity that confront analysis when it begins to take seriously the challenges of those representations/discourses for which (knowledge of) identity is, at the very least, a trouble (feminist, ethnic, aesthetic, post-structuralist, Heideggerian, Wittgensteinian, Kristevan, Freudian). And complementing this, the demand for analysis to make the "reflexive turn" (which these and other critical practices impose) requires it to confront the technoscientific context within which it seeks to "take place"; it is required to treat seriously the possible instrumentalising effects of this context for its own work. For making explicit through a reflexive constitution of the terms of its own practice, real-ising as the very matter of theoretical practice, the instrumentalising of analysis (its "place" as a technical special-ism within a technical division of labour, its necessary permeation by the interests of the institutions (market, governmental, academic, media) which maintain its "place"), already equivocates the certainties and confidence that analysis had to have about its traditional work of representation.

A recognition of the ways the concerns of reflexive and identity-ambiguating discourses overlap begins to open up possibilities for a mutant analysis – one which might begin to undo, multiply, decompose and disseminate itself in the face of its deformation by technoscience. Can cultural analysis(es) live on, to one side of identity-constitution (its own included) and outside the instru-mental frame of calculative thought? In the technoscientific culture, where calculation and identity inter-penetrate to define the terms of life, everyday life, perhaps the only kind of life left for analysis is a half-life, a half-life within which its strategy has to be to lead an unplaceable double (multiple) life. For the half-life lived within the appropriating "shelter", and apparently on the terms of, the culture's institutions would have, somehow, to represent at the same time, in its writing practices, that which is other to their calculative identifying interests. This after-life of analysis (post-analysis, para-analysis, cata-analysis) would have to become a practice of allegoresis, a double writing. The representation of some "thing" through another has to practise within and rests itself on the "final" (there is no "last analysis") undecidability of "meaning". Semiosis is bound to specific interests and contexts of interpretation which "re-produce" themselves "inside" the analytic

160

text itself. Para-analysis's way is a hovering in-between, in which others' truths (the truths of everyday life including those of the everyday life of technical knowledge discourses) are undone, occulted, without being replaced by another technoscientific certainty.

The cata-analytic text thus rests its always uncompletable case on the possibility, latent in every practice and representation, of an-other meaning, an alternative reading that shows that "things" could have been otherwise. Post-analytic practice thus celebrates the multiple, difference(s), as the groundless "condition" of all practice; it offers itself as a permanent undoing which, in its refusal to substitute positives (technoscience's re-constitution through its "objects of knowledge" of "what is the case"), can only have an exemplary role for everyday practices. It seeks neither to make common sense more "rational" (instrumentalism) nor to be an additive (more information) to common sense. Its resistance to the fixing of meaning can only be an exemplary performative, a model practice, the constant rehearsal of a "vision" of the relation between writing and praxis. In this it would be precisely "difference" that was rehearsed – what para-analysis takes to be the other of common sense in a culture where common sense is the "place" under the sway of technoscience, where technoscience "takes (over the) place", makes common sense its own. The difference of cata-analysis is neither that of the masterful control over things displayed in technoscientific representation (secure in its lack of self-doubt), nor the taken-for-granted acceptance of common sense practices (equally secure in their lack of self-questioning).

Post-analysis cannot join either of them in the hope of reforming them; rather it can only work perennially to display their attempts to become all-embracing binding ties. It seeks to establish, however fleetingly, an in-between where, in working its way out of both of them, it is without identity, beholden to neither, a site where difference may almost be representable. This is the hope of cathanalysis: a para-practice trying to re-mind us of the possibility of real difference without seeking to legislate either its specific qualities or how it should be achieved. For that would be to relapse, in thrall to the violently masterful appropriations of technoscience with its offers of method(ologies), into common sense.

Well, there you are! Thanks for not interrupting the flow. That's how everyday life under the technoscience of technocapitalism appears (in theory) to cathanalysis. I'm afraid you'll need to be beside yourself to practise it. But I suspect from your comments about EuroDisneyland, the mine-hunting dolphins, and the mutant practices of the biotechnologists, that that's where you are already.'

'Perhaps you're right. All that sounds OK *in theory*, Dad, but what about the relation between theory and practice? What *is* practice?'

'Now those really are questions you'll have to save for your mother . . .'

10

UNFIXING THE SUBJECT[1]
Viewing *Bad Timing*

David Silverman

INTRODUCTION

Alec McHoul has persuasively argued that there is no principled reason why conversation analysis (CA) cannot be used on fictional texts.[2] As Hammersley and Atkinson have demonstrated, a preference to work with 'naturally occurring data' is just that.[3] No data can ever be said to be more 'natural' than any other – no data are untouched by human hands. So telephone conversations, for instance, are not intrinsically better sources of data than, say, research interviews, official statistics or fictional texts. In principle, it would seem, there are only good and bad methods of analysis – not good and bad data.

McHoul illustrates how we can use methods from CA by taking an extract from Mervyn Peake's novel *Mr Pye*.[4] I will not reproduce the extract here but merely say that it deals with a short exchange between Mr Pye and a ticket-vendor. Using a paper by Drew,[5] McHoul shows how this exchange involves a negotiation of blame based on a direct challenge rather than the more common invitation to a speaker to do a self-correction.[6]

However, McHoul goes beyond this standard CA work on the sequencing of talk. He shows how the negotiation of blame is given a particular force by the descriptive apparatus used by one of the speakers. More specifically, McHoul is concerned with Mr Pye's reference to the ticket-vendor as 'my friend'. Here is what McHoul has to say about the matter:

> The challenge . . . manages a distinct effectivity by the addition of the tag-positioned address-term 'my friend'. The utterance form [CHALLENGE + FRIENDSHIP] works disjunctively insofar as the membership category 'friends' . . .

does not routinely carry with it a category-bound activity like challenging . . . 'Friends' more routinely carries with it 'support' and reliance on shared presuppositions.[7]

McHoul's analysis of the use of 'friendship' draws on Harvey Sacks's account of description.[8] Sacks argues that any number of descriptive labels may adequately describe a person or an activity. Choosing any particular label (or 'membership categorisation device' (MCD)) carries with it many implications. For instance, it implies:

- the sort of activities in which a person so described may engage (e.g. friendship is associated with the activity of 'giving support'; thus 'giving support' may be heard as a 'category-bound activity' linked to such persons as 'friends');
- the kind of role-partners associated with the description (e.g. 'friend/friend' or 'child/parent' both of which constitute 'standardised relational pairs');
- the collection of categories from which other persons may appropriately be named (e.g. 'friendship' or 'family').

Like McHoul, Sacks himself uses a text to illustrate the power of such analysis, drawing upon a children's story which begins 'the baby cried, the mommy picked it up'. However, there is no reason why the method cannot be used on other kinds of material. For as McHoul suggests we do not need to erect boundaries between the categories 'fiction' and 'non-fiction'. How such categories are actually deployed to describe texts then becomes a topic for investigation rather than a tacit resource.[9]

Take the following example of a conversation:

[BT:10]
1: Husband?
2: no
1: relation?
2: no
1: er boyfriend?
3: ( )
1: look what connection do you have with her?
2: you could say I'm a friend

The first speaker (1) is seeking to elicit 2's description of his relationship with a woman. Each description that he offers implies

164

a particular set of role-partners associated with certain obligations and activities, appropriate to standardised relational pairs (SRPs). For instance, husbands can be expected to have greater obligations than relations. In addition, certain SRPs, like husband–wife or relation–relation, can be heard as engaged in stable, routinised activities based on fairly clear-cut obligations. This is less true of other SRPs, such as boyfriend–girlfriend, where the expected obligations are less stable and associated with more delicate activities such as 'wooing: being wooed' which in a potentially unstable way constitute the material and sexual status of the relationship. Now note two features of this conversation:

- 1 hesitates ('er') before producing the MCD which can be heard as the most delicate description of 2's relationship.
- 2 chooses an MCD ('friendship') which avoids the delicate implications of 'boyfriend' by bracketing any issues of sexual involvement, i.e. one can have 'friends' of either sex. Unlike any of the three MCDs offered by 1, all of which imply specific obligations and activities, 'friendship' is much vaguer and ill-defined.

Now consider another conversation:

[51A WH1]
1: any particular reason why you decided to (0.3) be tested again? (0.6)
2: um (0.3) well the the person my partner (.) wanted to be tested
1: okay
2: he had never been tested (.) so I came with him

This exchange also involves an appeal to the descriptive apparatus of MCDs, although, in this case, 1 does not offer a direct invitation to 2 to describe a relationship. Now we can note three features in how the description gets done:

- As in the first extract, a speaker offering a description of someone with whom he is involved initially elects to use a neutral term to describe him ('the person').
- Speaker 2 ultimately offers a further description ('my partner'). This now carries more implications about the speaker since the use of the pronoun 'my' underlines the appropriateness of a hearing in terms of the SRP. However, compared to the many possible descriptions that 2 might have used to describe his relationship (e.g. 'my boyfriend', 'my lover'), we note that the

165

term he uses carries relatively few implications that might be perceived as 'delicate': it implies a 'steady' relationship but, unlike the other descriptions, fails to specify the nature or kind of sexual involvement.

- Nonetheless, there is a delay in the delivery of the term 'my partner' that 2 uses to describe his relationship (the 0.6 second pause before 2 speaks, followed by a hesitation, a further pause and finally a self-correction (or 'repair') before 2 finally delivers the description ('my partner').

Striking similarities have appeared between the two conversational fragments. In both cases, a speaker hesitates before delivering a description which is relatively more delicate than the ones that precede it. Again, in both cases a speaker's first preference in a self-description is for a category that is relatively 'neutral' ('person' here, 'friend' in the earlier extract).

As readers may have guessed, the second extract was taken from a tape-recorded, naturally occurring session of AIDS counselling. The first extract occurs in the film *Bad Timing*. I believe this underlies McHoul's point about the availability of 'fictional' material for analysis which is more normally applied to 'naturally occurring' talk.

In principle, having made out the case for doing so, I could continue this chapter by further MCD analysis on dialogue from the film. At this stage, I need to explain why, while not abandoning MCD work, the chapter goes off in other directions. Given the range of 'fictions' (both in film and in written texts) I first ought to explain why my gaze fell on *Bad Timing* (hereafter BT).

WHY BT?

I first saw BT in the late 1970s soon after the film was made. At that time, together with Brian Torode, I was writing a collection of papers on language use that eventually became *The Material Word*.[10] That collection established a certain critical distance from conversation analysis narrowly concerned with the sequencing of talk – at the time we overlooked the possibilities of MCD analysis. This had two implications relevant to the present chapter:

- A concern to resist Garfinkel's suggestion that the 'documentary method of investigation' is the only conduit through which social organisation proceeds.[11] This meant a critical distinction between what we called 'interruption' and 'interpretation' which will be discussed shortly.

– As we sought to widen our conceptual apparatus, we read extensively work written in the semiotic post-structuralist tradition. So our understanding of 'interruption' took on board elements of Barthes's discussion of signifying practice, Derrida's account of 'deconstruction', and Laclau and Mouffe's version of 'rearticulation'.[12]

The rich seam we now were mining made no distinction, of course, between 'fictions' and 'naturally occurring' data. So in *The Material Word*, Torode and I switched, without concern, backwards and forwards between our field data from classrooms and clinics and 'literary' texts by Kafka, Robbe-Grillet and Perrault. I also started to read *Screen* and to take on board the methods of semiotic analysis to be found in its pages.

In particular, the work of Stephen Heath seemed incisive and powerful. Reading his *Questions of Cinema* suggested to me how an analysis of a film could be conducted by using concepts like 'suture' and 'cut' which seemed almost synonymous with 'interpretation' and 'interruption'.[13] Following post-structuralism's rejection of any non-textual or 'authentic' subjects, Heath offers an account of 'suturing effects' which join the subject in structures of meaning.[14]

As Heath points out, the term 'suture' derives from surgery where it denotes a stitching or tying of the lips of a wound. In cinema, the frame establishes the joining or suturing of constituted subjects (characters) into structures of meaning.[15] These structures will unfold as successive frames establish a smooth narration in which, as in surgery, the trace of the original cuts (the scars) fades into oblivion.

Heath shows how this framing reconstitutes the signifier as a symbol representing a signified. Through narration, the images are laid out in a way which supports the frame against its excess (signifiers which will never be reduced to a signified). Narration suggests laws to hold the movement of the viewer's gaze, to ensure continuity. These laws exemplify the economy of narration which involves both a movement from beginning to end and a constant surveillance, or checking, of the images.[16] Surveillance operates by: 'prescribing a reading as correlation of actions and inscribing a subject as, and for, the coherence of that operation carried through against possible dispersion'.[17]

Despite (because of) the attempts at surveillance, a film is not a closed unity, determined in a mechanistic way, but the site of an unfolding and partial containment of a set of contradictions. As Heath notes, it is precisely in the movement of these contra- dictions that can be grasped the set of determinations (or closures) expressed in the film. This appeared to offer a fruitful version of the role of film (textual) analysis. However, Heath's treatment of what he calls 'the critical role of art' I did not find so persuasive.[18]

Heath writes of the emergence of a 'conception of a practice of cinema . . . in terms . . . of a production of contradictions against the fictions of stasis which contain and mask structuring work'.[19] As examples of this practice, he cites Brecht and, later, the avant garde cinema of Michael Snow where, he says, 'the play is never unified in a pattern . . . the apparatus pulls apart'.[20]

This appeal to the conceptions of the avant garde seems to involve at least two dangers. First, it masks the contradictions that may exist between avant garde preachings and avant garde prac- tice. Second, it deflects analysis away from the 'production of contradictions' within popular cinema. As Heath has shown else- where, we can learn about the gaps in ideological attempts to recuperate the realms of the imaginary and the symbolic through a close analysis of the workings of popular cinema.[21] BT provides an example of a movie made for a general audience which none- theless highlights issues of narration and articulation present in all story-telling (fictional and non-fictional).

QUESTIONS OF METHODOLOGY

In what follows, I gradually move away from the earlier focus on spoken language to a concern with images and, on one occasion, to the relation between sound and image (the songs played on the soundtrack of the film). This reflects the trajectory of my analysis. This began with the spoken dialogue and only later took up the pictures.

My database was very crude. Initially, I made notes in a cinema while the film was shown and then later re-transcribed them. To simplify, I ordered these notes around what eventually became 89 numbered 'scenes' – these are the numbers which appear with each extract from the film used here. Later, when I had access to a video-recording, I was able to watch the film more carefully, to freeze frame and to develop a better set of notes, correcting some of my earlier transcriptions.

In principle, with access to the video, I could have transcribed using the conventions of conversation analysis (CA) applied both to talk and to body-posture and gaze. However, because my concerns are not primarily with sequential analysis, my transcription is far looser. My only attempt to present detailed transcripts is the inclusion, where I thought appropriate, of indications of pauses within or between turns (in the usual way, these are noted as seconds or parts of a second).

In the next section, I want to retrace the trajectory of the analysis by returning to the conversations heard in the film. Later, I will reintroduce an analysis of the visual elements. As I hope to show, my concern with the soundtrack alone and with how the film is put together as film reveal a common concern with the practices of interpretation (suture) and interruption (cut).

INTERPRETATION

In our usage, 'interpretation' refers to the practice of treating language as the mere 'appearance' of an extra-linguistic 'reality' presupposed by the interpretation . . . in pretending to uphold a non- linguistic and so neutral reality, the interpretation in practice imposes its own language upon that of the language which it interprets.[22]

In the following extract from the soundtrack of BT, Dr Alex Linden (a character played by Art Garfunkel – hereafter G) is being interrogated by a policeman (played by Harvey Keitel – K) about the circumstances of a phonecall. The call had been made to Garfunkel by a woman called Milena (played by Theresa Russell – R) who reported that she had taken an overdose:

[24]
K: poor silly girl (.) how old is this girl?
    (2.0)
K: just a question
G: twenty-four twenty-five
K: a nice age
    (3.0)
K: she had difficulty speaking? (1.0)
G: she seemed normal (.) it sounded like a joke

K: but it wasn't though

G: how do you know?

K: if someone rings you and says they're going to kill themselves now that isn't *normal* (1.0) at least for normal people (.) would you agree?

We could initially approach this extract by purely sequential concerns. First, note how G's failure after two seconds to provide an answer to K's first question is made accountable by K ('just a question'). Once K has formulated the character of his utterance, G completes the 'adjacency-pair' by offering a recognisable answer. Now, through the 'chaining-rule', the floor is returned to the questioner. However, K's next utterance ('a nice age') lacks the speech delivery characteristic of a question. So, although the 3.0 silence after the utterance is completed offers G a slot to take a turn at talk, G is only obliged to speak when K asks a further question ('she had difficulty speaking?').

It is MCD analysis, however, which will be more relevant for our present concerns. Notice how both K and G trade off members' knowledge of category-bound activities, for instance in the play between them about what constitutes 'a joke' or being 'normal' in the context of a telephone conversation. More particularly, note how K offers descriptions with highly specific implications which link stage of life categories to personality characteristics ('poor silly girl', 'a nice age'). G, on the other hand, initially resists offering any description by his failure to answer K's first question. He then fails to take up the slot available after K's description 'a nice age'. Throughout, he confines himself to descriptions which carry minimal implications (giving a possible age and describing his caller as 'normal') and, thereby, minimises both his local knowledge of the person being described and anything unusual about the circumstances of the call.

Although G is not describing himself, he is implicated in these descriptions through the mechanism of standardised relational pairs. For instance, if he had assented to K's description 'poor silly girl', this would have opened up the possibility of a description of himself as involved with and perhaps exploiting 'poor silly girls'.

There are also category-bound activities present in the policeman's descriptions. K's questions depict a situation ('silly girl', someone who 'says they're going to kill themselves', 'not normal') in which the preferred response is to take immediate action. The long period of time that seems to have elapsed between Russell's phonecall and G's calling for an ambulance thus constitutes the 'bad timing' which K tries to recuperate.

As we have just seen, we can describe this exchange in terms of MCD analysis. However, the concept of 'interpretation' offers another, albeit related, line of attack. Throughout, K's utterances seek to constitute a non-linguistic reality beneath the appearances of G's answers. So 24, 25 becomes 'a nice age' and making certain kinds of telephone calls is not 'normal'. As in the documentary method of interpretation, this reality is both presupposed and reconfirmed by K's reading of 'the facts'. Like the viewer of the film, K's role is to interrogate the narrative in a doomed attempt to overcome 'gaps' and 'distortions' in the accounts offered.[23]

This role is set up early in the film, when we see Garfunkel buying Russell a popular puzzle game in a bookshop [12]. The game involves relating colour cards to numbers. Although we are not told, it seems that it is a form of 'personality' test. So G stands by, ready to interpret the colours that R has selected. But Garfunkel is also professionally interested in personality. The film, after all, is set in Vienna. And we learn that he is Dr Alex Linden, a psychiatrist.

Mechanistic readings of psycho-analytic practice use it to reduce every act or word to a pre-defined metalanguage. Such readings are popularised in everyday discussion of 'Freudian slips' and in the quizzes which enable the subject to 'meet himself as he really is'. Through these means, the unconscious is put into place. It becomes a way of fixing subjects; not a play of signifiers but an appeal to a reductionist essence.

Garfunkel seems to be at home with such reductionist interpretations. So we see him in a seminar where he offers an entirely reductionist reading of a kiss. When the seminar finishes, Russell enters. Beneath a picture of Freud, Garfunkel fondles her. Then he is shown lecturing to students. In a bland, glib manner, he informs them that 'secrecy' and 'spying' are basic to human personality. Despite what we learn later, he denies that he himself is also a spy. He prefers to call himself an 'observer'.

Such an 'observer' claims to be apart from practice – a non-subject viewing subjects. He observes the 'unconscious', categorising and relating others' actions and words. Yet he himself remains unconscious of the interpellation of subjects within a discourse of 'truth' which provides for his own practice.[24]

INTERRUPTION

The practice of interruption seeks not to impose a language of its own but to enter critically into existing linguistic configurations and to re-open the closed structures into which they have ossified.[25]

As Heath points out, the economy of narration involves a constant surveillance which *prescribes* a reading and *inscribes* a subject against possible dispersion.[26] Using the language of *The Material Word*, this surveillance represents the practice of interpretation.

In BT, Garfunkel's descriptions of 'personality' and the policeman's interrogations display the work of surveillance or interpretation. In such work, the dream world of static symbols or ideals is more satisfying than the uncertain material world of signifying practice. In BT, this is seen at its clearest in the dialogue between Garfunkel and Russell. Early on, we see the two of them in bed together [13]. He is reading a passage in a novel to her. We are, thereby, reminded of the play of texts which write a narrative. But the provision of such fictions is also a way of inscribing a subject. The fiction seeks to fix a subject by an appeal to dreams. The fiction offers a mythical 'outside' which deflects attention from the work of inscription 'inside' the text. As such, the appeal to another text is reductionist.[27]

But the figure of Garfunkel inhabits such a fictional dream world. Dreaming about fictional, idealised realities, his ideal is that life should imitate art. At his first meeting with Russell, he rejects her advances:

[8]
G: Why spoil the mystery? If we don't meet there's always the chance it could have been perfect.

But Russell openly rejects domination by this idealised dream world. She physically bars his way with her leg. While Garfunkel is immersed in ideal signified concepts ('romance', 'perfection'), Russell reintroduces the material reality of the signifier.[28] Yet Garfunkel persists in his reductionist readings. In his practice, signs are always to be read in terms of fictional ideals. The film opens in an art gallery in which Garfunkel is gazing at a Klimt painting of a man enveloping a woman:

[17]
R: (looking at the painting) They're happy.

172

G: That's because they don't know each other well enough yet.
R: *C'mon* you don't really believe that do you?

For Garfunkel, the painting, like his previous conversation with Russell, must be reduced to an expression of pre-defined forms or dreams. For him, as for the Marxism of the Second International, a pre-defined movement of history reduces discursive practice to empty mouthings. Surveillance must hold dreams and the unconscious firmly in its grasp. Its look is never open. It does not want to discover but to fix; not learn but reduce. Inevitably it is jealous about alternative readings. Its look desires to possess all it surveys.

Jealousy and the desire for possession are exemplified throughout Garfunkel's dealings with Russell. His look is always directed at signs of unfaithfulness. For the confirmation of unfaithfulness is deeply satisfying, fixing Russell's practices within stereotyped motives and allowing a stereotyped response. So when Garfunkel sees Russell kissing another man in a scene in a café, we see him scanning every detail. Like the elderly woman who is also observing the scene, we then see him expressing disapproval. The ambiguity that seems present in the kiss – only a casual display of affection perhaps – is not satisfactory. He must go beyond and outside the kiss in order to fix both kiss and subject:

[19]
G: (looking at the man Russell has just kissed) Asshole
R: I suppose he has one

Notice how Russell undermines the force of Garfunkel's expletive by implying that it can also be heard as a physiological description. The fact that R's comment can be heard as a 'joke' implies that this play on words serves to re-open a closed structure without attempting to impose a language of its own.

Throughout BT, Garfunkel encounters resistance to his attempts at coercive interpretation. Russell's playful responses to Garfunkel's descriptions contest his attempts to fix or suture her within a structure of meaning. But interpretation cannot accept a world of play. Trying to fix Russell's marital status, he is perplexed by her failure to offer a definitive answer in terms of some MCD:

[59]
G: Milena either you're married or divorced (.) you can't be in between (0.5) to be in between is to be no place at all (0.5) I don't get it

173

Failing to receive any answers that he would regard as satisfactory, Garfunkel takes to spying outside her flat. Early one morning, he sees her returning home and wants her to confirm that she has been sleeping with someone else. She spots him sitting in his car and the exchange proceeds as follows:

[64]

1. R: Fuck *off*
2. G: You're drunk
3. R: Disappear
4. G: I want to explain Milena
5. R: Tell it to your students
6. G: It's just that I can't stand to think of you with anyone else
7. R: Please I'm tired I had too much (2.0) I need sleep just go
8. G: It's fucking daylight (.) Milena I love you
9. R: Do you want me to tell you I slept with someone is that what you want (.) and fucked? Would you believe that? Is that what you want to believe? What do you want to *know?* The truth? (2.0) no you don't (.) call it a lie (3.5) What do you want us to do? To go up and make love to go up and fuck? You want us to do that? You want me to do that? What is it you want? (2.0) Okay (.) I love you (.) I don't love you what do you want me to say? What do you want me to do because of that? Kill myself? (1.0) Would you be sure then? Huh? Would you?
10. G: I want you to be mine
11. R: I don't want anything to be mine
12. R: Want me to give you a great big present Alex? Yes, I did it. You made me do it.
13. (G slaps R)

Each of Garfunkel's interventions involves reductionist interpretations of Russell's actions. She is held to be 'drunk' and, in any event, to be held accountable for being out on the streets at dawn ('it's fucking daylight'). These interpretations each constitute a fixed subject (or slave) defined by reference to another's (a master's) fantasies. Following Russell's long string of questions at 9, then, Garfunkel correctly expresses the desire that is implicit in his gaze: 'I want you to be mine'.

Russell's response is initially to avoid dialogue (1, 3, 5 and 7). However, when pressed by Garfunkel, she interrupts his discourse, revealing that he has already constituted her as a subject. She enters the voice of I to mimic his treatment of her in terms of what he 'wants'.

She is not prepared to offer a fixed account of her own dispositions ('I love you. I don't love you'). Nor does she want to fix another subject ('I don't want anything to be mine'). Only within Garfunkel's speech is she reduced to a fixed subject. But, as she says, to accept this speech would be to kill herself or to reduce herself to a symbol (at 9, the unfaithful woman). Unwilling to recognise the possible irony at 12 (telling him what he wants to hear versus what actually happened), Garfunkel gratefully accepts the proffered symbol and, coming to life within a renewed symbolic order, expresses his mastery of that order by slapping her.

SYMBOL/SIGNIFIER

In one sense, 'gaps' and 'contradictions' are the very stuff of popular cinema. Without them, the film would be over as soon as it started. The pleasure of the viewer depends upon the knowledge that all will not be revealed at the start but in due course. Gradually, pleasurably, as in a strip-tease, the plot unfolds and, slowly, things fall into place.

BT appears to offer itself to us very much in this form of a puzzle slowly dissolved. The film opens with shots of a couple (Garfunkel and Russell) on an outing. Immediately, puzzles are created as subsequent scenes, moving around in narrative time, show Russell unconscious in an ambulance, leaving another man (Denholm Elliott) and removing her wedding ring and then on her own, drunk in a bedroom. Why does she drink? To which man does she belong? How did she get hurt? What is the history of her relationship to the two men?

Within a few seconds, the narrative poses such questions for the viewer and, through a series of flash-backs, works on and through the puzzles it has created. In the popular cinema, such puzzles are created and resolved by reference to what Heath calls the 'novelistic'. Questions and answers are derived from 'within the limits of existing social representations' and in the context of 'fictions of the individual'.[29] A rich assortment of puzzles can thereby be generated.

In this film, for instance, is there a link between unfaithfulness (two men), deceit (removal of wedding ring), moral decline (drunkenness) and injury (being carried unconscious in an ambulance)? These 'novelistic' forms of connection immediately suggest themselves. In the dreams of everyday and 'fictional' narratives, we seem already to have encountered such women. Like the reader of tabloid newspapers, we lick our lips knowing that all will slowly, deliciously, be revealed: the juicy details, the moral ending.

The resolution of the puzzle provides for two central characters of doubtful moral stature (the scarlet woman and the jealous man). As in all good moral tales, we demand that they get their due. And, indeed, Russell suffers violence and near death, while we learn in the closing shots that Garfunkel is destined to lose the woman he desired to possess. In the final scene standing on a bridge, he peers down into the water below, apparently pondering his fate, learning his moral lesson as we have learned ours.

BT is replete with symbols. The first shot of a Klimt painting seems to prepare the spectator for a story of a passionate, enveloping relationship turning on the themes of possessiveness and possession. Then we discover that the film is set in Vienna, the city of Sigmund Freud and of Harry Lime (from *The Third Man*). Both symbolise what is hidden or unconscious: Freud explores the unconscious and the crooks and spies in *The Third Man* work underground, in the city sewers. However, BT is not prepared to allow the spectator merely to note the presence of these symbolic fields. It wants to work these fields for all they are worth. As if the Viennese setting were not enough in itself, we learn that Garfunkel is himself a psychiatrist and a part-time spy, hired by American Intelligence to report on Russell and her Czech husband.

The density and unity of symbols in BT seem to take up more and more of the visual field. As passive spectators, we only need a limited use of symbols to establish the space which the narrative will occupy. But instead of allowing the narrative to wash over us, the symbolic field threatens to take over from it. BT is over-determined by symbols. BT is thus 'about' the possibilities and limits of symbolic readings of texts. It establishes a set of symbols which then rotate and multiply to an impossible extent. One is reminded of the nausea and seasickness that Joseph K. experiences when he is close to the over-determined symbolic field of the court.[30]

But BT is also 'about' the possibilities of a reading which refuses any escape into a signified but instead enters into a play of signifiers. When, for instance, in only the third scene of the film, Russell removes her wedding ring, she sheds her last connection with symbolic objects. After that disavowal of the symbolic, she is connected only with images that refuse any simple link with a symbolic field. In many scenes, she is seen wearing a range of jewellery, often in the form of a brooch. But the brooches carry images that are not immediately retrievable in the closure of the symbolic. We see on them a woman's hand, a brightly coloured parrot and then a woman's face. But, like the painting in her flat, the face is open and offers no clues about motivation or personality.

BT thus reveals the possibility of a practice which is not obsessed with interpretation. Unlike Garfunkel, whose gaze is always turned towards symbols and metaphors (the Klimt painting, the symbolic and erotic paintings and statues in his room), Russell displays a practice involved in signifiers without any immediate signified. At the art gallery shown in the opening scene, where Garfunkel is immersed in his Klimt scene of the man enveloping a woman, she is looking at another less retrievable painting. Her gaze can offer no resource to the narrative: her preferred painting plays no further part in the unwinding of the narration. Like the spectator who is not immersed in the narration's relentless progress towards retrieving a set of signifieds, Russell's gaze is mobile and active. 'What about this?' she says, 'Look where we are' [54].

Nowhere does this suggest any pure discourse of truth apart from signifiers. But while Garfunkel, like the spectator, is professionally concerned with articulating dreams into a finite sequence, generating closures and silences, BT also shows how symbols can rotate within an inflationary symbolic economy which disarticulates expected sequences and interrupts closures.

We will examine this disarticulation by means of Heath's analysis of the 'look' and of 'suture'.

LOOK/DESIRE

Classically, cinema turns on a series of 'looks' which join, cross through and relay one another. Thus: (1) the camera looks (a metaphor assumed by this cinema) . . . at someone, something . . .; (2) the spectator looks . . . at – or on – the film; (3) each of the characters in the film looks . . . at other characters, things.[31]

We can start to understand the 'inflationary' character of BT by examining the central role that the 'look' plays in it. The most powerful image in the film is of Russell's unconscious body as seen from the point of view of Garfunkel, at first sprawled out and then as rearranged by him preparatory to rape. So Garfunkel looks at the body and we look at Garfunkel's look. This look wants to scan, define and close. For Garfunkel, the look defines a desirable object made accessible through being rendered passive or unconscious. This desire is a desire for mastery and mastery is attained by fixing a subject as an object in a system of equivalences which leaves no surplus.[32]

For the viewer, too, desire is satisfied by this fixing. As voyeurs, we can derive pleasure from the symbol of a subject-become-object and hence directly accessible to our fantasies. In the same way, as passive viewers, we are satisfied by a text rendered submissive via a symbolic order, as signifiers are fixed to a signified.

For this viewer, the scene offers the expected resolution of the puzzles established by the narrative's posing of an enigma. Within what Barthes terms the 'hermeneutic code', a site of tension and fantasy is established between reality and appearance.[33] Consequently, the spectator cannot avert his gaze lest he miss clues until the final revelation. Finally, for Garfunkel, the rape is the culmination of his attempt to fix Russell within a symbolic structure. While conscious, Russell continually resists and subverts Garfunkel's interpretive work. When unconscious, through an overdose, she offers a perfect target for the unfettered expression of his fantasies.

Like the passive viewer, Garfunkel is interpellated as a symbolic subject, a subject at home with symbols. Even as he arranges Russell's unconscious body, he stops to puzzle over the images present in the paintings and photos in her apartment, searching for a symbolic order which will still more firmly fix the subject of his desire (as an object of his gaze). Every time Garfunkel is with Russell, he turns to images as if to restock his fantasies. The gaze at the painting in the art gallery is matched by his stare at a painting of a unicorn when, some time later, he is in bed with Russell. Shortly afterwards, his eyes turn towards photos of her with Elliott. In the very next scene, he is on a bus still looking at photographs of her when she walks by.

In his looking, Garfunkel mirrors the look of the viewer or spectator who himself will be looking for symbols to fix the object of his desire. Like the spectator, Garfunkel turns his gaze towards what is enclosed within a frame. The 'series of looks' described by Heath is completed by the look of the camera which provides such a frame and thereby fixes what can be viewed. The fantasies which constitute subjects are products of specific practices and apparatuses (in this case of camera and frame); they do not spring from nature. Once again, like the spectator, Garfunkel does not receive his images in a direct, unmediated way. They are viewed within frames or, in other cases, through a kind of lens, as when Garfunkel observes Russell through glass.

A view through glass, like a view through a frame, is invariably associated with an attempt to fix a subject.[34] Thus, after their car breaks down in Morocco and they are given a lift by two Arabs in a truck, Garfunkel peers through a glass partition, puzzling about Russell's ambiguous relationship with the men on each side of her in the front of the truck. A little while later, back at home, he observes Russell talking to a man outside the window of a café in which he is sitting. In both cases, the glass frames silent images which, like the ambiguous photographs of Russell, function for Garfunkel as clues to be decoded by data drawn from the conscious mind (official records, files) and from the unconscious – the fantasies present in the Klimt painting already mentioned and in the erotic statue which we see in Garfunkel's bedroom.

Garfunkel's look shares with that of the spectator a particular version of desire and sexuality associated with mastery and closure. Such desire wants to risk nothing by fixing another subject without setting itself into question. So Garfunkel is only really happy when locating Russell in a satisfactory symbolic order. In the rape scene, this happens through his arrangement and penetration of her inert body in line with a fantasy. The link between the desire for mastery and passive looking or voyeurism (in this case, Garfunkel's watch over Russell's body) is made clearer in the activities of the policeman who investigates the rape. In early scenes, we see him puzzling over clues. Like Garfunkel, his sexuality is associated with imagining a world fixed according to a fantasy. For instance, as he enters Russell's bedroom, the policeman licks his lips at the sexual fantasy that he imagines.

Both Garfunkel and the policeman display a form of sexuality which relies on fixing the object of desire. Garfunkel is aroused when he is able to reduce Russell to a symbol (a 'slut', an expression of a Klimt painting). The policeman is excited when he reduces the appearances of Russell's room to a stereotyped picture of a sexual encounter.

The fixing of meaning of discourses via an appeal to symbols exemplifies the practice of interpretation. Alternatively, interruption can set up a playful relation between discourses. We saw this earlier, when Russell plays with readings of Garfunkel's MCD 'asshole'. On other occasions, Russell passively enacts the imaginary subject that Garfunkel proposes. Her passivity, however, serves not as a confirmation but as a contestation of Garfunkel's closures. Throughout, Russell shows that she is merely playing a part dictated from outside. Consequently, she shows no sign that she has mistaken this imaginary subject for reality. Without internalisation, the subject is only a dummy. In the first of these two scenes, we see her rooms cleaned and tidy – quite unlike their normal state. Garfunkel enters and is greeted by:

[48]
R: I'm being nice to you
(Garfunkel is delighted by this reconstituted 'tidy' subject that fits his fantasies. However, his advances are rejected by Russell. When reduced to a fiction, she experiences no desire:)
R: Not now (.) I just don't want to.
(Appearing to realise the emptiness of his mastery, Garfunkel says he has to leave and Russell asks:)
R: What if we'd made love? Why are you lying to yourself all the time? You've got to understand who I am.

Garfunkel's look/the narrative's look always lies because it seeks mastery by its practices of prescription and inscription. It only wants to inscribe subjects as coherent unities; it is never prepared to 'understand' the multiplicity and play of signifiers ('who I am'). For Garfunkel, however, the only perceived problem is Russell's wilfulness and perversity. For him, she is still a unitary subject – a selfish person:

G: You do everything when you want to.
(Faced with this coercive interpretation, Russell reverts to her earlier strategy of role-playing. Standing on the stairs, she flaunts herself:)
R: You want me? Here it is Alex. Fuck me right here and now.

Once more, Garfunkel is turned on by the offer of the subject of his desire. But she clearly does not enjoy the sexual act that follows.

She returns to her rooms crying and starts throwing objects around, disturbing the tidiness of the room/subject which Garfunkel had desired.

A final site of these challenges to interpretation occurs via Russell's playful version of Garfunkel's fantasies. This time Russell offers him symbols of romance: candles are lit all over his flat – and of male sex objects – she is dressed like a tart in an orange wig. This juxtaposition of sweetheart and whore destroys their individual symbolic power. Russell has gone over the top: she wears a bra over her sweater. She offers herself to him through a display of his symbols and a use of his language (the language of possession):

[68]
R: You can lock me up. I'll always be yours. We are celebrating the death of the lady you don't want and the birth of the lady you do want.

Russell interrupts Garfunkel's discourse by revealing the language of mastery that it involves. By setting his symbols in contradictory play, she shows the way in which they construct fictional, imaginary subjects. Faced with this interruption, Garfunkel cannot cope. He storms out of her flat. Russell, however, continues to interrupt his language of mastery:

R: Don't go, fuck me. That's what you want isn't it?

Locked into a relentless need to narrate, Garfunkel, however, can only treat images as clues as part of the narrative's constant surveillance. Instead of looking around or playing, he will only seek certainties. The kind of looking which Russell proposes can never be freed from discourse or presuppositionless (Husserl's mistaken dream). Garfunkel and the policeman engage in reductionism not because they engage in fantasies (what are 'truths'?) but because they employ fantasies to secure closures or suturing effects.

This helps us to move towards a reworking of our understanding of interruptive practice and of forms of desire. 'Interruption' is now revealed as an intervention which seeks to juxtapose or revolve fantasies (discourses) to prevent the forms of closure established by attempts at discursive mastery. The desire of interruption is for productivity and play; the desire of interpretation is for closure and silence. Moreover, as Hegel showed, a discourse of mastery is bound to fail in its object.[35] For, by constituting others as slaves, the recognition they give can count for nothing. And this perhaps explains something of the relentless movement of narration within the conventional film or text or the desire for ever new pornographic objects. Denied recognition by the very practices that were supposed to achieve it, interpretation can only thrust forward once again in its (self-defeating) task of imposing its fantasies.

CUT/SUTURE

A concentration on dialogue may seem to imply that BT is concerned only with verbal interruption. Through an analysis of 'cutting' (from one scene to another), we will conclude by establishing the nature and practice of visual interruptions in BT. Now, of course, the cut from one scene to another is part of the basic machinery of narrative cinema. As Heath points out, the major enemy of such a cinema is 'boredom'. By switching the site of the spectator's gaze through cutting away, interest can be maintained, so the cut – to a sub-plot, or an earlier, later or simultaneous time in the chronology of the narrative – is basic to narrative cinema.

There are elements of this kind of cutting in BT – particularly in the moves backwards and forwards in narrative time which, although complicated, are no more intricate than in many conventional films. The cuts which distinguish BT, however, serve to pull apart the fictions and symbols which ordinarily are used to make narrative and subjects cohere. This drive for coherence depends, in part, upon a certain essentialist treatment of the people we view.

In the narrative cinema, people are cast as imaginary subjects, grounded in familiar fictions. As they flicker before us on the screen, their only substance is derived from such fictions. In BT, this suturing effect is contested and the wound unstitched, by the repeated cutting between different versions of the body: the mythical body invested by fictions and the material body subject to cuts and suturing effects. Five times the film cuts away from the dreams of the subject to the material practices in which bodies are inscribed as subjects. Each time involves a cut from the smooth unfolding of the narrative to a shot of Russell's body in hospital being treated for her overdose, as follows:

Cut 1 In the second scene of the film, we move away from the fictions of the Klimt painting to a shot of Russell in an ambulance.

She is unconscious. Yet her fixing as a clinical object is unsettled by the low-cut gown in which she is dressed. The play between clinical/sexual object is unsettling and will be repeated rather than overcome.

Cut 2 Some scenes later, we see Garfunkel signing a statement for the policeman [27]. The practice of surveillance is stressed by the policeman's query about his subsequent movements. The film now cuts to a view of Garfunkel peering into a river, imagining making love to Russell [28]. Through surveillance and the recourse to the imaginary, the narrative coheres. But this scene itself disappears and we cut to the operating theatre where we see Russell being given a tracheotomy. We witness the bloody cuts and the attempts at suture concealed beneath the fictions of coherent narration.

Cut 3 Shortly afterwards, we cut from the bedroom scene where Garfunkel is questioning Russell about her marriage [35], back once more to the hospital where she is being given an electric shock to revive her [36]. Garfunkel's interrogation is juxtaposed to another violent practice and is relocated in a material, bodily reality away from dreams of the imaginary. As in cut 1, however, the two realities are shown to intersect: during the administration of the shock, Russell's breasts appear out of her gown. Her body is not to be fixed as a property of either the clinical or Garfunkel's sexual gaze. Both gazes are interrupted and a disturbing rotation or revolution of discourses takes place.

Cuts 4 and 5 On two further occasions [42–3 and 58–9], the film cuts from bedroom scenes to views of injections and catheters in the operating theatre. These unsettling shifts of the camera's gaze destroy the stability and coherence that narrative cinema demands and through juxtaposition of scenes reminds us of the discursive constitution of the body.

The lack of stability of the narrative gaze is emphasised in the penultimate scene of BT where Garfunkel gazes at Russell's empty apartment and sees it first tidy, then untidy [87 and 88]. The practices which ordinarily generate stability have failed to do their proper work. So, finally, we see Garfunkel in New York, catching sight of Russell getting out of a taxi [89]. The camera closes up on her body and reveals a tracheotomy scar on her neck. For BT, both cut and suture are visible. And, for once, this is not an empty display of directorial cunning (the emptiness of the avant garde) but a learning experience – an invitation to dialogue rather than closure.

Fittingly, given these troubles, the film ends with a blues sung over the credits. As Heath points out, in this way sound is 'contained . . . as the safe space of the narrative voice' [120–1]. Sound focuses, underlines and links images for the sake of a smooth narration: it is central to the work of suturing. Only the possible irony present in the words of the song ('It's the same old story . . .') gives the slightest hint of the suturing in progress – the narration of 'the same old story'. But the ironicisation and hence distancing is far less than, say, in Altman's *The Long Goodbye* which follows a brutal killing by an ending in which the murderer skips up the road dancing to a recording of 'Hooray for Hollywood' played on the soundtrack.[36]

Viewed in this way, *Bad Timing* pays tribute to the 'good timing' of the narrative as, in Heath's words on the nature of film, it successfully rewinds 'a tangle of memories . . . as the order of the continuous time of the film' [127]. And yet the interest of this film is that these very suturing effects, which fix the subject as part of the narrative, are themselves put in issue. Like any film or text, *Bad Timing* never entirely incorporates every excess or contradiction. Images, for instance, are introduced, like Russell's striking jewellery, which are never taken up in the narrative and so constitute an untapped surplus in its economy.[37] Unlike many other films which operate within the conventions of popular cinema, however, BT interrupts and disrupts this economy. Unlike 'monetarist' cinema, which is concerned with fixing and limiting the production of surplus signifiers, the work of this film is specifically 'inflationary', encouraging productivities which can only endanger a sound currency.[38]

CONCLUSION

Ultimately however the struggle is not between one person and another but rather between ways of speaking and writing.[39]

The way I have used the behaviour of the fictional characters, Alex and Milena, may imply to the casual reader that I have been concerned with a 'struggle . . . between one person and another'. This, then, might look like an essay in gender politics in which it is demonstrated, once again, how a man exploits a woman.[40]

Why, however, should we define Milena in terms of her gender?

Surely, this would be to fall prey to the same essentialist, interpretive project which we have described above. Instead of trying to fix Milena as one kind of subject or another, the point has been to analyse verbal and visual processes of fixing (suture) and unfixing (cut). This has meant that we have gone beyond 'ways of speaking and writing' to ways of looking and cinematic forms of representing looking. In doing so, it may be argued that my use of concepts has become uneconomic. Somewhat foolhardily, I have tried to merge MCD analysis – deriving from CA – with accounts of suture deriving from semiotic discussions of film.

Perhaps, however, these two traditions are not so far apart as we might believe. We already know that semiotics insists that our focus must not be on the authentic character of subjects but on how subjects are constituted within discourses. However, this argument is implicit in Sacks' account of MCDs. More recently, it has been made explicit in Schegloff's discussion of how we may appeal to context as an explanation.[41] Fully in line with Stephen Heath, Schegloff argues that analysts' characterisations of persons in terms of features such as gender, ethnicity and class are only legitimate if such features can be shown in participants' own orientations.

I began with McHoul's demolition of the unthought polarity between 'fictional' and 'naturally-occurring' data.[42] Building on his contribution, this chapter has sought to encourage rethinking of our attachment to polarities between 'schools' of analysis.

ACKNOWLEDGEMENT

This paper was first published in *Continuum*, 5,1 (1991), pp.9–31, and reproduced with kind permission of the Editor.

NOTES

1 I would like to acknowledge the helpful comments of Tom O'Regan (Murdoch University) and Anssi Perakyla (Glaxo Research Fellow, Goldsmiths' College).

2 A. McHoul, 'An initial investigation of the usability of fictional conversation for doing conversation analysis', *Semiotica*, 1987, vol. 67, no. 1–2, pp. 83–104.

3 M. Hammersley and P. Atkinson, *Ethnography: Principles in Practice*, London, Tavistock, 1983.

4 M. Peake, *Mr Pye*, Harmondsworth, Penguin, 1972.

5 P. Drew, 'Accusations', *Sociology*, 1978, vol. 12, pp. 1–22.
6 E. Schegloff, G. Jefferson and H. Sacks, 'The preference for self-correction in the organisation of repair in conversation', *Language*, 1977, vol. 53, pp. 361–82.
7 McHoul, op. cit., pp. 98–9.
8 H. Sacks, 'On the analysability of stories by children', in J. Gumperz and D. Hymes (eds), *Directions in Sociolinguistics*, New York, Holt, Rinehart & Winston, 1972, pp. 216–32.
9 H. Garfinkel, *Studies in Ethnomethodology*, Englewood Cliffs, NJ, Prentice-Hall, 1967.
10 D. Silverman and B. Torode, *The Material Word*, London, Routledge & Kegan Paul, 1980.
11 Garfinkel, op. cit.
12 R. Barthes, *Image, Music, Text*, London, Fontana, 1977; J. Derrida, *Of Grammatology*, Baltimore, Johns Hopkins University Press, 1977; E. Laclau and C. Mouffe, *Hegemony and Socialist Strategy*, London, Verso Books, 1985.
13 S. Heath, *Questions of Cinema*, London, Macmillan, 1981.
14 Ibid., p. 106.
15 Ibid., p. 13.
16 See also J. Vagg, 'The productivities of realist and modernist texts', unpublished PhD thesis, University of London, 1981.
17 Ibid.
18 Heath, op. cit., p. 7.
19 Heath, op. cit.
20 Heath, op. cit., p. 128.
21 In Heath's sense, the 'imaginary' refers to the specific function of the subject in the symbolic realm. Ideological practice involves fixing a relation between the symbolic and the imaginary. See Heath, op. cit., pp. 105–6.
22 Silverman and Torode, op. cit., p. 8.
23 There are parallels here with modernist texts like the Robbe-Grillet novel analysed in Silverman and Torode, op. cit., Ch. 8. The scenes of interrogation there also shows the practices of surveillance at work.
24 As Anssi Perakyla has pointed out to me, there is an alternative version of psychoanalytic practice in which the patient's fixed patterns of interpretation are made visible and become the subject of a dialogue.
25 Silverman and Torode, op. cit., p. 6.
26 Heath, op. cit.
27 There are parallels here with Robbe-Grillet's *Projet pour une révolution à New York* where the interruptions of Laura are challenged by readings from her brother's library, well-stacked with pulp novels. See Silverman and Torode, op. cit., Ch. 8.
28 Although Russell's gesture might suggest the symbol of an 'easy' woman, the film as a whole reveals the contestation of this, or any other, symbolic reading.
29 Heath, op. cit., p. 125.
30 See Silverman and Torode, op. cit., Ch. 4.
31 Heath, op. cit., p. 119.

32 This parallels Laclau and Mouffe's account of practices of closure in political discourse. See Laclau and Mouffe, op. cit.
33 R. Barthes, *S/Z*, London, Cape, 1975.
34 Arthur Penn's enigmatically named *Night Moves* (moves in the dark/ the elliptical moves of the knight in chess) makes a great play with views through glass (a glass-bottomed boat, a scene viewed through a car window).
35 A. Kojeve, in A. Bloom (ed.), *Introduction to the Reading of Hegel*, New York, Basic Books, 1969.
36 Altman's films are distinguished by the way in which image subverts sound. See, for instance, the bland play overheard on the radio by the lovers in *Thieves Like Us* and Geraldine Chaplin's trite broadcast commentary from a car junkyard in *Nashville*. Altman's films also use overlapping dialogue to good effect. In all cases, sound is not allowed to become a mere substitute for the image.
37 Vagg discusses the role of unused surpluses in Stendhal's *Le Rouge et le Noir*. See Vagg, op. cit.
38 This use of 'economic' terms follows Goux's suggestive paper. See J.-J. Goux, 'Marx et l'inscription du travail', in *Tel Quel, Théorie d'Ensemble*, Paris, Seuil, 1968, pp. 188–211.
39 Silverman and Torode, op. cit., p. 6.
40 Pursuing this line further, it might be argued that the (male) director of *Bad Timing* is exploiting women by the vivid depiction of rape in the film.
41 E. Schegloff, 'Reflections on talk and social structure', in D. Boden and D. Zimmerman (eds), *Talk and Social Structure*, Cambridge, Polity Press, 1991.
42 McHoul, op. cit.

11

GOING SHOPPING
Markets, crowds and consumption

Don Slater

Concepts of 'the market' stand in a difficult relation to those of 'culture'. The problems are clearly reflected in economic theory where 'the market' denotes a set of abstract, formally rational relationships rather than concrete cultural forms of encounter: the hidden hand of market forces should not be affected by whether they are at work in an open market, shopping mall or global electronic futures market. This abstract, disembodied sense of the market is in marked contrast to the concretely spatio-temporal original meaning of 'a market': a physical place where buyers and sellers meet at particular times, a word for the actual 'building, square, or other public place for such meetings' (*Chambers Dictionary*). The market, in this older sense, *is* the town square on the first Saturday of each month, the floor of the Stock Exchange between 9.00 and 3.00 on weekdays.

In this chapter, I want to return to the concrete sense of 'the market' as a place and event, using the term to refer to any actual gathering of large numbers of buyers and sellers – medieval and early modern markets, open and covered, periodic or daily, fairs, exchanges and bourses, arcades, department stores, shopping malls, shopping streets and precincts. By looking at the 'empirical' market we can reconnect the idea of a market (and along with it, shopping, corporate marketing and consumerism) with culture in at least two strong senses. Firstly, focusing on the empirical market stresses agency and emergence – a market must itself be culturally reproduced as a meaningful event in order to be an embodied actual market (rather than an abstract economic construct). Secondly, we can reconnect the abstract economic notion of the market with the cultural image on which it decisively depends, and which has borne an enormous ideological load throughout the modern period, and again today: the image of a thriving civil society, the boisterous, dynamic and autonomous pursuit of private interests by large numbers of individuals – market or enterprise culture. The abstract economic construct *assumes* the empirical existence of that vibrant culture of the market place.

Economic theory defines market behaviour as a process of abstraction from all cultural content: buyers and sellers evince market behaviour when, abstracting from their specific qualitative desires (the realm of use value and utility, the cultural content of demand), they calculate relative quantities. The appearance of culture *in* the market (rather than outside it, as its precondition) indexes a pathology. For example, advertising is an 'embarrassment'[1] to neo-classical economics because through it firms operate directly on cultural content, which thus allows manipulation of market forces. Monopoly theorists and neo-Keynesians therefore aggregate cultural 'factors' such as advertising, marketing and design into the category of 'non-price competition', which they set alongside 'institutional features' as forces which disrupt or rigidify the formally rational dynamic of the market. The notice Galbraith,[2] for example, pays to advertising and design is part of an argument that the market no longer exists: in his 'revised sequence' control over demand, exercised through the cultural reproduction of the consumer, replaces markets with management and with the corporate plan.

This view of the relation between markets and culture has long been reflected in critical and cultural theory, particularly in the manifold theories of mass culture and mass society. The appearance of culture in the market indicates that autonomous civil activity has been subordinated to the logic of the commodity and the planning principles of the firm; that culture has been rationalised and functionalised. In this view, the mass production of goods (occasioned by technological expansion and reorganisation) has as its necessary corollary the mass production of consumers: all the forces of cultural reproduction are now effectively hitched to the engine of commerce. Hence the culmination of the enterprise culture of nineteenth-century bourgeois capitalism is the eradication, by monopoly capitalism, of the civil society on which it depended. Economic reproduction of an autonomous culture *through* the market has been replaced by the market as a tool for the cultural reproduction of the capitalist mode of production.

The image of a bustling market indicates the presence of a thriving and dynamic civil society. Walter Benjamin condenses this image of civil energy into a snapshot of 'the crowd':

> A street, a conflagration, or a traffic accident assemble people who are not defined along class lines. They present themselves as concrete gatherings, but socially they remain abstract – namely, in their isolated private interests. Their models are the customers who, each in his private interest, gather at the market around their 'common cause'. In many cases, such gatherings have only a statistical existence. This existence conceals the really monstrous thing about them: the concentration of private persons as such by the accident of their private interests.[3]

This image of the crowd contains two dialectically related (hence irreducible) terms: on the one hand, autonomous activity – people moving about according to their own self-determined logic. The crowd is not called into being as a whole, but because a number of individuals coincide – accidentally, in a causal sense – in turning their gaze towards a particular focus. Even their interest in the same object is not identical. Hence the independent second term: a focus – a spectacle, an event, an object of interest or desire. This focus may be unplanned – as with the 'conflagration' – or planned: the regular and expected display of large numbers of goods, the presence of showmanship, entertainment, advertising, the hawker's call – the attempts to 'attract a crowd'. These attempts are eventually rationalised into the idea of 'marketing' – the regularised focusing of autonomous individuals upon commodities. However, given the dialectical logic by which the two terms are connected, crowds 'happen' – they cannot be coerced into existence. However rationalised, indeed however *successful* marketing may be, what it attracts is still a crowd: a contingent, unstable and emergent entity, one of whose terms is always *agency*, however compromised that agency may be.

Hence, the stress on the crowd's 'statistical existence' is crucial: the crowd is a probabilistic event, expected perhaps but not predictable in a causal sense. A crowd is formed around a common but not shared stopping point, a brief halt in a multitude of independent trajectories. We can only 'account for' a crowd by specifying the unique interest which each individual finds in the current object or spectacle, as well as the steps taken by each individual to have arrived at it. 'We were just walking down the street to my friend's house and came upon . . .'

As a dialectic of action and focus, both poles must be maintained. 'Masses' represent a reification of the crowd in which autonomous action is collapsed into the spectacular focus: when talking of masses, we are saying that the movements of the former crowd are reducible, without residue, to its point of focus; that we can 'account for' the gathering by analysing the power of the focus which attracted it. Twentieth-century fears of scientific advertising (Vance Packard[4] is exemplary) move in this direction: advertising as a spectacular and scientifically grounded focus determines the action of consumers en masse, as a reified entity with scientifically ascertainable laws of motion. Benjamin himself[5] discerns in this collapse into spectacle the spectre of the fascist masses of the 1930s: totalitarian states, the above passage goes on to say, deploying the power of public signification, can 'rationalise' the crowd into 'permanent and obligatory' masses.

The dialectic of the crowd can collapse in the other direction – the absorption of spectacle into unregulated and unfocused action: the 'mob'. Here the impulses of the actors, uncathected to even the most fetishised external object, are entirely anarchic, uncontained and hallucinatory, producing a gathering which cannot be satisfied but only quashed or exhausted.

For Benjamin, the urban crowd is modelled on the gathering of customers at the market: in fact, market, crowd and city are inextricable terms. As Braudel[6] puts it, 'Without a market, a town is inconceivable', while a 'crowd' is inconceivable outside towns or markets (which can be a sort of temporary town). The market attracts crowds to the town, makes of it the geographical focus of networks of commercial enterprise and interest. The market square was the natural focus of social life, of its communication networks, activities and identity: Braudel[7] notes that market days saw a rise in all forms of activity (for example, land sales, marriage and dowry contracts). As it grew, the permanent shops and houses built by prosperous merchants dominated the town centre, while the permanent civic structures designed to house the market tended also to house the town hall, thus uniting political, social and commercial centres. Only in the largest commercial cities and those which identified themselves less with merchant culture (e.g. Paris) were political and commercial activities hived off into separate civic spaces. Yet even non-commercial gatherings created markets: in the seventeenth century the old Palais in Paris (much like Westminster Hall in London) was the site of the Parlement and of the commercial law courts, yet along with the crowds gathered there, primarily for legal matters, were gossips, merchants, prostitutes and strollers catered for by 'stalls selling everything from ribbons to mirrors or purses to plumes'. It was referred to as the 'Palais Marchand', a kind of 'luxury shopping centre'.[8]

Because of its relation to crowds, to the focusing of heterogeneous activities, the market is never just a market. For example, exchanges and early bourses, like the Royal Exchange (1567) in London or the Bourse (1513) in Antwerp, were permanent enclosed structures built to house the activities of international merchant and banking networks. They included large, enclosed courtyards for gathering merchants, stalls in arcades around the centre for displaying and warehousing samples; on the upper stories, shops and refreshment stands selling unrelated goods, such as books, pictures, luxury clothing, spices and rarities; inside and around the exchange might well be rentable apartments. The crowd attracted to the exchange included not only merchants, but people keen to obtain information about international affairs; hawkers and prostitutes; a general public for whom the exchange like any market evinced the exotic in the form of goods and people from far-flung lands.

The arcades which Benjamin explored embody within a single image the idea that a market is, culturally, a gathering place for crowds, offering diverse points of focus for diverse and contingent interests. Constructed in major capital cities throughout the nineteenth century, the arcades were covered passageways – glass and steel roofs covering pedestrian streets, originally crammed between buildings, closed to traffic, policed, and lined by architecturally uniform shops as well as 'cafés, brothels, luxury stores, apartments, displays of food, fashion and furniture, art galleries, book stores, dioramas, theatres, baths, news stands, gambling houses, private clubs'.[9] The Palais Royal (which Benjamin does not specifically discuss) built in Paris from 1780 contained the first arcade, and is emblematic in showing the roots of modern consumerism in the urban, spectacle-focused crowd. It represents the 'unity'[10] of crowd functions gathered into one space: market, 'society' and city crowds (from all social strata) were focused on to a spectacle in which there was 'a direct connection between business, consumerism, entertainment, politics and information'.[11] The Palais Royal contained 'reading rooms, bookstores, small food markets for the cosmopolitan palate . . . furniture stores, jewellery and fashion shops, souvenir shops, pottery, tobacco, perfume and antiques. It had restaurants of all categories, cafés, gambling rooms, a stock exchange, a real estate agency, betting offices, brothels for all inclinations, and countless apartments and attic rooms for rent. It also contained theatres, picture galleries and other exhibitions.'[12] On to the Palais Royal was focused the emergent public sphere of the revolutionary period; the emerging consumer groups; emerging capital from stall-holders to international speculators; the emerging artistic bohemia: all the scattered dynamism of civil society focused on one physical space.

At least three historical forms of crowd-gathering can be mapped on to the 'unity' of the Palais Royal: the pre-modern market, the leisure gatherings of 'society', and the city itself. Firstly, although the Palais Royal contained shops, it contained them within the form of the older markets and exchanges. Pre-modern shops exemplified medieval *personalised* relationships (the seller was also the craftsman, the producer and member of the guild; the relationship between client and craftsman was one of patronage and commission in which even entering a shop involved an obligation to buy); by contrast the market, and the congregation of shops within an arcade, was based on *depersonalised* relationships – the individuals who here and there constellate into crowds are not only autonomous but *anonymous* and therefore democratically freed from personal obligation. The depersonalisation of market relationships is crucial to the history of shopping: the separation and *mediation* of production and consumption in the rise of middlemen; the replacement of haggling with fixed prices; not least the very idea of the (eventually *mass*) manufacture of goods for an unknown and generalised market. Above all, the anonymity of the marketer as opposed to shopper is linked from the earliest of markets and fairs to the idea of the hedonistic release of desires. The theme of the Rabelaisian, the carnivalesque, the spectacular, of utopian gratification in consumption (more specifically in shopping, in the market place itself) has been revived recently[13] and particularly in relation to the reassertion of the body in cultural experience,[14] and this must certainly be crucial in countering the formal and overly cognitive abstraction

of the market in most social discourse. That the arcade, as proto-
type of the future of shopping, reaches back to the market rather
than the shop, emblematises the continuity of a certain kind of
relation between action and focus (i.e. the crowd), one in which
economic activity continues to be wrapped up in the carnivalesque
and the exotic, in showmanship and the attraction of desire. It
points to both the libidinal nature of the relation between people
and spectacles in shopping (the paradox that it is so utterly
intimate precisely because it is so thoroughly depersonalised); and
to the way in which this libidinal environment takes the form of
such a wide range of amenities, so many forms of focus.

The second form of gathering contained in the 'unity' of the
Palais Royal was the gathering of 'society', the beau monde of the
fashionable, the promenading social elite. To some extent, too
much has been made of the role of social emulation in the
development of consumerism, the aping of society fashions (and
the very derivation of the idea of fashion from 'society').[15] I would
rather derive the sense of play in modern consumerism from the
culture of commerce itself, from the libidinal crowd, rather than
from the diffusion of aristocratic lifestyles. Nonetheless, the structures for gathering developed by 'society' over the eighteenth
century certainly directly promoted the growth of specific consumer infrastructures, for example the modern shop and the
commercialisation of leisure. What is most interesting however are
the crowd-like qualities of 'society' itself: 'society' took over or
created loosely enclosed public spaces (malls, parades, squares,
streets such as Regent Street) for the purposes of gathering and
circulating, lobbying and politicking, arranging love and
marriages, seeing and being seen. The well-dressed promenader in
the Cours de Reine or Tuileries was halted in his or her tracks by
the equivalents of 'a street, a conflagration, or a traffic accident' –
though it might be the sight of a royal, a courtesan, or a scandal.

'Society' as an element in the history of shopping emphasises
that the idea of 'a public space' is as important to actual markets
as the buying and selling *per se*. This space could be commercially
exploited – many of the activities around which society focused
carried a price tag, while buying emerged gradually as a major
activity in its own right – but all the forms in which it was institutionalised and commercialised had to preserve the essential
element of 'gathering' amorphously and on the basis of one's own
desires and impulses: the promenades and avenues were them-

selves catered for by cafés, performers, the ubiquitous prostitutes; the pleasure gardens and coffee-houses, the leisure towns (spas like Bath) all had to preserve the free flowing nature of crowd-like encounters.

In fact, the relation between the carnivalesque market and the commercialisation of leisure could be quite direct: late medieval fairs, like St Bartholomew's, Mayfair or Foire St Germain, were periodic gatherings of merchants from all over Europe. The range of people and activities it attracted made of the fair another city, a simulated city: the incoming population often dwarfed and took over the town itself. The range of activity was astonishing: at the centre, the goods to be displayed and sold came from around the world, were themselves an exotic spectacle; on one side of this, the meeting of merchant bankers behind closed doors to settle debts on an international scale; on the other side, a panoply of Rabelaisian activity from gaming and prostitution, through animal baiting and theatricals, to refreshments, and the lure of the crowd itself. However, if the market was never just a market because it was also a spectacle and amusement, so it could evolve into pure spectacle, as was the case in the eighteenth century with both St Germain and St Bartholomew's 'where the cloth-selling booths gradually disappeared and puppet-shows, plays, rope-walkers, waxworks, menageries, fire-eaters, jugglers and Punch and Judies took over'.[16]

Thirdly and finally, in addition to being a market place for the crowd and a leisure centre for society, the Palais Royal was also a simulated city. The list of the Palais Royal's amenities shows that it contained a city-like range of crowd-focusing attractions. It also simulated the city by virtue of the crowd that it gathered: catering to a sophisticated bourgeois market segment, nonetheless the presence of a panoply of social types – 'financiers, gamblers, bohemians, *flaneurs*, political conspirators, dandies, prostitutes, criminals, ragpickers'[9] – rendered it a fit setting for a Balzacian *Comédie Humaine*. This crowd, like the members of 'society', assembled among other reasons in order to be a crowd, to be at the centre of networks of display, communications and spectacle. Finally the spectacle of the goods themselves signified cosmopolitan urbanity: like the range of social types and their activities, the mixing of identities and origins to be found in the city, such a market could claim to represent the world, its wealth and its diversity.

But the arcades which developed along the lines of the Palais Royal simulated the city in a deeper sense which Benjamin expresses in terms of their 'ambiguity of space': 'The passages were buildings, closed interiors, yet their three-storey high, glass roofs let in the sky and gave the illusion of an exterior space, a street lined by shop façades.'[9] Were these spaces interiors or exteriors? The glass and steel roofs did more than keep the elements out: they kept a 'reality' in, moulding it and shaping it while cutting it off from the city outside, containing the ambience of market and city like a genie in a bottle. 'What is really at work in the arcades is not, as in other iron constructions, the illumination of inner space but rather the subduing of external space'[17] with the result 'that such an arcade is a city, indeed a world, in miniature'.[18] A simulacrum: 'constructions or passages that have no outside, like the dream'.[19]

The arcade is a 'dreamscape'. This is Benjamin's term, but Rosalind Williams[20] demonstrates that the metaphor of consumption as 'dreamworld' dominated nineteenth-century discussions of consumption. The arcade, the department store, the world exhibition – these were all places of transport, and this possibility of transport hinges on the crucial ambiguity which Benjamin identified in the interiorisation or containment of the market which both preserved and intensified its crowd qualities. One entered the arcade as if into a dream: new experiences loomed out of the hazy space as one walked, due to the flickering gas-lighting, the punctuation of spectacle by spectacle, and to conscious architectural ploys such as poured glass shopfronts, and the arcade's 'wealth of mirrors which extended spaces as if magically and made more difficult orientation, whilst at the same time giving them the ambiguous twinkle of nirvana'.[21]

The range of amenities, wares, spectacles and activities – of focal points for gathering crowds – is not peculiar to the Palais Royal, but universal to the idea of a market. Geist's exhaustive catalogue shows that all arcades would have many of the following attractions in addition to shops: cafés, restaurants, bars; brothels, gaming rooms; hotels and pensions; clubs, meeting rooms; theatres, vaudeville, concert halls, cabarets, later cinemas; showrooms; panoramas, dioramas, cosmoramas, panopticons; bazaars, picture galleries, reading rooms; baths.[22] The nineteenth-century department store, too, would want to boast reading rooms and rooms for ladies to write letters and relax, tea-rooms and restaurants, concerts and other theatricals.[23] Williams[24] vividly evokes the modelling of nineteenth-century Parisian department stores on the North African bazaar, producing a style she dubs the 'chaotic-exotic': extravagant shop displays rapidly became a crowd-attracting spectacle in their own right, in which both the profusion of goods and the use of props to place them in exotic settings turned the 'market' into something of a theme park. Williams[24] notes that at the 1900 Paris exposition, 21 of 33 major exhibits involved a 'dynamic voyage of illusion', '*visions lointains*': a trip down the Nile or across the Alps deploying every contemporary tool of magic, including film of mountain landscape back-projected on to the windows of real (and shaking) railway carriages. Further back in time, dioramas and panoramas were a central spectacular craze of the early modern period and were offered by most arcades.

This nineteenth-century coincidence of hedonistic drifting, geographically focused gathering and wide-ranging attractions all contained within an enclosed space in a such a way as to 'have no outside, like the dream' is virtually identical to the kind of consumer markets which are now considered archetypally postmodern. Consider, for example, Jameson's[25] description of the Bonaventura hotel as emblematic of 'a mutation in built space'. The Bonaventura – like so many similar developments – houses a profusion of shops, cafés, financial facilities, landscapes and waterfalls, residences (albeit temporary) and amusements, all lining the street-like walkways the whole of which are contained within reality-excluding glass and metal canopies. Jameson notes that the entryways are almost backdoor affairs, the 'membrane' between inside and outside being effaced to increase the sense of being within a self-contained world: it 'aspires to being a total space, a complete world, a kind of miniature city'.[26] 'It does not wish to be a part of the city but rather its equivalent and its replacement or substitute.'[27] Like the arcade, this space replaces the city by simulating it. Consider the current convergence of shopping mall and theme park (like that between fair and leisure park or pleasure garden in the eighteenth century), in which the former attracts crowds increasingly through entertainments and the latter survives by selling goods. Consider the film *True Stories*, in which the shopping mall has once again become the town centre, the simultaneous focus of social, economic and cultural life. Consider too Willis's[28] description of how the formerly functional, factory-like,

197

'modernist' supermarket is postmodernising itself through the provision of theme park-like 'theatricals'.

Market culture is tied to the production of crowds, a constellation of people who are freed from personalised restraint to be wafted along by individual desire; who are legitimated in their pursuit of leisure by a collective sense of public gathering; and who are provided with a public place of contained and intensified representation, a stimulating but safe spectacle which excludes while it distils the enervations of the 'reality' on which it is modelled.

However, the idea of containment, the interiorisation and intensification of the market experience into the managed 'dreamscape' of modern shopping, is generally regarded as a lever by which crowds were disciplined into masses. We noted earlier that Benjamin discerned the fascist mass in the ur-image of the crowd. The arcade was, for him, a 'fossil', its consumers 'dinosaurs', precisely because it preserved an image of an ur-form of consumption which was destroyed by department stores and exhibitions, by the concentrated forms of capital which assembled masses and linked them to overriding mass identities such as capitalism, nation, race. The dialectic of the crowd – its ability to use the output of mass production as vehicles for dreaming its own dreams – was shattered as its interests were regulated and rationalised in relation to the now all-determining mass production of commodities and the commodification of all the crowd's points of focus: they become means to the end of regulating and controlling consumption. Thus, for Rosalind Williams, the mid-nineteenth-century department store appears to have become a place of manipulation by spectacle, the 'dreamworld' (defined dialectically by Benjamin) has become instrumentalised into a generator of *mass* consumption.

We can isolate several features of such a story of the move to mass marketing. Firstly, the market – punters and stalls – is incorporated and literally *interiorised* within ever larger and more rationalised and integrated forms of management. The department store, shopping mall and so on interiorise the crowd and market spatially – within a unified architecture and logistics – and organisationally; all aspects of shopping are subject to rationalisation: range and supply of goods, shop display, movements of people around the commodities, payment and billing. The market can be cost-accounted on a per item basis. The entire spectacle of focused desire can be placed under one roof – under the control of unified management – and subjected without residue to the rationality of profit.

Under the rationalising logic of routinisation and the commercial logic of high turnover with low unit price, the residual fripperies which formerly attracted the market crowd fall by the wayside until in the end we reach the supermarket, the hypermarket, the discount warehouse: the impulsive crowd is subjected to the unitary logic of planning. These are Taylorist machines for selling, in which buyers and sellers are both ergonomically measured for maximum throughput. Function and process dictate form and movement: unambiguous, evenly lit commodities differentiated by category on cost-accounted, highway-like shelving; check-outs like toll-booths at the end of the road or like the time-clock at the entrance to the assembly-line. Modernism in production – Taylorist rationalisation of all movement to standards of efficiency – is met with the mass production of consumer desires as standardised and predictable as the goods which supposedly fill them. This is the 'myth of mass culture': the fear of unitary organisation (vertically integrated monopolies with price-fixing power) and unitary principles of control (the psychology of persuasion, the power of the media). This is not a market.

Secondly, the assembled crowd is turned into a mass by being 'named', in Benjamin's terms. By the mid-nineteenth century, arcades, markets, department stores, international exhibitions were hitched to the twin juggernauts of nationalism and global modernity. The arcades up to the mid-nineteenth century were private speculations which depended on serving public needs. After this point, Berlin, Milan and Brussels, for example, built – for the first time with major public financial and political participation – monolithic arcades which were designed as symbols and ideological engines of national unification, national pride and modernity. Moscow's New Trade Halls, later GUM department store, was the giganticist culmination, clearing an entire section of the city for a statement of modernising nationalism which suited the productivist avant garde (Mayakovsky and Rodchenko did the advertising) and Stalinist bureaucracy as well as the modernising elite which actually built it under the Czar. The department stores, too, claimed to be national institutions and linked themselves to the world expositions, marrying nationalism, modernity and

199

consumption. The world exhibitions, according to Benjamin, turned the market into a social and political phantasmagoria – an advertisement for modern industrialism.

Thirdly, the interiorisation and 'ideologisation' of the market can be understood in Foucauldian terms as the disciplining of congregated bodies. In the narrative of oppressive modernism, the arcade is a direct ancestor of twentieth-century social engineering. Emblematic for Benjamin of the 'dream-world' of consumerism, they were also Fourier's model for the phalanstery: these were envisaged as large self-contained 'communities' of 2000 people, divided into 'clans' and living on arcade-style corridors – flats taking the place of the shops – linked by covered and heated passageways, with a communal dining hall which could serve the whole community at once, and 'one shop for buying and selling goods would replace the 300 parasitic and competitive businesses. In short, a uniform economic plan . . .'[29] Fourier had in mind the Palais Royal, but turned its atomic crowds into masses organised in detail. Geist notes close architectural and historical connections between the arcades and prisons and other Foucauldian carceral and public buildings. John Havilland's American prisons were influenced by the Parisian arcades from 1822 onwards. The arcade is actually the original panopticon: arcade and prison are a 'total traffic system, with surveillance and a very high density of cells/shops'.[30]

The interiorisation of the market appears as part of the story of the social engineering of cities and dwellings under bureaucratic socialism and welfare capitalism, with a stopping point first in the utopian modernism of the avant garde – simulations of the city as a 'machine for living' which crowd out the very dynamism of civil society they were designed to house. Drive through miles of housing developments served by a single supermarket in East Berlin, or around Prague, and you wonder where people will find the space for 'markets', for wide ranges of diverse enterprise in direct contact with a demanding public.

After oppressive modernity, postmodernity presents itself as a reaction and a return to first principles. The shopping mall returns architecturally to the arcade and the market in its diversity of shops, its range of amenities and entertainments, its provision of public spaces for gathering and browsing, its simulation of the city street, its planned organicism. The central theme in postmodernism is precisely the return from the mass back to the crowd: instead of replacing the chaotic movement of individuals with the uniformity of efficient movement, it addresses the bizarre, organic, lunatic ways in which people move about. It starts from the spectacles which attract them rather than the functions into which they must fit. Such is the promise anyway: that distraction rather than discipline is the order of postmodern space. Certainly the labels of 1980s consumerism highlight this: the move from mass, national markets to market segments; from standardised mass production to small-batch targeted design; the move to designed environments and a 'shopping experience', to 'consumption communities',[31] lifestyles and identities which 'are not defined along class lines', a heightened hedonistic individualism which constellates groups by the accident of their shared desires. All this addresses the 'crowd' in terms of the very concrete situations of the persons whose attention must be gained to constitute it (and translate it into sales).

While it unarguably expresses real tendencies in the unstable dialectic of the crowd, the central problem for the massification argument, in any of its forms, is that it presumes the complete collapse of that dialectic. Can the movements of people really be reduced to the manipulation of the spectacle, the commodification of culture? The disappearance of civil society into an administered one and the irredeemable character of commodity culture – these were specifically at issue between Benjamin and Adorno, with Benjamin perceiving a potential for reforming the imagination in the way we appropriate the products of new industrial nature. Where critical theory looked forward from the heyday of bourgeois capitalism to the totalisations of its monopolistic form, postmodernism looks back on mass modernism from the vantage point of its cultural and social – if not economic – fragmentation. From either perspective massification is presented as an 'epochal' category: an 'age' of the mass modern when massification was actually accomplished rather than, perhaps, attempted.

An example might be useful: a number of commentators on advertising[32] rely heavily on the argument that recent years have seen a shift from marketing based on product differentiation to marketing based on lifestyle and consumer segmentation. This distinction keys into broader postmodern arguments about post-Fordism. Product differentiation is a Fordist, mass consumption strategy which makes an appeal to a mass of consumers to recognise the difference and superiority of one product over another. Segmentation relies on identifying and targeting precise consumer lifestyle groups to whom new products or reformulated old ones are made to appeal. In fact, though Fordism refers to an undeniable historical configuration of actual production and marketing practices, 'post-Fordist' segmentation always subsisted alongside it – in the car industry itself, Sloanism[33] arose in the 1920s as a philosophy by which General Motors introduced ranges of cars, differentiated by price and specifications, each targeted on different consumer lifestyles. Cosmetics similarly has always been based on targeted ranges.

Moreover, the idea of mass market differentiation (like scientific mass advertising) appears an ideologically opportunistic formulation of advertising and marketing practice: it was purveyed largely by pundits and promoters of modern marketing who wanted specifically to be seen as modernisers and spoke the language of cultural (not economic) modernisation: the possibility and desirability of scientific management and planning. If one looks at the actual practice of marketing and advertising up to World War Two,[34] the story is different: marketing consisted of the collection of mundane marketing information, generally in the form of demographics which separated out consumer and readership groups according to segmented profiles. Indeed, as Marchand documents, lack of knowledge of crowds was thematised during the 1920s as a major problem for advertisers. One could say that mass marketing was carried out in default of real marketing knowledge and was tied to a sense of failure: advertisers, it was said, suffered from 'deskitis' – stuck in the office they only knew their public as a mass. Where industrialisation led technically and economically towards the large-scale production of standardised goods, marketing was *always* moving in the opposite direction – towards specific cultural relations between discrete consumer groups and highly specific goods. In any case, in marketing differentiation and segmentation are *logically* inseparable: it does not take a black belt in semiotics for a marketing manager to know that a difference between products must be a difference *for* someone and that these someones must be identified through an at least rudimentary demographics.

Marketing relies on a knowledge which follows and exploits the logic of the crowd rather than organising the masses. It is the antithesis of Taylorism: rather than defining norms of movement by standards of efficiency it measures crowd movements for cost-efficient exploitation. Modern marketing starts from the multiple impulses of the composite crowd rather than the laws of motion of the mass: not how to manufacture gatherings, but how to attract and exploit them in an orderly, rational, forecastable way. As the advertisers say in all seriousness, marketing is about having what the consumers want rather than making them want what you have. Yet it is still very much *planned* movement: an infrastructure which unobtrusively contains, focuses and controls the random movement of the crowd. It nudges and draws people in by their desires and impulses rather than by a disciplinary space. The history of the market as it moves from open stalls to massive shopping malls certainly demonstrates a process of rationalisation, but the principle of this rationalisation is not that of massification. However well planned the spectacles and allures – from advertising through shop displays through architectural planning – what is at stake is the intensification of an experience which belongs to crowds not masses.

The theme park probably exemplifies the highest development of this crowd management: we are engineered through an experience in which all contingencies have been taken into account; focus on ambience and atmosphere rather than functionality; on the eccentric logic of the individual rather than the systemic reason of the process. The theme park carries this embodied logic to new heights of subtlety: it shows how, although this approach is not unitary reason, it is highly rationalisable. Throughout the Parc d'Asterix, near Paris, placards in Kodak yellow with the Kodak logo are stationed at strategic, photogenic sites. Labelled 'picture points', they have a hole in them through which to insert your camera lens. Some people earnestly took photos at every point; others laughed at the idea – as they photographed through the hole. I wanted to photograph the outrageous roller coaster: each time I walked backwards, trying to frame the whole view, I found myself next to a yellow post. They knew the logic of the situation and of my desires before I did.

The notion of crowd-based rather than mass marketing provides an alternative line of interpretation of the history of shopping. The interiorisation of market, crowd and 'dreamscape' within the simulated city is not about the increasingly direct control of bodies *en masse*, but rather about the ways in which firms can profit from attracting and containing the crowd within rationalised frameworks.

Markets have always been contained and bounded social spaces which is to say that they have always been regulated. It has often been noted that even the creation of modern 'free' markets requires enormous government intervention and regulation. In the pre-modern market, the restriction of trade to particular times and places was designed to protect revenues, to maintain public order, to harness market trade to furthering urban power and prosperity. This regulation and containment of trade, which funnelled all goods to the town market, created the exotic bazaar, the crowd experience, and at the same time ensured the safe provisioning of the town through its control over the surrounding region, or its attraction of wider trade networks. For the consumer, the market was also internally regulated and policed: from the earliest medieval markets, stalls were set up in numbered places, allotted in advance, registered and paid for with the local authorities. Most importantly for the crowd, the market was a place of regulated supplies, prices and quality assurance. Officially, markets have always been regulated through on the spot policing of prices and quality. Braudel[35] notes that in Sicily traders could be sent directly to the galleys, and in England to the stocks, for selling over the odds. Given the early modern obsession with adulterated goods, these too were punishable on the spot: 'A seller of bad meat might have it burned under his nose while he stood in the pillory. Bakers were often in court for selling undersized or poor quality loaves.'[36] The sense of safety afforded by the contained market is best appreciated perhaps by contrast with the intense hatred of middlemen and 'private traders',[37] who got round supervision of markets by going directly to farms or holding court in inns. They are excoriated throughout the medieval and early modern period as parasites and profiteers, hated for their ruthlessness and for disrupting market supplies: they were the outlaws of the sphere of circulation.

The modern interiorised market is built on the same paternalistic principles: the simultaneous provision of security and stimulation. Department stores, for example, first attracted crowds not only because of their scale and the range of their goods but because they offered their clientele a series of assurances which differentiated them from other forms of shopping. Foremost, as in the medieval market, was on the spot regulation of prices and quality: Paris's Bon Marché (from the 1850s) was one of the first markets with a declared and publicised policy of fixed and labelled prices: there was no haggling, while the financial structure of low margins, high turnover tended towards reasonable prices. Shop assistants, socialised into a clear and draconianly policed occupational structure, got their commissions on fixed price sales from management rather than bidding up the customer, guaranteeing the latter an experience focused on desire for objects rather than sharp-witted bargaining. This was coupled with a policy for the exchange or full money back return of unsatisfactory goods and guarantees of quality on higher priced goods. The Bon Marché also took care of customers through a daily delivery service, regular hours, catalogues and a huge secretariat devoted to customer correspondence. The department store also preserved another essential feature of the market: the anonymous, impersonal, 'democratic' nature of the crowd: one could come in and *browse*, with no obligation to buy, and could wander the Bon Marché without being personally targeted or identified.

The department store was crucially a safe place for the dreaming crowd. Miller's[38] history of the Bon Marché argues that the very scale of its operation and bureaucracy, its modernity, appeared to the bourgeoisie as destructive of the traditional values of *gemeinschaftlich* society. The Bon Marché answered these worries with a policy of paternalism. The aim of its regulatory, rationalising innovations was not massification and disciplining the crowd, but rather disciplining the *sellers*, about making the market safe and convenient, a place for dreamy indulgence rather than vigilance. The Bon Marché instituted close regulation in order both to routinise its provision of crowd-satisfying experiences and to assuage the moral doubts attached to the place of public indulgence it produced. And given the class composition of its key clientele, the department store was mainly concerned with containing the chaotic energies of the crowd within a space that was not just safe but *respectable*. Emergent places of public gathering regularly attract moral suspicion: this goes for the pleasure gardens and assembly rooms of 'society' as much as for commercial gatherings and the city streets themselves. All these crowds typified unregulated hedonism – how was any moral order possible in a collectivity organised around desire and distraction and no longer regulated by traditional, person-based forms of scrutiny?

Miller traces the history of kleptomania, topicalised in Parisian debate and psychiatry from the 1850s onwards: it was clearly ascribed to female sexual disorder (hysteria) and focused moral fears of shopping as unbridled and unabashed desire. These fears extended to shopping as a female addiction, stories of women abandoning children and ruining husbands because of the enticements and the moral anonymity of the crowd, the possibility of living out a secret life in these public places. Such fears were furthermore projected on to the shop staff, with worries about shop girls leading licentious lives. The Bon Marché consequently policed their employees' private lives (cohabitation was grounds for dismissal), and at work provided separate dining rooms for men and women.

Miller is concerned with precisely that time of transition from early to modern consumption when Benjamin's arcade consumer becomes a dinosaur and Geist's 'unity' in the functions of public space is shattered. However, the transition that Miller evinces in great detail is not one from crowd to mass. The issue for the Bon Marché was precisely how to maintain the *gemeinschaftlich* values and culture of the early bourgeoisie in the context of that modernising rationality which I have here condensed into the idea of interiorisation. The astounding thing is that the department store did so by preserving the essential attractions of the market crowd: the exotic yet contained dreamscape of the bazaar filled with many goods; the internal policing and regulation of shopping; the anonymity of the members of the crowd within their desires; the sense of the market as a public meeting place and amenity for 'society'. The rationalising modern bureaucracy managed and contained this crowd experience, intensified it through its instrumentally rationalised surveillance of this crowd and its relation to the goods on offer, but it did not reduce that crowd to a scientifically managed mass. Indeed that was the very opposite of both its aim and its significance.

It does not need arguing that over the modern period the processes of cultural reproduction have become increasingly tied to the buying and selling of industrial products, of commodities. People must go to the market, must go shopping, in order to sustain and develop their culturally specific forms of meaningful life – their lifestyles, their identities, their specific social membership. So long as one does not attempt to argue, as do massification theorists, that this process of cultural reproduction has come to be dominated in its entirety by the logic of those industrial products and their producers – by the logic of the commodity – then one can see a market culture still in operation, one which I have characterised as a culture of the crowd, a culture poised on a dialectical knife-edge between the desires of the consumer and the rationalisation of the (commodified) spectacles on which those desires are focused. The two sides are irreducible, and each side is, moreover, a condition of existence of the other. Thus at one level this chapter simply takes a different route (through the market itself, rather than its produce) to the same destination reached by much recent work[39] on various aspects of consumers and audience: a reassertion of the rebellious and creative subject, of the resistant consumer who is able to come up with new meanings, if not under conditions of their own making, a sense that while the liberal myths of sovereign consumers and autonomous subjects are neither analytically tenable nor politically desirable, the old oppositional myth of the total triumph of the system is analytically wrong and politically tantamount to taking masochistic pleasure in seeing oneself as victim.

By considering the market as a specific kind of experience – that of being a place where crowds of desiring individuals are presented with the most diverse objects of stimulation – with a long cultural history and dynamics we can see that this rebellious and creative subject can be found not only at the moment of consumption, but prior to that in the market itself. In going to the market for the material means to sustain and develop ways of life, we become embroiled in the game of distracted and playful hedonism. Indeed, and ironically, the market as a place of desire without obligation, of intimate fantasy in the midst of impersonal anonymity, of spectacle, entertainment and play, as a place where dreams can flow across a multitude of objects without yet being fixed permanently on any one probably still provides the single most potent space in Western societies in which one dreams alternative futures and is released (utopicly) from the unthinking reproduction of daily life.

NOTES

1 D. Smythe, 'Communications: blindspot of economics', in W. Melody (ed.), *Communications and Dependency: The Tradition of H.A. Innis*, Norwood, New Jersey, Ablex, 1980, p. 112.

2 J.K. Galbraith, *The New Industrial State*, Harmondsworth, Penguin, 1972.
3 W. Benjamin, *Charles Baudelaire: A Lyric Poet in the Era of High Capitalism*, London, Verso, 1989, p. 62.
4 V. Packard, *The Hidden Persuaders*, Harmondsworth, Penguin, 1977.
5 Benjamin, op. cit., p. 63.
6 F. Braudel, *The Structures of Everyday Life*, London, Fontana, 1981, p. 501.
7 F. Braudel, *The Wheels of Commerce*, New York, Harper & Row, 1982, p. 30.
8 M. Girouard, *Cities and People: A Social and Architectural History*, London, Yale University Press, 1985, p. 169.
9 S. Buck-Morss. 'Walter Benjamin – revolutionary writer', *New Left Review*, 1981, vol. 128, p. 66.
10 J. Geist, *Arcades: History of a Building Type*, Cambridge, MIT Press, 1983, p. 458.
11 Ibid.
12 Ibid.; see also S. Schama, *Citizens: A Chronicle of the French Revolution*, London, Penguin, 1989, pp. 134–6.
13 M. Featherstone, *Consumer Culture and Postmodernism*, London, Sage, 1991.
14 B. Turner, *The Body in Society*, Oxford, Blackwell, 1985.
15 See N. McKendrick, J. Brewer and J.H. Plumb, *The Birth of a Consumer Society: The Commercialization of Eighteenth-century England*, London, Hutchinson, 1983.
16 Girouard, op. cit., p. 184.
17 D. Frisby, *Fragments of Modernity*, Cambridge, Polity Press, 1988, p. 241.
18 Benjamin, op. cit., p. 158.
19 Frisby, op. cit., p. 240.
20 R. Williams, *Dream Worlds: Mass Consumption, in Late Nineteenth Century France*, Berkeley, University of California Press, 1982.
21 Frisby, op. cit., p. 241.
22 Geist, op. cit., p. 110.
23 A. Adburgham, *Shops and Shopping: 1800–1914*, London, Barrie & Jenkins, 1989; M. Miller, *The Bon Marché: Bourgeois Culture and the Department Store*, London, Allen & Unwin, 1981.
24 Williams, op. cit.
25 F. Jameson, 'Postmodernism, or the cultural logic of late capitalism', *New Left Review*, 1984, vol. 146, pp. 53–93.
26 Jameson, op. cit., p. 81.
27 Ibid.
28 S. Willis, *A Primer for Daily Life*, London, Routledge, 1991.
29 Fourier quoted in Geist, op. cit., p. 32.
30 Geist, op. cit., p. 28.
31 D.J. Boorstin, *The Americans: The Democratic Experience*, New York, Vintage Books, 1973.
32 W. Leiss, S. Kline and S. Jhally, *Social Communication in Advertising*, London, Methuen, 1986; D. Pope, *The Making of Modern Advertising*, New York, Basic Books, 1983.

33 E. Rothschild, *Paradise Lost: The Decline of the Auto-Industrial Age*, London, Allen Lane, 1973.
34 Pope, op. cit.; R. Marchand, *Advertising the American Dream: Making Way for Modernity – 1920–1940*, Berkeley, University of California Press, 1986.
35 Braudel, 1982, op. cit., p. 30.
36 A. Adburgham, *Shopping in Style*, London, Thames & Hudson, 1979, p. 18.
37 Braudel, 1982, op. cit., p. 39; R. Porter, *English Society in the Eighteenth Century*, Harmondsworth, Penguin, 1983.
38 Miller, 1981, op. cit.
39 For example, D. Miller, *Material Culture and Mass Consumption*, Oxford, Blackwell, 1987; D. Hebdige, *Hiding in the Light*, London, Routledge, 1988; D. Morley, *Family Television*, London, Comedia, 1986; Willis, op. cit.; S. Buck-Morss, *The Dialectics of Seeing: Walter Benjamin and the Arcades Project*, London, MIT Press, 1989.

12

MANET AND DURKHEIM
Images and theories of re-production

John A. Smith

A common prejudice links many communities of theorising, including the 'posterities' of recent practice: representation is taken as a second-order derivative if not wholly negative mediation. Of what? Leave that open for the moment: reality, presence, economy, essence? Whereas – concealed amongst a number of less interesting pretensions – the proposed theorising of Durkheim – 'sociology' – the unique theorising of organic[1] community, reflexive upon itself, begins with re-presentations, that class of uniquely social phenomena that are '. . . capable of exercising upon the individual an external constraint . . .';[2] constrain, that is, individuality as membership. Moreover, in the injunction to take social phenomena as 'things', representations are taken as first-order, irreducible – not derivative mediations but the sui-generic phenomena that generate the possibility of sociology as a specific discipline.

In other words, Durkheim's sociology begins by admitting the original representation of nature in terms of the social but then insists on the radicalness of this absolute and unrecoverable trans-formation: the difference and not the origin of the difference becomes the ontological foundation of membership, as or in, social phenomena.

More radically, the notion of the organic ramifies the status of these transformations, saying that we neither live through our original modifications of nature nor the expectation of repeated resemblance that is characteristic of the mechanical. Then the ontological foundation of specific kinds of organic membership is doubly differentiated, from nature and from all other forms; organic membership begins and exists in irrecoverable deter-minate differentiation – which, in turn, might be taken as the notion of representation that informs this writing.

Put slightly differently, the theoretic prejudice against 'phenomena' – the insistence that they are *merely* phenomena, therefore contingent, conventional, etc, and the associated unrealisable desire of theorists to escape their locatedness by demonstrating it – may be taken to militate against the theoretic objects of sociology: those representations that structure, shape, constrain the specific courses of membership. A prejudice, then, directed not simply against the objects of sociologists' enquiry but against the specific forms of members' practices; it is precisely exemplified in the irony of Socrates who (as Kierkegaard argued)[3] came not to 'save', inquire into, arbitrate, nor develop human order, but to condemn it, as a whole. It would seem, then, that Durkheimian sociology stands in implacable opposition to the community of theorists invoked by Socrates.

With whom may Durkheim stand in forging the new theoretic community his work (at least) implies? Specifically with that form of membership Socrates reviles most: the artist, the forger of representations in their most extreme and culpable form – the image; more generally, with the embedded theorising of the Sophists – a tradition of convincing rhetorical performance, embedded and convincing, that is, in relation to securing a specific sense and shape of membership that 'will be able to exercise a constraint upon the individual'.

I take, then, that however implicit or tentative our commitments, that if we propose a sociology of art, then analytically there are at least two specific sets of phenomena, location, membership, that we cannot be too 'liberal' about – that we cannot take as contingent but, on the contrary, as both binding and inaugural: art and sociology. That is to say that we welcome the constraint implied by these disciplines – and so the endless worries about transcending 'locatedness' are postures that cannot grasp the notion of representation as irrecoverable specific differentiation. Yet, from the point of view of sociology there still remains an unhappy conjunction with art that threatens to make this implicit solidarity self-cancelling. We as sociologists are prone to employ a metaphor, or better, a cliché that treats art as in some sense a reflection of society and in that usage we continue to suggest an imprisoned, correspondential passivity (wholly unlike ourselves) in which the artist is not only a dupe but complicit, through a tradition of 'inauthentic' criticism that emphasises individuality, talent, genius over social context.

211

That is why Manet's *Olympia* is finally so challenging: not because it fits the stereotype of neo-classic or romantic 'genius' (like, say, Michelangelo or Delacroix); nor will it lie easily with common (should we say Socratic?) usage: the image as the mundanely inauthentic substitute. *Olympia* – however irredeemably it is related to social order – is also unquestionably *special*, an image that both at the time of its production and subsequently has brought the tradition of painted representation into the sphere of reflexive controversy. And unless that is misunderstood, let me reiterate: its undiminished 'specialness' is therefore absolutely social.

Are we then agreeing that *Olympia* is a good painting, and no more? Or, is there concealed in that agreement – and every agreement that a painting is 'good' – an altogether explosive analytic issue that is nevertheless routinely suppressed in our tendency to think images and paintings as a whole? – in other words, mathematically, as formally differentiated units in an apparently equally formally identified whole. Of course both that whole and its parts are actually defined purely commonsensically in the routine absence of any specific formulation: something you do with paint and brushes. Of course, no artists with the slightest seriousness would have anything to do with that!

As a consequence – of what can at best be described as a sort of gross cultural negligence and at worst as deliberate violence – very rarely do we agree as sociologists to speak qualitatively of painting, which is decidedly queer and insular, since that is the only way painting ever speaks of itself – manifestly because that is the only way it actually enters real social inter-relations. Perhaps it is that we still envy Socrates for his disinterest in mundane social order (a difficult position for sociology) but fear the implicit moral and political alignment of a more Sophistic commitment to a certain set of preferences. Of course, that would make sociology in some measure an agent of a certain mundane social order – a dangerous position; one can in a sense understand sociologists' reluctance. One cannot forgive, however, the failure to see that Manet is anything but reluctant, no passive co-respondent, but a reforming zealot. There is one greater failure, however, and that is to mistake the blatant fact that a sociology of Manet's painting is being asked to address precisely that committed activity and so one's reluctance is beside the point: any formulation is unavoidably 'aesthetic' in the widest sense – qualitative and never quantitative.

The matter may be raised more precisely: to the question, 'Is a sociology of art possible?' Manet ('Olympia') would appear to say no – not because discourse about *Olympia* is impossible (it has hardly ever ceased) but because it refuses to sit mutely alongside other 'art' or 'paintings' in those formal categories; alongside 'paintings' such as those of his academic predecessors, the history painters, which suddenly then (and now) appeared not to be authentic painting at all.

If this difference is not to be taken seriously, then an implicit developmental-correspondential model falls silently into place, which if made explicit would draw objections even from the most moribund. Sketched broadly, it would say this: Manet is better because he is newer (more politely, 'a man of his time'), or, social order has changed so that the means to value Manet exist at the expense of the devaluation of his predecessors. Which, roughly translated, is the elevation of 'I don't know much about art but I know what I like' to the status of sociology. No, the matter cannot be safely left as 'Manet is a better painter' because that assertion was never safe in the first place. It is rather that he, amongst others, makes the formal category explicitly contradictory, forbidding inclusion even of work that is arguably the equal of his own – Chardin's or even Corot's, except as painting 'of the past'. One could, of course, dispute his inclusions and exclusions, but at the inevitable price of recognising sociology as an active agent in the controversy and in the specific sense and shape of the resulting agreements and disagreements which, as the terms of membership, 'will be able to exercise a constraint . . .'.

Contrasted with his interventions, then, the question 'Is a sociology of art possible?' indicates a kind of verbal habit that looks specifically, if unconsciously, platonic – the assumption that art has a form of which painting is an instance, of which Manet's painting is a further instance. If that were true – or if that sort of formal mathematics were in any way adequate – Manet could not possibly have caused the furore he did. Then either that was an illusion, or the apparent sense of 'a sociology of art' is instead the illusion. Or, to put it another way, Durkheim's interest in the phenomena of re-presentation as sui-generic and irreducible to some common form presents not so much a fresh subject matter, namely, 'sociology' inserted, as it were, within ordinary 'platonic-academic' usage but a massive intervention in usage, a reform of the language no less far reaching than Manet's devastation of the visual language of his predecessors. Durkheim, in short, re-produces the possible shape of utterance; not, as he at times suggests, through acceptance, development or modification of Kant's analytic limitation of representation qua 'merely the phenomena of appearances' – nor, as he also suggests, through the espousal of Kant's 'critical' empiricism – but through the entire reappraisal of the notion of phenomena: not the contingent consequence of a collision between sensory data and a transcendent but individual subject but the necessary and intersubjective origin of every socially organised cognitive possibility. Where Kant's phenomenon is always the singular 'effect' and so 'could have been otherwise', Durkheim's phenomenon is concerted, causal, inaugural.

Plato's prejudice – modernised by Kant – is dependent on a hierarchy of representation, whose apex was noetic 'understanding', whose middle strata were composed of its representation in philosophical speech, and whose base was the ostensibly degenerate representations of poetry, art and ordinary usage. That there may be no realisable difference between 'understanding' and 'philosophical' speech generates a kind of awkward compression – which, nevertheless, is nothing compared to the unsustainably volatile compression that Durkheim's interest in social phenomena or 'ordinary representation' achieves. For neoplatonism (in which must be included all phenomenological analysis derived from Kant) expectation is always, as it were, mechanical rather than organic: neoplatonists expect that the instance has some correspondential accord with the category; they expect to be able to talk about 'art' and not be too concerned with whether the quality or commitments of the instance concur with the category: it 'ought' to fit. Moreover, unless we actively seek to disrupt the ordinary flow of speech-habit we do not hear the further elision that is quietly, if not silently, taking place: it is not a matter of whether the noun 'painting' (with a few specifics attached, such as 'Manet's painting') will lie easily with the category but rather that a wholly different way of representing, namely painting, in which the categorial mode is arguably absent is being represented in and as speech. Platonists expect that to be all right.

Durkheim's reform, transformation, revolution, consists first in destroying that expectation – for example, in this form: the ostensibly real relationships between the instance and the category are better represented as one of the solidarities that certain kinds of academic speakers share in 'realising' formal speech. On the other hand, Manet (in contrast to, say, Ingres) finds formality and generality to be anathema; exactly his objection to history painting: it occupies no specific history. And when M. Manet 'realises' a re-presentation according to his reflexive inquiries on the nature of painting there is no a priori reason that the result should in any way concur with re-presentations realised in formal speech. So when Durkheim announces the series of irrecoverable, foundational differences that he names organic solidarity, he makes sociology both one of the many specialised means of representation and – perhaps impossibly – also the representation of their unity. In effect, where Plato elides noetic understanding with philosophy as speech, Durkheim provides no realisable difference between solidarity and reflexion.

It is interesting that contemporaneous criticism of Manet recognised but somehow lost the salience of this point; it was painting that was being newly realised, newly specified in 'Olympia' and whilst it was possible to speak 'about' it – there was also a kind of threat, or better, an explicit tension that the painting made manifest between itself and its representations in speech – as though for the first time painting insisted on the radicalness of its own forms of solidarity and so threatened its intelligibility for speech.

Faced for the first time with *Olympia*, critics could no longer invoke neo-classical vocabularies of perfect or instructive form; nor again the sublime constellations of spectacle, action and significance that is expected in the romanticism of Delacroix or Gericault. Clarke instead documents references to ugliness: 'a sort of female gorilla, a grotesque in india rubber'; to corruption: 'her body has the livid tint of a cadaver displayed in the morgue'; to dirt: 'she is a coal lady, never outraged by water'; to her occupation: 'the little fabourienne, woman of the night from Paul Niquet's . . .'[4]

We therefore appear to be caught between an aesthetic programme which in formal terms is interesting and intelligible enough and what seems to be an almost deliberately perverse realisation. The programme, essentially Baudelaire's and itself a critique of the Académie for ceaselessly depicting the past, opposes 'general beauty' with 'particular beauty . . . the beauty of circumstance' and in particular, the circumstances of Parisian life.[5] But the realisation is blatantly, obviously, a prostitute.

Given the somewhat greater distance of time and acclaim, Clarke offers a more sociological replacement for the critics' outrage: *Olympia* makes hay with our assumptions as spectators . . . but this very negation is as something produced in the social order, happening as part of an ordinary exchange of goods and services. The painting insists on its own materiality . . . but does so in and through a prostitute's stare, a professional and standardised attentiveness . . .[6]

Quite so; most convincing; most sociological. But the problem is that *Olympia*'s specificity (even for sociologists) does not consist in its being a picture of a prostitute (there are thousands of pictures of prostitutes). It is rather an enormously important painting (of a prostitute) that has had an overwhelming effect on the course of the history of pictorial re-presentation – an issue beside which the lady's occupational status is somewhat secondary. In that sense, Clarke's substitute for the critics' outrage is a not dissimilar spluttering: 'She is a prostitute!' they all seem to say – and so she is, and there the matter will stay so long as it is a matter of what 'she' was and what 'M. Manet' painted. On the other hand we might reflect that such an approach altogether ignores the independence of the social phenomenon of painting as a re-presentative tradition that cannot in any sense be spuriously 'restored' to M. Manet or the occupations of his models, nor to the verbal-sociological definition 'prostitute'. Most sociological? No – or not at least in the sense that Durkheim's organicism proposes. Of course, both the transformations and so also the restorations would be unthinkable under mechanical solidarity.

But she *is* a prostitute and that in a deep sense is the 'cause' of her portrayal; after all, the subject is not isolated; think of Zola's 'Nana'. Isn't that the very standpoint of sociology? Conventionally yes, and the sooner it is abandoned the better on the grounds of its inadequacy. For to insist that 'her' prostitution is in any sense whatever 'causal' is to refuse to engage, to become voluntarily blind, to two profoundly important dimensions of intelligibilty.

The first is the ability to view (to read, or listen, etc) critically in the aesthetic sense, to discern the 'quality' of a representation. To say that this is difficult for sociology is true enough – but if that were cause to ignore it it would be analytically equivalent to saying that the sphere of aesthetic judgement is unintelligible to sociology. Then a sociology 'of art' would be an illusion; but further, it would be a grotesque irony to argue for the unintelligibility of aesthetic judgement in the narrow sense whilst at the same

216

time citing the all too obvious intelligibility of 'prostitution' – an aesthetic judgement in the wider sense.

The second is the simple, explicit and readily visible fact that the conditions of production of the social phenomenon (for example *Olympia*) are in no sense determinant of its future uses. To cite a somewhat savage example, there is no a priori socio-logical reason why *Olympia* should not be burned, and for a variety of sociologically 'authentic' if conventionally undesirable reasons: as fuel for a fire, as heresy, as a byproduct of an act of war or terrorism. To cite a less savage but related case, our museums are full of 'art treasures' (for example Egyptian reliquary) that we use as 'art' in a quite different sense from that which determined their making. And that is not to cite a falsehood but a power: the sovereignty of social phenomena, in Durkheim's sense, that refuse to be second-order or restored to some presumed first-order cause or dimension.

Then, prostitution cannot be in any sense a cause of *Olympia*, or else sociology is a kind of elaborate charade founded on a pretence that these two routine yet fundamental dimensions of intelligibility were in fact unintelligible.

In truth, prostitution was left behind when the project of representation was conceived. But that is rather imprecise; let me say instead that it is the manner of Manet's conception that makes prostitution irrelevant. We are again, therefore, in the midst of questions related to quality, for had his intention (conscious or not) to be merely to make a picture of a prostitute, a sort of recognisable sign that was, as it were, 'used up' and itself made irrelevant once that content was grasped, then the primary, causal matter would indeed be prostitution. But then again we are being imprecise because the question of quality is immediately so per-meated with subsequent interpretations that to talk of 'Manet's' intentions (assuming they were establishable) becomes a kind of little farce in which we fail to hear our own; a farce characteristic of sociology in its conservative and radical forms – again the habitual blindness to issues of quality and subsequent usage.

'My' response (I don't think I'm alone – I believe I speak as a member of a concerted critical tradition) is to find the quality of the re-presentation of so much more interest that it displaces the 'original' presence as the origin of inquiry. Moreover, I cite that both as a position within a tradition of art-criticism and as a position within sociology: the irreducibility of social phenomena to other primary causes whether biological or psychological is Durkheim's fundamental delineation; but the sovereignty of subsequent interpretation, usage, consumption, 're-production' suggest also an extension of that principle that the independent intelligibility of one social phenomenon demonstrates that it cannot be reduced to a second-order manifestation of some other social phenomenon. If gender cannot be reduced to a question of biology, 'Olympia' (the present wrested intelligibility of the painting) cannot be reduced to M. Manet, the incidence of prostitution, or Paris, or 1865. That is to sorely confuse the relatively private conditions of production and its subsequent public availability for reproduction. It is perilously close to being both the crudest form of determinism and at the same time citing the conditions of a biography as the primary sociological dimension. In that sense, the determinist reduces the processes of cultural reproduction to the expectation of mechanical resemblance; his task, ironically, is to find ways to deny the 'organic' action of other subsequent forms of intelligibility. Like Plato he finds them inauthentic: 'Olympia' isn't really a painting at all because painting isn't a true act; it is reflection, the virtual set against the real. Simply put, for determinism, there cannot be cultural reproduction, only replications whose apparent differences are nothing. I see that prejudice as a call to mechanical solidarity in unconscious opposition to organicism, a call rooted in the failure of professional academic usage (itself a phenomenon of organicism) to realise the salience of Durkheim's transformations.

To repeat, that salience consists in asserting the organic as the sphere of re-productive difference and as the ontological foundation of membership. Or again, organic membership – as opposed to behaviour in the bio-psychological sense or resemblance in the mechanical sense – begins in irrevocable re-productive difference.

Olympia is extraordinary – it insists on its re-productive rather than replicative status on several counts. The first of these is the reference to prostitution – as we have seen already, it is secondary not because it was unimportant at the time but because it is superseded by the density of more compelling references to the processes of painting, rather than the processes of prostitution. Ravenel catches this tension beautifully: 'Painting of the School of Baudelaire, freely executed by a pupil of Goya.'[7] The subject matter – a prostitute – is arguably 'School of Baudelaire' but the manner of its subjection, if not precisely Goya's, is at least in keeping with Manet's constant painterly references to him and to the Spanish tradition. So that a series of current, certainly interesting, but doctrinal positions codified by Baudelaire under such terms as 'particular beauty', the 'beauty of circumstance' are realised in and through the reflexive idioms of Goya and, equally importantly, Velasquez. It goes without saying that this shift occurs at the expense of the then current French tradition – which with the enormous benefit of hindsight we dismiss as 'academic', which is to say that we have no concept whatever of its status at the high point of its influence before Manet's intervention. It also goes, but not quite without saying, that the spectacle of the founder of modernism reaching backward without irony to a tradition whose roots lay in a quite different national, political and technological milieu in order to realise visually a number of persuasive, modern, doctrinal positions cannot easily be squared with any extant sociology, recent practice included.

My sense of Manet's indebtedness to Goya is touched on by Clarke's reference to the prostitute's 'stare'. I prefer to think of it as an almost explosive admission of visibility; that the painter and (in this case) the model are complicit in a kind of composition that has nothing to do with neo-classical notions of design. It is rather entirely both spatial and social; the painter and the model – or perhaps the viewer and the model – agree to stare at each other on either side of the socio-spatial medium of the picture plane and all of its attendant conventional devices, the paraphernalia of painting. It is one thing to say that this visibility which Goya pursues so harrowingly in his etchings and portraits depends upon jettisoning the baggage of neo-classic 'correctives' that, for example, so plague Ingres's painting. It is quite another to find in painting the means, not the obstacle, to visibility, to find the 'conventions' of painting inaugural in that sense. Of course, the former merely confirms all the Platonist prejudices of most sociology: convention as an occasion of narrowing and obscuration which should therefore be eclipsed. The latter, however, is equally a narrowing – a most profound one no doubt, but in many senses as crushing a limit, which writers in particular find irksome.

So I am inclined to see Clarke's reference to a prostitute's stare as a kind of reflex evasion which in giving the writer room to work with words (the importance of prostitution in Paris, 1865, etc) also evades the transformations that are going on in the agreement to make a painting. I say this not to chide Clarke but to indicate that he (no doubt correctly) feels squeezed out, perhaps even demeaned by this emphasis on visual re-production; after all painting may well be presented as somewhat marginal to the processes he seeks to analyse. Squeezed out reciprocally, then (from the artist's point of view), is prostitution – and indeed by Manet's very painting of a prostitute – unless *Olympia* is to be reduced to a kind of foreplay.

I say again there are representations of a similar subject matter that are precisely intended as foreplay; to define *Olympia* as a painting of a prostitute comes analytically close to confusing it with these. The problem is not that old chestnut, placing high art next to soft pornography – but the failure to grasp differentiated purpose; or again, the reduction of one set of social phenomena that are sufficient to claim serious critical attention in their own right, namely Manet's painting, to the status of second-order derivatives of another, namely, prostitution. It may be that one would sooner talk about prostitution than painting. Fair enough, but I should not; and I cannot see that the contrary preference has anything to do with the sociology of art.

Returning, then, to the confines of visual project, visual desire, the epiphenomena of absolute, specific visibility-for-painting are everywhere: the choice of so much black contrasted against such enormous illumination of the body, the palpable ambiguity of so many aspects of the 'subtext', such as the cat, the face of the negress, the unresolved hair – all conspire to make the face and body the nexus of all sustained attention. It is in this context that what is for me the greatest passage occurs: the extraordinary line that begins, almost horizontal, at the left breast, distinguishing from it the left arm and the soft, plunging line of the stomach, steepens to a vertical to constitute the thumb and flexed fingers, then to define the overlap of the legs.

Let me formulate it negatively: it is merely the provisional horizon of a series of forms. Constructed with great verve, accuracy, potency – yes – but nevertheless in itself merely the consequence of two sets of elections; one fairly simple, the exigencies of the relative position of painter and model, the 'visual edges' so produced; the other less simple and inclusive of the first, namely, the tradition of which the topicalisation of 'visual edges' as lines (which they are not) is merely a part: the generalised post-Renaissance project of representation in painting and drawing. Outside of this desire, it is nothing; and is in many senses so slight that to grasp its traces as the signature of something else is to lose sight of it altogether. So the issue, whether presented negatively – or, as I take it, as one of complete fascination – is this re-productive desire: to commit the subject matter, the object of interest, to a process of introspection, reflexion and inquiry which, however exalted those words ring, is grounded in the mundane, routinely organised desire to fashion an image of an object in an alien though traditonal set of materials.

Nothing, perhaps – or does the world wish to be represented in painting or other kinds of visual fashioning? Is the social organisation of sight-through-painting a fundamental characteristic of social interaction that makes Baudelaire's and Manet's modernistic programmes look altogether more serious? Of course, Platonism will only see that as a loss: sight corrupted through a style of representing, be it painting, sculpture, the novel. For Durkheim there could be no such loss; 'sight' is only ever socially memorable in and as the various shapes of its reflexive re-presentation: if sight were not re-produced (and for the Platonist, debased) it would be invisible to itself. In that sense the 'impossibly' heightened visibilities of Goya and *Olympia* refer instead to – or are 'possible' as – a traditional inquestive action of sight upon sight; in no way do they refer to an original literalness, as it were, 'over-wrought'. That is why critical outrage – or sociological interest – stimulated by 'a picture of a prostitute' is quite beside the point; that line (to cite but one aspect), an entirely qualitative issue, already inextricably tied up with the conventional, inaugural relationships of seeing-for-painting, has shifted the considerations elsewhere. Its 'origin' is an entirely spurious concept except as a feature of the transformative relationship itself; precisely Durkheim's notion of social phenomena: treat social phenomena as things.

Bataille has an apparently similar argument with Valéry:[8]

Valéry: . . . given over to absolute nudity she makes one think of all the remnants of primitive barbarism and ritual animality which lurk beneath the routine of prostitution in great cities.

Bataille: It is possible (though questionable) that this was initially the text of Olympia . . . but . . . the text is effaced by the picture. And what the picture signifies is not the text but

221

the effacement . . . the 'scared horror' of her own presence . . . a presence as simple as absence. Her hard realism . . . consists in the painter's determination to reduce what he saw to the mute simplicity of what he saw.

I am a little disturbed by that argument: 'the mute simplicity of what he saw' seems a little disingenuous (to say the least) when one considers the vast edifice of painterly 'determination' that both precedes and follows from it. No – this is a work of art: sophistry rather than simplicity.

Zola is similarly enthusiastic, unwittingly confused, and amply demonstrates what is at stake. On the one hand: 'Ask nothing more from him than an accurately literal translation. He knows how to paint, and that is all.'[9] On the other: we should understand that the 'shockingly nude woman' – a reference to *Le Dejeuner sur L'Herbe* where 'she' is placed between two clothed men – derives only from the demands of colour, design, composition, '. . . a pretext to . . . paint a bit of flesh'.[10] In the first case we are invited to find the transformations of painting invisible; in the second, only the transformations are visible.

But the difference remains visible, addressable, troublesome. Modernism's most radical response was to attempt abolition. Maurice Denis's constriction is one occasion: a painting is essentially a plane surface . . .[11] Only a difference of emphasis perhaps, but contained within it the possibility of a complete subversion of Manet's re-presentative project. Then occurs the critical absurdity of 'painting itself' which haunts, especially, post-war American criticism as a parody of a categorial imperative. One can only say that art might have been spared this foolishness if Durkheim had been read more seriously: there is *nothing* 'essential' about painting either as a plane surface or as a category of acting if by the 'essential' is meant something other than the social occasions of its use. Or, more pointedly, the 'essential' – as opposed to the 'social' form, the form that claims solidarity – can only occur in and as the refusal to take the social phenomenon seriously. Consequently, the 'essential' understood as the intention to ignore the various forms of solidarity gathered around the materials and traditions of painting is bound to subvert not only Manet's figuration but any other form of solidarity at all. In short, it is the political standpoint of Socrates. It is also a characteristic of modernist formalism because both exhibit a predilection to suppress representation-as-difference. Neither can have any part in post-Durkheimian usage.

It may be thought that I speak as a recipient of the emancipation – the 'posterity' – that flows from the collapse of modernism taken as a series of spurious constraints in which Manet is at least implicated; I am free to analyse his work as something other than a fragment or way-stage in a greater imperative. In short, I am able to consider whether his project claims my/our solidarity rather than engage in the excusing pretence that our solidarity is really founded upon some compulsive essence. The question, then, concerns the desirability of Manet's work and in the formulation, description commitment to that set of desires, there will inevitably also be complicity, rejection, even a kind of 'repression' (if that is the right word). In short, specificity; though no one expects the specification to be closed, a determination voluntarily entered into is no less determinate for all that.

In this context of voluntaristic determination it becomes clear that 'posterities' repeat the same disastrously unresolved stance toward that entire plane of difference that finds its ontological foundation in the specific acts of cultural re-production (rather than replication) that are the profound characteristic of organic solidarity. That lack of resolution is further reflected in that the notion of posterity ostensibly belongs to both sociology and philosophy.

First, so far as 'posterity' is intended to connote a displacement of the 'real' by social phenomena – the 'virtual' – then its consequence could only pass for sociology in the context of a farce. Such a connotation, then, is properly understood as philosophy in the specific sense of a refusal to engage sociology or its objects at all – precisely Socrates's position. The 'real' means here (for example) biology but not gender, production but not value, thought but not language, language but not speech. It also means philosophy but not sociology, nor their supposedly easy coexistence: the (neo-)Platonic philosopher-guardian has the principal duty of exclusion. And those exclusions are not simply to be directed against sociology but against any act of cultural re-production that disputes its virtual status and so threatens the altereity of the ostensibly real. That position need not detain us more than to say that the topic of cultural re-production is both forbidden and impossible within its confines.

Second, so far as 'posterity' is intended to connote a displacement of what once firmly was, by a subsequent 'presence', defined primarily in terms of not-being and indeed revealing its ante-cedent in questionable guise – for example modernism and post-modernism, or equally, Hegel's historicism and post-historicism – then we have a deeply ironic inversion of an imagined or superseded 'reality' coalesced into the 'actually' virtual. A less pointed rejection of the social in favour of some imagined reality, it demonstrably has philosophic precedents and decays into similar forms: the socio-virtual masquerading as real to its members, set against the ostensibly greater 'analytic' speech of some other members-at-a-distance that dis-covers its status. The difference rests on a characterisation, or better, a caricature: (absurd, conventional, narrow, unreflexive) commitment set against (rational, critical, informed, reflexive) detachment; again, the persistent standpoint of especially, but not exclusively, phen-omenology; the conventional standpoint of the Academy in its current (and incorrigibly modernistic) notion of guardianship: immediate horror of convention. (Postmodernists included.)

Similarly, John O'Neill writes: '. . . postmodernism celebrates the neutralisation of all conviction from which even mimicry derives.'[12] But that is to represent a conviction, and an important one: that the conventions of modernism were actually false, and therefore so is O'Neill's premise. Given that the premise is a characteristic falsehood of postmodernism that 'we' (citizens of the postmodern theoretic community) are supposed nevertheless to believe (as O'Neill demonstrates), one can only say that we are being invited to feign unawareness that our conviction – for con-viction it must be – like any other is wholly exclusive of its theoretic opponents. But the failure to recognise that conviction (or should we say convention) is wholly determinate – 'the neutralisation of all *other* conviction' – does not erase determinateness, nor suppress its consequences.

Let me in opposition, then, say that the last thing I want is the neutralisation of Manet's figurative project; that in my conviction of his worth I am prepared to risk that the celebration, espousal, promotion of Manet's work (if it were ever taken seriously) might equally lead to the re-invigoration of interest in his figuration or to an extremely mannered or limited visual project, whether as painting or criticism. Of course, that is exactly what happened to Manet through subsequent modernist 'discipline' – but the pre-tensions of postmodernism's false liberality invite us not only to conceal our convictions from ourselves but also to be blind to the difference between the qualities of (Manet's) modernism and the weakness of its subsequent course. In that sense, the risk of decay and failure that will necessarily be a part of any renewed critical interest in Manet (for example) will be transformed into certainty by the intervention of convictions that are, so to speak, 'self-cancelling'. Such a position would, without exaggeration, absolutely renounce all critical social faculties. And so O'Neill's self-cancelling sentence does not so much point to the logical principle of non-contradiction but the ridiculous spectacle of, say, Warhol, Rushdie, the descendants of Khoumeni and whoever is the hardest-liner in Peking these days, speaking together in mutually assured postmodernity (an image Rushdie so disastrously essayed). Suffice to say that the postmodern 'age' is rendered explicit, determinate, exclusive and limited not least by those who refuse to live within its confines.

The frank acceptance that a visual project is necessarily determinate – one is speaking entirely of *pictorial possibility* – is sociologically preferable to the erosion that begins with Manet's no doubt 'repressive' modernism and somehow forges from that exposed illusion – through the intervention of the self-cancelling conviction of postmodernity – the 'social phenomenon' as a pure formality, as the virtual commitment that makes no difference other than a sea of contingent inflections in the monad of historical interaction. Rather than the scourge of the Académie, Manet, in the name of this sort of postmodernity – the basis of my/our supposed emancipation – then becomes the idle doodler, the ironic zealot. And we are supposed not to notice that this lax, ironic posterity is not new, lax or ironic at all, but a most practised, recognisable and ignominious convention that is as old as it is violent: modernism's teeth drawn by Socrates in a new suit.

The dominant paradigm of this violence is again mathematics: the one set against the many at the expense of the subject matter of sociology, namely, phenomena whose primary characteristic is intelligibility, not number. Again, the ensuing speech could only pass for sociology in the context of a farce. I do not contest the original theoretic intention; as Rosen has[13] it – the desire to construct a 'speech about the whole'. It is occasioned, accompanied and compromised, however, by a failure or refusal to imagine that 'speech about the whole' may be impossible or, more importantly, to admit the corrosive action of its concomitant, namely, the a priori mathematisation of the 'units' of the whole (as though speech about it were possible) which immediately strips away their intelligible qualitative relationships. (For the 'whole' cannot be premised upon a finite set of intelligibilities, but must include 'all such occasions' imaginable or not.) In this sense, discourse about cultural reproduction can only occur as a matter of frequencies of displacement; no concept of membership is possible, or is already assumed, delineated and confined to a question of number: aggregated individuals, 'mechanically' equivalent.

In this sense, the irresolution of posterities occurs as inattention to the difference between philosophy and sociology:[14] interest in speech about the whole contrasted against the refusal to countenance the inevitable reduction of its 'parts' – the intelligible world of qualitative membership – to instances of mathematically equivalent action. Into that chasm of equivocation, the entire edifice of contemporary phenomenology rapidly disappears.

The freedom to practise only mathematics is rather a specific constraint. More interestingly, the freedom to practise sociology thus also occurs as the renunciation of mathematics or philosophy – which is to say that an argument about freedom is an inadequate way to engage the specificity of the sociological or artistic enterprise. Consequently, the ancient, modern and postmodern academy's unmitigated horror of 'ordinary' convention looks startlingly like a misplaced family resemblance. Stated in slightly different terms, Durkheim's organicism or Manet's visual militancy are invitations to consider the ontological force of determinate re-productive actions; for philosophers these are unambiguously inauthentic constraints – they obscure the whole; for Durkheim's sociology and for art they occur as determinate but inaugural openings in which the desires and interests of membership are forged. And so it is not a question of the freedoms connoted in 'posterities' but rather of the inaugural openings that sociology makes possible (which philosophers dismiss as mundane). The essential question is this: is it possible to gather a kind of theoretic community, a solidarity, around sociology in that sense? Is it possible to agree to practise abstinence from the mathematical usage of philosophy? For only in that abstinence can the replete world of membership become the object of inquiry.

Or is the language of the theoretic community denoted by the word 'sociology' so permeated by mathematics as the avoidance of too close an inter-penetration with political and aesthetic solidarity that the discipline denoted by that word will consist of no more than a series of ritual demonstrations that such contacts are, in general, too close for academic propriety; and that Durkheim, in particular, risks the collision of theory with desire?

NOTES

1 I hope it is clear that my, and arguable that Durkheim's, sense of the organic refers primarily to difference and not to what Lyotard calls 'the paradisic representation of a lost "organic" society' (J.F. Lyotard, *The Postmodern Condition*, Manchester, Manchester University Press, 1986, p. 15). For me, 'organic' difference is at least as likely to lead to chaos as to cohesion – marked with the requirement of concerted, wrested realisation, which, whilst not a guarantee of truth, is nevertheless a guarantee of determination, in both senses.

2 E. Durkheim, *The Rules of Sociological Method*, New York, Free Press, 1964, p. 13.

3 S. Kierkegaard, *The Concept of Irony*, Bloomington and London, Indiana University Press, 1965, p. 198.

4 T.J. Clarke, *The Painting of Modern Life: Paris in the Art of Manet and his Followers*, London, Thames & Hudson, 1985, pp. 88–96. See also G.H. Hamilton, *Manet and His Critics*, New Haven and London, Yale University Press, 1954, pp. 65–80.

5 P. Gay, *Art and Act*, New York, Harper & Row, 1976, pp. 88–9. See also C. Baudelaire, *The Painter of Modern Life and Other Essays*, trans. and ed. J. Mayne, London and New York, Harper & Row, 1965.

6 Clarke, op. cit., p. 78.

7 Ibid., p. 88.

8 Ibid., pp. 137–8 (footnote).

9 Hamilton, op. cit., p. 95.

10 Ibid., p. 97.

11 'It is well to remember that a picture – before being a battle horse, a nude woman, or some anecdote – is essentially a plane surface covered with colours assembled in a certain order' (see H. Chipp, *Theories of Modern Art*, Berkeley and Los Angeles, University of California Press, 1968, p. 94.

12 J. O'Neill, 'Postmodernism (Postmarxism)', in H.J. Silverman (ed.), *Postmodernism – Philosophy and the Arts*, London, Routledge, 1990, p. 70.

13 See S. Rosen, *Nihilism*, New Haven and London, Yale University Press, 1969; *G.W.F. Hegel*, New Haven and London, Yale University Press, 1974.

14 These terms are not intended as conventional definitions but as analytic invitations to reflect, in particular, on how certain modalities of language-use efface the objects of sociology, in Durkheim's sense. Here the focus is a distinction between a universe and a community of possibilities.

13

THE ROLE OF IDEOLOGY IN CULTURAL REPRODUCTION

David Walsh

From its very inception in the work of Marx himself, Marxism has assigned a central role to ideas and forms of consciousness in the formation, legitimation and preservation of the institutions of society. As an expression and reflection of the interests of the ruling class within society and generated in productive practices and in that sense ideology, ideas and forms of consciousness act both as an ideational and material force which stabilises society (sustaining and reinforcing the status quo) by reproducing the relations of production through the way in which ideology clothes the economic order and assigns specific roles to individuals within the economy which turns them into economic and political agents of it. Consequently, within society, a dominant ideology emerges as a hegemonic culture which incorporates and institutionalises the interests of the dominant class and serves as a social cement which binds the whole social order into a particular and prevalent pattern.

Marx's own conception of ideology needs to be placed within his discussion of the relationship between consciousness and material conditions. As a materialist, Marx necessarily rejects the pre-eminence which Hegelian thought had given to consciousness. As Marx puts it: 'it is not the consciousness of man that determines their being but, on the contrary, their social being that determines their consciousness.'[1] Moreover:

> consciousness can never be anything else than conscious existence and the existence of men in their actual life process . . . Men, developing their material production and their material intercourse, alter, along with their real existence, their thinking and the products of their thinking. Life is not determined by consciousness but consciousness by life.[2]

But this does not mean that consciousness is a simple mechanical reflection of material conditions which is produced by those conditions as an automatic product since, as Marx puts it:

> What distinguishes the worst architect from the best of bees is this, that the architect raises his structure in imagination before he erects it in reality . . . At the end of every labour process . . . we get a result that already existed in the imagination of the labourer at its commencement.[3]

For Marx, then, consciousness is not just a mere reflection of material reality because reality is not just a given object but includes the subject's activity. It emerges out of practice in the sense that consciousness is conscious existence which is the life processes of human beings as they engage in the actual activities of production, i.e. the production of their own livelihoods. These actual activities are intentional activities and are forged in historical life processes which determine them. As Marx puts it, productive activities are historically located and history is nothing more than human beings in pursuit of their ends yet 'men make their own history but they do not make it just as they please, they do not make it under circumstances chosen by themselves but under circumstances directly encountered from the past'.[4] Reality, then, is historical reality but it is not just an objective datum but human productive activity (the historical product of the reproductive practices of human beings) which has an objective existence. For Marx, then, the relationship of consciousness to reality is one of practice and he looks at real individuals, their activity and the material conditions under which they live which include not only those which they find existing but those which they produce through their activities. In their productive activities, human beings produce forms of consciousness since their activities are intentional, purposive and creative and it is through these activities that the world in which they live is transformed and made. What then are these productive and reproductive practices? Marx argues that they are practices of material production which produce a particular division of labour between human beings that forces them into a particular sphere of labour and which places conditions upon them which become the historical circumstances in terms of which they make their world. As such these practices are both historical and collective, and because of this, consciousness which is forged in the context of such is 'from the very beginning a social product and remains so as long as men exist at all'.[5]

What, then, for Marx is the nature of ideology and how does it emerge from productive and reproductive practices? Here he argues that, as practice creates the social conditions of existence for human beings, it creates a contradictory reality and the rule of a particular class who own the forces of production. These contradictions generate ideology, i.e. as contradictions emerge they are given distorted solutions in the mind and projected out as ideology. Ideology is a solution in the mind to contradictions which cannot be resolved in practice so it conceals consciousness. 'If the conscious expression of the real relations of these individuals is illusory, if in their imagination they turn reality upside down, then this is the result of their limited material mode of activity.'[6] But, as the conditions of production are always controlled by a ruling class (who own the forces of production), the ideological hiding of contradictions is always in the interests of that class.

> The ideas of the ruling class are in every epoch the ruling ideas, i.e. the class which is the ruling material force of society, is at the same time its ruling intellectual force. The class which has the means of material production at its disposal, has control at the same time over the means of mental production, so thereby, generally speaking, the ideas of those who lack the means of mental production are subject to it.[7]

This ruling class regulates 'the production and distribution of the ideas of their age; thus their ideas are the ruling ideas of the epoch'. So ideology is a condition for the functioning and reproduction of a system of domination. It works in an insidious way by hiding the real relations of the ruling class and this it does by presenting the interests of the ruling class as universal and rational since each class represents 'its interests as the common interest of all members of society, that is, expressed in ideal form; it has to give the ideas the form of universality, and represent them as the only rational and universally valid one'.[8] As contradictions are historically given and the greater they become in society so ideology becomes the greater and is increasingly deliberately created by the ruling class, but still it is contradictions in productive and reproductive practices that are the basis of the illusory and distorted nature of ideology rather than conscious deception.

230

However, it is class domination that is required for ideology to become successful.

Marx now moves to the specific productive and reproductive practices of capitalism and here he introduces the concepts of the economic base and the legal and political (cultural) super-structure of society to examine the ways in which the ideology of capitalism serves to underpin and legitimise the structures of capitalist society by disguising the relationship between the essence of its nature and the appearance which it presents. As he puts it:

> the economic structure of society is the real basis on which the juridical and political superstructure and to which definite forms of thought correspond; the mode of pro-duction of material life determines the general character of the social, political and intellectual processes of social life.[9]

His interest at this point becomes one of showing the detailed correspondence between the ideological forms and the concrete forms of economic activity to see how the productive and repro-ductive practices of capitalism lead to the domination of material conditions over individuals. What Marx does at this point is to develop political economy, and he looks at capitalist practice as it is objectified in commodity production. 'We have proceeded from the presuppositions of Political Economy. We have accepted its language and laws . . . From Political Economy itself, in its own words, we have shown that the worker subscribes to the level of a commodity.'[10]

> The commodity-form and the value relation between the products of labour which stamps them as commodities, have absolutely no connection with their physical properties and with material relations arising therefrom. It is simply a definite social relation between men, that assumes in their eyes, the fantastic form of a relation between things . . . This I call the fetishism which attaches itself to the products of labour . . . it has its origin . . . in the peculiar character of the labour that produces them.[11]

Surplus value (the difference between the cost of labour necessary to produce a commodity and what it fetches on the market) is disguised as the selling price of commodities over their cost so the profit which is extracted from the surplus value of the labour of the worker and which is the real fact of capitalism goes unrecognised by everybody. Wages (presented as a fair contract between capitalist and labourer) disguise the division between the value and the price of labour power. Basically capitalism hides the fact that it is all based on the pursuit of profit which is generated by the extraction of surplus value from the labour power of the worker so that objectified economic forms – prices, wages, profits, etc – present themselves in external forms (appearances) that conceal their actual and essential nature as objectified and distorted forms of human relationships.

> The social character of men's labour appears to them as an objective character stamped upon the product of that labour; because the relation of the producers to the sum total of their labour is presented to them as a social relation, existing not between themselves, but between the products of their labour . . . There it is a definite social relation between men, that assumes in their eyes, the fantastic form of relations between things.[12]

Economic relations, then, are seen on their surface instead of in their essential nature and the conceptions which human beings, particularly capitalists, have of them and through which they try to understand them are the reverse of their real but concealed nature. 'The practical capitalist, blinded by competition as he is, is incapable of penetrating phenomena to recognise the inner essence and inner structure of this process (the working of capitalism) behind its outer appearances.'[13] So:

> the final pattern of economic relations as seen on the surface, without real existence and consequently with the conceptions by which the bearers and agents of these relations seek to understand them, is very much different from, or indeed quite the reverse of, their inner but concealed essential pattern and the pattern corresponding to it.[14]

Within capitalism, and at the level of their essential nature, social relations have become inverted and this leads to a twisting and inversion in consciousness – consciousness accepts the inverted phenomenal forms and so is ideological. It fetishes the world of appearances and separates them from their essential nature in reality and this is the essence of all the forms of consciousness and institutional structures that develop within capitalism. As Marx puts it, 'the distorted forms in which the real inversion is expressed is naturally reproduced in the views of the agents of the capitalist mode of production'.[15]

So, to summarise, Marx's conception of ideology, then, is formed in men's engagement in the productive and reproductive practices that produce it and, in that sense, has an objective foundation in these practices and is not just a subjective illusion. What Marx does is to move through an analysis of the nature and function of ideology with relation to society. He begins with an historicist conception of ideology which treats it as illusions of thought which give ideas an independent existence as though they were actors on the historical stage to a later scientific stage which treats ideology as the opposition between essence and appearance that allows him to examine the general nature of consciousness in a capitalist world. But always his conception of ideology remains basically the same, viz, that contradictions that cannot be resolved in practice give rise to distorted forms of consciousness. These distorted forms of consciousness serve to represent and legitimate the interests and rule of the dominant class by universalising and naturalising their interests so preserving the structures of the world over which they rule and cementing that rule itself. There is, then, for Marx, no solution to ideology but the overthrow of the distorted practices which produce it, viz, the overthrow of the productive and reproductive practices of capitalism itself, which only the penetration of appearances to an understanding of the nature of the essence which underpins capitalism can generate. This is precisely the task which Marx set himself in his own theoretical and empirical analysis of the structures of capitalism. But in his theorising, which is of necessity conducted within a materialist mode, the problem arises that, necessarily, priority is assigned to the economic order in the analysis of culture as ideology which comes with it – particularly in the distinction which Marx makes between economic base and legal and political super-structure – the danger of a kind of economic determinism that reduces culture to structure and structure to economic determin-ation which leaves no place for consciousness or praxis without which the conception of revolutionary activity as a transforming practice makes little sense. Agency is lost in structure.

Gramsci seeks to restore the praxiological basis to Marx's thinking in his reconstruction of the Marxist tradition. He specific-ally rejects the vulgar and orthodox Marxism of the 2nd International and that espoused by the Soviet Union, which he saw as turning Marxism into a form of economic determinism which rejected dialectical thinking and replaced it by scientism. Criticising this orthodoxy he argues that:

> the claim presented as an essential postulate of historical materialism, that every function of politics and ideology can be presented as an immediate expression of the structure must be contested in theory as primitive infantilism, and combated in practice with the authentic testimony of Marx.[16]

Such Marxism reduced the historical flow of events to a predetermined evolutionary pathway which was dictated by autonomous economic forces without reference to either particular historical circumstances or the role which human beings play within the course of actively determining the direction of affairs. Returning to the early Marx instead, Gramsci seeks to develop a philosophy of praxis which reasserts the role which human beings play in changing their historical circumstances and bringing about revolution.

> Man does not enter into relations with the natural world just by being himself part of it but actively by means of work and technique. Further; these relations are not just mechanical. They are active and conscious . . . Each of us changes himself, modifies himself to the extent that he changes and modifies the complex relations of which he is the heart.[17]

Gramsci argues that historical change is produced by the subtle interplay of objective material conditions and the creation of subjective forms of consciousness that activate human beings to take charge of situations and direct them through particular programmes of political action. The process is dialectical and he argues that:

> the true fundamental function and significance of the dialectic can only be grasped if the philosophy of praxis is conceived of as an integral and original philosophy which opens up a new phase of history and a new phase in the development of world thought. It does this to the extent that it goes beyond both traditional idealism and traditional materialism if the philosophy of praxis is not considered except in subordination to another philosophy then it is not

possible to grasp the new dialectic through which the transcendence of old philosophies is effected and expressed.[18]

In this he rejects scientistic forms of Marxism which work with statistical laws since:

the fact has not been properly emphasised that statistical laws can be employed in the science and art of politics only so long as the great masses of the population remain essentially passive in relation to questions which interest historians and politicians. But in science and the art of politics (the extension of statistics) it can have literally catastrophic results which do irreparable harm. Indeed in politics the assumption of the law of statistics as an essential law operating of necessity is not only a scientific error but becomes a practical error in action.[19]

Consequently, for Gramsci, the role of consciousness is crucial and he quotes with approval Engels' remarks that the reflections of struggles in the minds of participants also exercise their influence upon the course of historical struggles in many cases having a preponderant effect in determining their form. So ideology is crucial because it is a necessary superstructural expression of contradictory social reality. Ideologies are reflections of the whole assembly of the social relations of production and have an objective reality through which human beings achieve consciousness of their positions and goals – through ideology human beings become conscious of fundamental conflicts in society – for this reason, then, Gramsci largely treats capitalism as a cultural phenomenon rather than just an economic one.

Addressing the role of ideology in civil society, Gramsci argues that the ruling class largely engineers its control of the state and society by consent rather than by coercion, and it does so by establishing a hegemony of its own ideas and forms of consciousness which come to dominate society as the 'common sense' which all sections of it accept as their own and act upon. The ruling class, then, assume a moral and intellectual leadership over all other classes in which the ideas that they espouse and propagate are accepted by all other classes in society and it is this hegemonic ideology which is essential for the survival and success of any ruling class. 'A social group can and indeed must already exercise "leadership" before winning governmental power – but even if it

235

subsequently holds it firmly in its grasp, it must continue to "lead" as well.'[20] In 'Twentieth-century Bourgeois Capitalism', he goes on to argue that:

> the normal exercise of hegemony is an area that has become classical, that of parliamentary regime, is characterised by a combination of force and consensus which vary in their balance with each other, without force exceeding consensus too much. Thus it tries to achieve that force should be supported by the agreement of the majority, expressed by the so called organs of public opinion – newspapers and associations.[21]

To achieve such hegemony, the ruling class must be prepared to accept a degree of compromise *vis-à-vis* the interests and tendencies of those groups over whom hegemony is achieved. This entails making sacrifices but not, in the end, over essential interests. It does mean, though, that the ruling class must be prepared to co-operate with other groups and partly respect their interests and concede their demands and this is achieved by intellectuals making use of intellectual processes to harness popular sentiment to the dominant ideology and by making limited concessions to the masses. In this way the ruling class need only resort to force in crisis situations.

The effect of the dominant ideology on the proletariat for Gramsci is very much, then, as Lukacs suggests in *History and Class Consciousness*, that it prevents them from transforming themselves from a class-in-itself to a class-for-itself which contains revolutionary potential and prevents it from acting. Such a change, Gramsci argues, can only occur with the emergence of consciousness in the form of an ideology of its own which rejects and replaces the dominant ideology. This in turn opens up the role of the Communist Party and the role of intellectuals within it in the process of revolutionary struggle. The Party's role is to dissect and understand the particular historical situation, educate the masses for power and lead the political struggle for revolutionary change through both its active and passive stages but not, importantly, from above. Here the issue of the role of the intellectual becomes crucial. For Gramsci:

> each man . . . carries on some form of intellectual activity, that is, he is a philosopher, an artist, a man of taste, he participates in a particular conception of the world, has a

conscious line of moral conduct and therefore contributes to sustain a conception of the world or to modify it, that is to bring into being new modes of thought.[22]

But human beings can only develop themselves and their surroundings if they have a class view of what possibilities are open to them and it is for the intelligentsia to provide a philosophy and ideology for the masses which allows them to exercise their own hegemony. But this must be an organic process.

> History is to be made not by intellectual elites separated from the masses [but by] intellectuals who are conscious of being organically linked to a national-popular mass [and] who struggle against the false heroisms and pseudo-aristocracies and stimulate the formulation of homogeneous, compact social blocs, which will give birth to their own intellectuals, their own commandos, their own vanguard – who in turn will react upon those blocs in order to develop them.[23]

Moreover, the intellectual must be a man of action. For Gramsci, then, it is the masses who must give rise to their own harnessing of popular sentiment where feelings and passions can become understanding and knowledge. In this a new hegemony, forged for and by the masses, will overturn the dominant ideology and propel the revolutionary overthrow of capitalism.

Gramsci, then, liberates Marxism from overt scientism and determinism through the role which he assigns to consciousness and ideology in the cultural reproduction of capitalism, but his analysis operates almost exclusively at the level of the superstructure and retains, as a result, the ordinary conception of base and superstructure in which the force of culture can only be emphasised at the expense of a weak sense of the structures to which it relates. Structure is lost in agency and the relation of culture to structure is hypostasised as a result. Althusser, in part, helps to redress the balance by treating ideology as structure as well as ideas and forms of consciousness. 'Relations of production presuppose the existence of a legal and political superstructure as a condition of their peculiar existence.'[24]

As a structuralist, Althusser argues for an epistemological break between the early humanistic and pre-scientific Marx and the later scientific Marx who develops a political economy of capitalism. Consequently for him he retains the sense of the economy as the final determinant in the sense that it determines what other structures dominate in society. However, the superstructure is crucial. But in this sense ideology is not an arbitrary and psychological creation of human beings – pure false consciousness which is subjectively determined – but a system of representations where:

> in the majority of cases these representations have nothing to do with 'consciousness'; they are usually images and occasionally concepts, but it is above all as structures that they impose on the vast majority of men, not via their consciousness.[25]

Ideology is the representation of the real nature of existence but necessarily a false one because it is 'necessarily orientated and biased'.[26] It is a 'representation of the imaginary relationship of individuals to their real conditions of existence'[27] and can be studied objectively. Ideology arises from the fact that human beings cannot live without a certain representation of their world and their relations to it, but this representation is given to the subject in the same way as their economic and political relations are given to them. What gives its character as a form of distorted thought is that:

> it is socially necessary as a function of the very nature of the social totality – as a function of its determination by its structure which is made, as all the social, opaque for individuals who occupy a place determined by this structure. The opacity of social structure makes necessarily mythical the representation of the world necessary for social cohesion.[28]

The central function of ideology is to act as a social cement which binds the whole social structure together and makes possible the adjustment and cohesion of individuals in their roles. It is necessary for society because it fills essential social tasks so:

> human societies secrete ideology as the very element and atmosphere indispensable to their historical respiration and life. Only an ideological world outlook could have imagined societies without ideology and cannot conceive that even a communist society could ever do without ideology.[29]

But, with class society, it has the further function of maintaining the domination of one class over another, class divisions overdetermine the opaque character of society increasing its mystification. What Althusser does, then, with regard to his conception of ideology is to take over the general role which structural functionalism assigns to the value-system of a society which is to produce social cohesion and align it with the particular role that Marx assigns to ideology which is that of class domination. So through the way in which it functions, then, ideology reproduces the relations of production in society by assigning specific roles to individuals within the economy thereby turning them into economic agents of it. Ideology, then, operates through the theoretical practices by which human beings represent reality and consequently engage in their activities within society and so it acts as a structural condition which constitutes them as subjects in the world.

Althusser goes on to construct a theory of ideology in general – which is its function to secure cohesion in society – and a theory of particular ideologies – which has to do with the function of securing the domination of one class over others. The latter theory refers to the emergence of specific ideologies in concrete historical social formations which depend on a certain combination of modes of production and a particular class struggle. In this sense all ideologies have a history. The general theory of ideology deals with ideology as a phenomenon which is endowed with a structure and way of functioning which turns it into an omnihistorical reality of all societies in the sense that structure and function are always there in the same form throughout the whole of history. It is the general theory which provides Althusser with a framework for examining particular ideologies in particular social formations. But, addressing the role of ideology in capitalism specifically, he relies on his general theory of ideology to address its particular nature, i.e. he examines how individuals accept the roles which capitalism assigns to them and so is able to address how the skills of labour power and labour power itself are reproduced in capitalist society. Such reproduction, Althusser argues, can only occur in the forms and under the forms of ideological subjection. But to understand this it is necessary to examine the nature of the state in capitalism and separate out the Repressive State Apparatus or RSA (bureaucracy, the judiciary, the military, etc) from the Ideological State Apparatus or ISA where the former functions through repression and the latter functions through ideology. The reproduction of the relations of production is largely determined by the exercise of state power in the state apparatuses in which the RSA secures the political conditions for the operation of the ISA.

The ruling ideology is concentrated in the ISA and specifically ensures the reproduction of the relations of production partly through the family but mainly through education. The educational system:

> takes children from every class at infant school and then for years . . . it drums into them . . . a certain amount of know how wrapped in the ruling ideology or simply the ruling ideology in its pure state. Each mass ejected en route is practically provided with the ideology which suits the role it has to fulfil in class society: the role of exploited, of the agent of repression or of the professional ideologist.[30]

So, in these terms, ideology projects not the real world but the relationship between the individual and reality in which the individual is 'interpellated as a [free] subject in order that he shall submit freely to the Commandment of the Subject i.e. in order that he shall freely accept his subjection'.[31] Individuals live with ideology by participating with certain practices within specific ideological apparatuses and through these ideological practices the individual is constituted as a subject because individuals are subjected to the ideology contained within them.

To overcome ideology, Althusser argues that one must turn to science which, unlike ideology, which is a pre-scientific mode of cognition, is a theoretical practice that elaborates its own facts through a critique of ideological facts. Science brings not just a different solution to problems (and this is its epistemological break with ideology) but poses problems in an entirely different manner so the solution is not presupposed in advance as with ideology. So science penetrates mystifications and reveals the distortions produced by ideology thereby showing the true nature of reality. It permits ideology to be overcome by breaking with it – by unmasking it although ideology can never be brought to an end because of its functional necessity. But this poses a precise problem: how can ideology end if it is a functional necessity because of the opacity of the social world and the need for mythical representation of it as well as the need for social cohesion? Is science a solution, if ideology is generated at the level of productive and reproductive practices whilst science is generated at the level of theory? Moreover, the materialist structuralism that informs Althusser's work is dangerously near to an economic determinism which denies the autonomy of culture in the reduction of representations to structural apparatuses that in the end have their foundation in the economy.

The general problem with the whole of the Marxist perspective with regard to the role of ideology in the process of cultural reproduction is that it reduces culture to ideology and ideology to structure, so culture has no autonomy of its own – it is simply superstructural however sophisticated the analysis of the superstructure. Moreover, in Marxism, a further reduction is always lurking in the background which is that of reducing social structure to economic forces. We can note here how, despite the devastating critique that Abercrombie *et al.*[32] mount of the dominant ideology thesis in Marxism it leads them eventually to the kind of economic determinism that the thesis was designed to defeat and which is the inevitable legacy of the materialist perspective of Marxism in that they ultimately argue that the reproduction of class society is best explained by the dull compulsion of economic relations rather than by any form of ideological cohesion. There is a way out, however, and it is to Mannheim that I turn for a beginning to this in the sense that he addresses culture and structure as a relationship allowing them to be seen as interacting with one another rather than them being seen as one determining the other.

Mannheim criticises Marx's theory of ideology on the grounds of its economic determinism and substitutes for it a sociology of knowledge that replaces a study of class interests with an examination of the world-view or *Weltanschauung* of social groups within society including classes. In this respect he examines the social determination and organisation of all knowledge in terms of how it arises out of the social location of particular groups within society and is an expression of their practical engagement with socio-historical circumstances in which these groups share the framework of a common fate, common activity and the overcoming of common difficulties.

> We are no longer accepting that the values of a given period are absolute, and the realisation that norms and values are historically and socially determined can henceforth never escape us. Thought and existence were still regarded as fixed and separate poles, bearing a static relationship to one another in an unchanging universe. It is only now that the new historical sense is beginning to penetrate and a dynamic concept of ideology and reality can be conceived of.[33]

The system of attitudes shared by a group as a perspective or standpoint on the world is only tenuously associated with economic interests and in most circuitous ways because 'competition' and 'generation' equally shape social knowledge. Generations influence thought and consciousness in a similar way to class because a common location in social and historical processes limits people to a specific range of potential experience and predisposes them to certain characteristic modes of thought. Competition between social groups for power produces different interpretations of the world as the result of the forms which it takes.

Developing a sociology of knowledge leads Mannheim to develop a radical historicist and neo-Kantian viewpoint that separates the world of nature from the world of culture by treating cultural products as requiring interpretation which involves locating them within a totality of which they constitute meaningful parts. Scientific knowledge, on the other hand, for Mannheim is not existentially determined but develops immanently through one question leading up to another with purely logical necessity. In this, however, he is both naïve and somewhat mistaken as science too has an existential location and can be treated as part of culture. But Mannheim sees his main task as understanding cultural knowledge by finding the factors in the historical location of social groups which determine and relativise the thought of these groups. He seeks to discover 'the relations between certain mental structure and the life-situations in which they exist'.[34] He calls this approach to the social organisation of knowledge relationism and distinguishes it from the determinism of Marxism and it is this which provides him with the methodological foundations for his sociology of knowledge. 'Relationism signifies that all of the elements in a given type of historical existence to which, for a time, it furnishes the appropriate expression.'[35] So Mannheim has taken Marx's conception of ideology as the existential determination of knowledge by social and political interests and widened it out into a general view which approaches an understanding of ideas in terms of how they represent the perspectival world-views of various social groupings in society that arise out of their socio-historical locations. In one sense, Mannheim is treating all ideas as ideology because they are perspectival, but this really mistakes his task and the specific definition he gives of ideology (in a Marxist sense) because his real concern is to argue that:

with regard to the possibility of intellectually formulating our knowledge . . . every perception is and must be ordered and organised into categories. The extent, however, to which we can organise and express our experience in such conceptual forms is, in turn, dependent upon the frames of reference which happen to be available at a given historical moment.[36]

Mannheim distinguishes between a total and a particular conception of ideology which allows him to define ideological thought (in the Marxist sense) as such. The total conception looks at the characteristics and composition of the total structure of the mind of an age or a group. It is sociological and not psychological and requires a radical historicism – really Mannheim is talking about culture here. In this respect no position is privileged as ideology – at this level ideology is not the exclusive property of any one group or class and Marxism, too, is ideological in this sense. The particular conception of ideology is more psychological and seeks to examine thought and knowledge as conscious deceptions which conceal particular interests not just as conceptual errors but as deliberate lies – this is ideology proper. Mannheim singles out three sources of bias from which such deceptions arise.

1 An ethical attitude can be ideological 'if it is oriented with reference to norms, with which the action in a given historical setting, even with the best intentions cannot comply'.[37]
2 Ideology occurs when ideas cover up real relations.

> This is the case when we create 'myths', worship 'greatness in itself', avow allegiance to 'ideals', while in our actual conduct we are following other interests which we try to mask by stimulating and unconscious righteousness.[38]

3 Ideology occurs when:

> a form of knowledge is no longer adequate for comprehending the actual world . . . knowledge is distorted and ideological when it fails to take account of the new realities applying to a situation, and when it attempts to conceal them by thinking in categories which are inappropriate.[39]

Finally, Mannheim distinguishes between ideological and utopian thought where the first is orientated towards the present and the second towards the future. The first is locked into the present order of things and conceals its true nature, whilst the second is thought which shatters the present order and exceeds its limits in a transformative way. The two cannot always be easily distinguished except historically with the realisation that genuine utopian thought is that which truly transcended the social order and was realised in practice even if it then went on to produce a new ideology which constituted the new order of things.

But how is the sociology of knowledge to proceed, i.e. how are world-views to be related to social structures? Mannheim offers a three-stage model for doing this. Firstly, the analysis proposes the determination of a style of thought referring to a general *Weltanschauung* with which many theories arise – the analyst constructs an ideal-type of thought by identifying its main and integral features by looking for the basic way of approaching the world which is the inner drive of the style of thought. Secondly, the analyst tests these many theories against one another to see if they belong within a *Weltanschauung* and this is used to produce a concrete picture of the course and direction of development which is actually taking place so that the history of a style of thought is revealed in all of its manifestations and its main theoretical principles are established in terms of its struggle with other forms of thought. Finally, the style of thought is traced back to the social forces or classes or groups which produced it and the analyst examines how the interests and aspirations of these are reflected in it and find expression through it – here the analyst looks at the social composition of the classes or groups within which styles of thought originate and the direction of the historical development of the structural situation. So, for example, Mannheim shows how German conservativism was a romantic protest of the aristocracy after the introduction of industry by the monarch and state bureaucracy in the absence of a strong indigenous bourgeoisie, the natural protagonists of industry, to institute it.

So, with relationism, Mannheim steers between determinism on the one hand and complete relativism on the other – knowledge must be related to its social base but this does not necessarily implicate its truth. What remains true is that all knowledge is partial and in that sense relative. Mannheim attempts to rescue the possibility of objectivity in terms of a free-floating intelligentsia who lack a social base and are thereby impartial arbitrators of knowledge. But the possibility that such a group could achieve an objective synthesis of knowledge is somewhat naïvely conceived and in the case of science mistaken since, as Popper and Kuhn have argued, it is not the impartiality of the scientist which guarantees the validity of science but the common methods that weld the community of science into a community – a shared method of enquiry rather than the value-free scientist is the guarantee of science. Nevertheless, Mannheim's conception of relationism releases the whole discussion of cultural reproduction from the grip of structural and particularly economic determinism which is there in the Marxist debate about cultural reproduction. It is now possible to see how structure and culture have an interactive relationship and to examine that.

But still, even in Mannheim's work, the emphasis and focus is more on structure than culture and it is Mannheim's mentor, Weber, to whom we must turn to be offered a more balanced sense of the relationship that recognises that culture can have an autonomy *vis-à-vis* structure with the sense that it may possess a dynamic of its own. Turning to the relationship between ideas and values and the economic order, Weber argues that 'very frequently the world images that have been created by ideas have, like switchmen, determined the tracks along which action has been pushed by the dynamic of interest'.[40] Now, this is not to say that Weber divorces culture from structure in a new form of idealism, but that he situates the relationship in terms of the dynamic between the two and recognises how culture has its own thrust. Famously in *The Protestant Ethic and the Spirit of Capitalism*, Weber shows how the culture of capitalism – its ethos – which is necessary to the production and reproduction of capitalism cannot be understood except with reference to changing religious values – the Protestant Reformation which helped to bring about the ethos. Thus, he claims to refute the doctrine of naïve historical materialism according to which religious beliefs can simply be treated as reflections of economic conditions, arguing that 'we must free ourselves from the view that one can deduce the Reformation as a historically necessary development from economic changes'.[41] What the development of capitalism needed, apart from the economic and political structural changes that took place historically within Western Europe – and which Weber documents extensively in his empirical work – was a profound change in the social psychology of the inhabitants of this civilisation. It needed an inner rationalisation of the life of human beings which only the Protestant Reformation could have supplied and without which the other processes of structural rationalisation in the West could not have conjoined and led to the rational organisation of economic activity which is, for Weber, the hallmark of capitalism itself. Widening out this thesis, Weber then goes on to show the importance of religion generally for economic development, arguing that, by comparison with other equally advanced civilisations, viz. India and China, that possessed the necessary economic, political, legal and administrative structures to make capitalism possible, capitalism did not emerge as it did in the West because the spirit of capitalism was missing because of their religious systems. Speaking of Hinduism – but what he says is equally true of Buddhism and Confucianism, but not Christianity – Weber argues that:

> the core of the obstacle [to capitalist development] did not lie in particular difficulties, which every one of the great religious systems in its way has placed, or has seemed to place in the way of the modern economy. The core of the obstruction was embedded in the spirit of the whole system.[42]

Weber goes further still to develop a thesis about Western civilisation and the process through which it achieved its modern form – a process, then, of modernisation – in terms of which its structure, institutions and ideational form can be seen as participating in a general process of rationalisation which has been the foundation of their production and continuous production. In this way, Western civilisation can be seen to have, if not a dominant ideology, a central core to its nature which is that of instrumental rationalism which sustains and is supported by a social psychology that Weber critically addresses and describes as one of 'specialists without Spirit, sensualists without heart'.[43] What we live in, according to Weber, in Western civilisation, is an iron cage of rationalism supported by and supportive of the bureaucratic organisation in which society is embodied – culture and structure are locked into one another in an homologous process or, in Weber's terms, through elective affinity.

Critical theory recharges the Weberian account of contemporary society in the West in its discussion of the ways with which late capitalism, as an economic, political and cultural entity, reproduces itself. In such a society, legitimation is achieved not only in terms of an ideological belief in the value and validity of the system but by steadily increasing material rewards and participation in parliamentary democracy where decision-making in the economic and political spheres have increasingly become a technical and bureaucratic exercise. Technocracy itself becomes not only the institutional means by which society is administered and the basis of how people participate in it, but 'a background ideology that penetrates into the consciousness of the depoliticised mass of the population, where it can take on a legitimating power'.[44] Through it the public are 'engineered for purposes of legitimation'.[45] So late capitalist culture preserves itself by depoliticising both political debate and the mass of the population by presenting the political decisions of the state, not as alternative courses of action, but as technical solutions to agreed problems and:

> the development of the social system seems to be determined by the logic of scientific-technical processes. The immanent law of this progress seems to produce objective exigencies, which must be obeyed by any politics oriented towards functional needs. But when this semblance has taken root effectively, then propaganda can refer to the role of technology and science in order to explain and legitimate why in modern societies the process of decision-making about practical problems loses its practical function and 'must' be replaced by plebiscitary decisions about alternative sets of leaders of administrative personnel.[46]

Truly technocratic consciousness makes the iron cage complete by creating the illusion that political decision-making is one in which people actually participate rather than, as it actually does, which is merely to secure their loyalty to the state by getting them passively to approve its decisions.

Marx's debate about ideology and cultural reproduction stimulates through its limitations a wider discussion of the whole relation between structure and culture through which the processes of cultural reproduction can be understood and in terms of which it is the interactional relationship between the two which stimulates the production and reproduction of social relations where one and now the other takes the lead, although often in conjunction in the process of generating and regenerating the social order of society. To restrict the processes of cultural reproduction to the role played in them by ideology alone fails to grasp that this is only one source of such and not always the dominant one.

NOTES

1 K. Marx and F. Engels, *The German Ideology*, London, Lawrence & Wishart, 1970a, p. 81.
2 Ibid., p. 47.
3 K. Marx, *Capital*, vol. 1, London, Lawrence & Wishart, 1974, p. 174.
4 Marx and Engels, 1970a, op. cit., p. 96.
5 Ibid., p. 51.
6 K. Marx, and F. Engels, *Selected Works*, London, Lawrence & Wishart, 1970b, p. 57.
7 Marx and Engels, 1970a, op. cit., p. 64.
8 Marx and Engels, 1970b, op. cit., pp. 65–6.
9 Marx, 1974, op. cit., pp. 87–8.
10 Ibid., pp. 80–1.
11 Ibid., pp. 77–8.
12 Ibid., p. 72.
13 Ibid., vol. 3, p. 168.
14 Ibid., vol. 3, p. 209.
15 Ibid., vol. 3, p. 232.
16 A. Gramsci, *Prison Note Books*, London, Lawrence & Wishart, 1971, p. 407.
17 Ibid., p. 352.
18 Ibid., pp. 428–9.
19 Ibid.
20 Ibid., pp. 57–8.
21 Ibid., p. 1638.
22 Ibid., p. 9.
23 Ibid., pp. 204–5.
24 L. Althusser, *Lenin and Philosophy and Other Essays*, London, New Left Books, 1971, p. 71.
25 L. Althusser, *For Marx*, London, New Left Books, 1977, p. 233.
26 L. Althusser, *La Filosofia como Arma de la Revolución*, trans. O. del Barco and E. Roman, Cordoba, Cuadernos del pasado y presente, 1970, p. 55.
27 Althusser, 1971, op. cit., p. 156.
28 Althusser, 1970, op. cit., p. 55.
29 Althusser, 1977, op. cit., p. 232.
30 Althusser, 1971, op. cit., p. 147.
31 Ibid., p. 156.
32 N. Abercrombie, S. Hill, and B. Turner, *The Dominant Ideology Thesis*, London, Allen & Unwin, 1980.
33 K. Mannheim, *Essays in the Sociology of Knowledge*, London, Routledge & Kegan Paul, 1968, p. 84.
34 Ibid., p. 71.
35 Ibid., p. 76.
36 Ibid., p. 77.
37 Ibid., p. 86.
38 Ibid.
39 Ibid., p. 253.

40 M. Weber, *The Social Psychology of World Religions*, New York, Free Press, 1948, p. 280.
41 M. Weber, *The Protestant Ethic and the Spirit of Capitalism*, London, Allen & Unwin, 1930, pp. 90–1.
42 M. Weber, *The Religions of India*, New York, Free Press, 1958, p. 112.
43 Weber, 1930, op. cit., p. 182.
44 J. Habermas, *Toward a Rational Society*, London, Heinemann, 1971, p. 105.
45 J. Habermas, 'What does a crisis mean today? Legitimation problems initiate capitalism', *Social Research*, 1973, vol. 40, no. 4, pp. 643–7.
46 Habermas, 1971, op. cit., p. 105.

BIBLIOGRAPHY

Althusser, L. and Balibar, E. (1975) *Reading Capital*, London, New Left Books.
Barrett, M. *et al.* (eds) (1979) *Ideology and Cultural Production*, London, Croom Helm.
Bennett, T. *et al.* (1981) *Culture, Ideology and Social Process*, London, Batsford.
Habermas, J. (1976) *Legitimation Crisis*, London, Heinemann.
Larraine, J. (1979) *The Concept of Ideology*, London, Hutchinson.
Mannheim, K. (1972) *Ideology and Utopia*, London, Routledge & Kegan Paul.
Marx, K. (1969) *Theories of Surplus Value*, London, Lawrence & Wishart.
Weber, M. (1948) *Economy and Society*, London, Bedminster Press.

NAME INDEX

SUBJECT INDEX